CAMP-FIRES IN THE CANADIAN ROCKIES

The Finest Mountain Goat Picture

TAKEN AT EIGHT FEET.

CAMP-FIRES IN THE CANADIAN ROCKIES

BY

WILLIAM T. HORNADAY, SC.D.

Director of the New York Zoological Park
Professional Member of the Boone and Crockett Club

ILLUSTRATIONS BY

JOHN M. PHILLIPS

Pennsylvania State Game Commissioner
Regular Member of the Boone and Crockett Club

WITH SEVENTY ILLUSTRATIONS AND TWO MAPS

B&C
CLASSICS
MISSOULA, MONTANA | 2014

CAMP-FIRES IN THE CANADIAN ROCKIES
BY WILLIAM T. HORNADAY

Originally published in 1906.

Reprinted in 2014 as part of Boone and Crockett Club's series, B&C Classics.

Paperback ISBN: 978-1-940860-06-0
eBook ISBN: 978-0-940864-89-4
Published April 2014

Published in the United States of America by the
Boone and Crockett Club
250 Station Drive, Missoula, Montana 59801
Phone (406) 542-1888
Fax (406) 542-0784
Toll-Free (888) 840-4868 (book orders only)
www.booneandcrockettclub.com

MESSAGE FROM THE PUBLISHER

THE Boone and Crockett Club was founded by Theodore Roosevelt and George Bird Grinnell in 1887. Two years earlier, Grinnell, then editor of *Forest and Stream,* wrote a critical review of Roosevelt's book, *Hunting Trips of a Ranchman.* Roosevelt paid him a visit to discuss the matter. During that meeting Grinnell presented a strong case about his concerns on the future of hunting and conservation. TR was in agreement, and thus began a lifelong friendship that lead to the founding of the Boone and Crockett Club, the first private hunting and conservation organization in North America. The two also went on to collaborate on numerous books about hunting, conservation, exploration, and adventure. Since its early days, B&C has had a strong tie with publishing and furthering hunting and conservation.

In 2012, we launched our B&C Classics series of hunting and adventure books, including works from TR and Grinnell, as well as William T. Hornaday, Charles Sheldon, Frederick C. Selous and other adventurers from the late 1800s through the early 1900s. Each title in the B&C Classics series is selected by a committee of vintage hunting literature experts and is authored by a Boone and Crockett Club member.

Unlike other reprints of these hunting and adventure books, the B&C Classics series has been meticulously converted resulting in high-quality, digitally remastered eBooks and paperback editions. Many are complete with vintage photos and drawings not found in other editions. This attention to detail helps transport readers back to a time when hunting trips didn't happen over a weekend, but were adventures that spanned weeks, months, or even years.

We hope you enjoy the books we've selected for this series. They will give you a strong sense of our hunting heritage and provide hours of entertainment for anyone who loves adventure and the outdoors.

JULIE L. TRIPP
B&C Director of Publications
MISSOULA, MONTANA

PREFACE

MY FRIENDS ARE CALLED UPON to bear witness that of the various hunting trips I have enjoyed in the late lamented Wild West, I have written of one only. That was twenty years ago. For so large a sum of outdoor enjoyment which might have been set forth in print, my sight drafts upon the reading public have been by no means extravagant.

Even up to the end of our hunt in British Columbia, I had no thought of bookmaking; but now that the hunt is over, and we are out of those wonderful mountains, a printed record seems worth while. The land looms up so grandly, its wild creatures seem so interesting, and Mr. Phillips's pictures so fine, it would seem churlish to refuse the labor that will place them before those who care to enjoy them. Moreover, detailed information of nature as it exists to-day on the summits of the Columbian Rockies is not so outrageously abundant that this volume is likely to be crowded off the shelf by other books on that subject.

One month ago to-day we scrambled out of the mountains of southeastern British Columbia, tired, torn, and travel-stained, but with the wheels of Time turned back about five years. Three months ago literary composition was unendurable nerve torture. To-night, however, with the roar of the mountain torrents, the whistle of the wind on the passes, and the tinkle of the horsebell in my ears, I begin the writing of these pages as cheerfully as if I never had known an official care. I am disposed to tell of the wonders of that mountain land where we found health and vigor while climbing after grand game. We feel like saying to the tired business man, the overworked professional man, and the sleepless newspaper man,—go, thou, and do likewise!

This is merely a story of recreations with big game with a few notes on nature. Next to the necessity of a strenuous trip into mountain wilds, my chief object was to get into the home of the mountain goat, and learn at first hand something of the strange personality of that remarkable animal. The most valuable result of the trip, however, is Mr. Phillips's wonderful photograph of a live mountain goat, secured at risks to life and limb that were really unjustifiable.

Until our mountain diversion was half over, I had not realized that so much of living interest in nature of good luck in hunting, of rare success in photography and unalloyed delight in camp life could be packed into the limits of one vacation hunting trip; but that experience established a new record. At first I could no understand how Mr. Phillips could find interest in going to the same region for five trips in succession; but now I know. It is the mystic Spell of the Mountains!

We dread the day of the ranch, the road, the railway and the coal-mine,—anywhere near the Elk and the Bull Rivers. We left behind us all those "improvements "on the face of nature, and went far beyond the last tin can of civilization. For many miles our men had to chop out a trail for the pack-train before we could get on. Some of our travel was laborious, and some of it dangerous; but there was no accident. In every respect both the outfit and the trip were ideal.

No doubt all persons who are interested in the photographing of wild animals in their haunts will desire to know how Mr. Phillips obtained the mountain goat photographs which are reproduced in this volume. They were made with a Hawk-Eye Stereo Camera, No. 1. Mr. Phillips never has used a telephoto lens. His series of photographs of the mountain goat represent what I believe to be the most daring, and also the most successful, feat in big-game photography ever accomplished.

WILLIAM T. HORNADAY.
New York, November 1, 1905.

CONTENTS

A GREAT DAY WITH GOATS

CHAPTER VIII
THE MOUNTAIN GOAT AS WE SAW HIM

CHAPTER IX
TIMBER-LINE AND SUMMIT

CHAPTER X
ALONE ON A MOUNTAIN

CHAPTER XI
MY GRIZZLY-BEAR DAY

CHAPTER XII
NOTES ON THE GRIZZLY BEAR

LIST OF ILLUSTRATIONS

Except when otherwise noted, all these illustrations are from photographs made by John M. Phillips, and have been reproduced without the slightest alteration or retouching.

PHOTOGRAPHS

MAPS

CHAPTER I

THE PILGRIMAGE TO GOATLAND

THE DELECTABLE MOUNTAINS—OVER THE GREAT NORTHERN—
THE SWEETGRASS HILLS—INTO THE ROCKIES—THE FERNIE
GAME-PROTECTORS—BRITISH COLUMBIA GAME-LAWS TOO
LIBERAL.

IN AN UNGUARDED MOMENT, MR. John M. Phillips, of
Pittsburg,—true sportsman, game-protector, mountaineer,
photographer and genial gentleman, all in one,*—told me of
some wonderful mountains in the far West. He said they are
well filled with game, and as yet wholly unspoiled by hunters.
There the mountain goat abounds, and can be studied to excellent advantage. There are grizzly bears and mountain sheep
which may be killed under license, and a few elk which may
not. In that wonderland of Nature no sportsman has yet set
foot without Mr. Phillips's consent and cooperation; for it was
discovered by him and his guides, and by them is carefully preserved from ruin.

Thoughtlessly, I voiced my long-standing desire to see

*Mr. Phillips is also State Game Commissioner, and the founder of the Lewis and Clark Club.

many mountain goats at home, in fine mountains; and straight-way my good friend graciously invited me to accompany him on his next trip. Before the invitation could be withdrawn and cancelled, it was accepted.

Being averse to deep snow as the basis of a pleasure trip, I voted for September as the month, and although Mr. Phillips thought that the chances for finding grizzlies in that month were not great, he readily consented. Never having gone through northern Montana from end to end, I bespoke the selection of the Great Northern Railway as our route from St. Paul, and we found that the panorama of Montana thus secured was delightful as well as instructive.

The country traversed by the Northern Pacific Railway is to me almost as familiar as my own door-yard; but what lay north of the Missouri? And wherein would it differ?

Through the level and fertile wheat-lands of northern Minnesota, there run so many parallels and feeders of the Great Northern system that the "main line "is almost a fiction of the past. The tenderfoot needs to be told which section he is riding upon. From St. Paul up to the latitude of Grand Forks, even a new trolley-line would seem to be an inexcusable extravagance.

A ride in August through the heart of our great north-western wheat-belt is an event. Mile after mile, and hour after hour, the sea of golden grain is being swept in by the harvesters, bound into millions of bundles,—with the least possible expenditure of labor, shocked, loaded and hauled to the threshers. Hither, yonder, anywhere, the steam thresher "'lights "for a few hours, and a section of the wheat-laden plain is thrust into its insatiable maw. No longer does the farmer and his labor-swapping neighbors toil and moil on the strawstack, as of yore. The automatic stacker does all that, while the farmer busies himself with gathering in the spoil. The straw-heaps dot the stubble-fields at near intervals, and with the baled product selling in New York at $18 per ton, these reckless north-western nabobs *burn their straw*!

In the days of the buffalo millions, this country was a part of the summer range of the great northern herd. And it was to these same smoothly shaven plains, in North Dakota, delightfully free from the sage-brush that pervades the lands farther south, that the Red River settlers, of what is now Manitoba, came every summer with their great caravans of carts, accompanied by their wives and children. They came to kill buffaloes, dry their meat, make pemmican and cure buffalo-hides for leather—all for use during the long and dreary winters that tried men's souls. The naked plains over which the Red River settlers joyously drove their carts are now covered with wheat. The creaky cart has given place to the locomotive. The steam thresher has taken the place of the halfbreed's rifle, while to the present generation pemmican is almost unknown.

And now, when at last we are surfeited by the abundance of the harvest, and worn out with thankfulness for the continued prosperity of the great wheat-belt, we glide on into Montana, and turn with even keener interest to a new panorama—the late lamented "Wild West."

Throughout the once great but now greatly diminished Sioux Indian Reservation, canvas tepees, log cabins, blanketed braves, broad-beamed squaws and paintless wagons abound. The Fort Peck Reservation, as it is called, begins near Calais and extends to Whateley, about eighty miles. The time was when the Sioux were picturesque, uncertain, and at times even thrilling. As tame Indians, with no more buffalo-herds to tempt them upon the war-path, the Sioux look commonplace. When I think how the souls of their hunters must yearn for the chase, and how even the excitement of horse-stealing is denied them, I pity them. It is no wonder that even with horses in abundance, parties of young Sioux of the "warrior "class used to go down to the Crow Reservation, two hundred miles or more, steal horses and run them up north of the Missouri, purely for the excitement of the chase.

South-east of Fort Assiniboin, about forty miles away, is a mountain mass of considerable magnitude. It is the Bear Paw Mountains, once good hunting-grounds for big game, but now" hunted out." All along the line of the Great Northern, from Minnesota to the mountains, there is an astonishing absence of sage-brush. It is so abundant along the Northern Pacific west of the Missouri that I expected to see a good showing of it farther north. But there is so little of it that it fails to count; and there is no other plains brush to take its place. South of the Sweet-Grass Hills, for instance, the prairie is like a smoothly shaven lawn. On hundreds of square miles of it, we see not a tree, nor a bush as thick as a penholder. More than this, there is no rank grass, and the earth looks as if it were covered with a vast and all pervading sheet of cocoa matting. Upon it, a jack-rabbit looms up to enormous proportions—or would if there were one left to loom.

It is from this smoothly shaven and almost level world of brown-gray that the three peaks of the SweetGrass Hills rise suddenly and sharply out of the plain, without a vestige of intervening foot-hills. Rising as they do, they seem lofty, steep-sided, black and even uncanny. From certain points you see that they stand on a wide and almost level bench, like three mineral specimens on a thin pedestal. Notice particularly the bench that joins the western side of the most westerly peak. Miles and miles to the westward, it rises very abruptly, and with its top almost level, it runs up toward the peak without the slightest break in its upper line. These Hills are about forty miles from the railway, and for fully one hour the train glides along seemingly due south of them.

The Great Northern reaches the main range of the Rocky Mountains at Midvale, and the transition from plains to mountains is made quite abruptly. Here the Rockies are not in the least like those crossed by the Union Pacific—so modest and uneventful you scarce know where they begin or leave off. You can plant your foot on the very spot where these begin; and from that spot they tower up to the heights of your imagination of what real mountains should be. The foot of these mountains marks the eastern boundary of what now is the great Lewis and Clark Forest Reserve, embracing the whole main range of the Rockies from the international boundary southward, one hundred and thirty-five miles, to the lower end of the Flathead Reservation.

As you glide smoothly along the south fork of the Flathead River, you are aware of much dead timber, both standing and" down." Unless you are an old campaigner, however, the sight of those tracts of "down timber" does not strike any terror to your soul. But wait! One week hence, and you shall learn, by wrench of joint and sweat of brow, by ups and by downs, just how terrible fallen tree-trunks can become.

From our first entry into the Rocky Mountains, at the edge of the Sweet-Grass plains, until a month later when we left them at that point bound east, we were never out of the highlands. The ride through to Rexford is a beautiful panorama of mountain scenery and vegetation. Hour by hour Mr. Phillips devoured it with his eyes, missing not even one rock or tree, or one emerald green pool of the clear mountain stream far below.

Like a hair-pin on the map, the Kootenay River comes down from British Columbia into the north-western corner of Montana, bends westward for a short distance, then turns and runs north again—as if it had found Montana an inhospitable country. At the extreme eastern angle of the big bend is the backwoods hamlet of Rexford; and be it known that the section of the Great Northern from Columbus Falls to Spokane direct is no longer the "main line," but a branch. The main line runs up to Rexford, and thence down to Spokane.

At Rexford, we changed to the branch line of the Great Northern which runs up the east bank of the Kootenay, into British Columbia. At Gateway we had the pleasure of seeing the mythical International Boundary, and standing astride it. It lies across the railway platform, and is painted white. Near by, a bronze monument has been erected to its memory.

This branch brings us to the Canadian Pacific Railway at Fernie, the metropolis of the great soft-coal mining district known as the "Fernie district." It is in the extreme south-eastern corner of British Columbia.

At Fernie, Attorney H. W. Herchmer, president of the local Game Protective Association, gave us a royal welcome, and turned over to us the two non-resident hunting-licenses which he had procured at our request. The licenses cost us $50 each. They conveyed full warrant of law for the holder to kill five mountain goats (sex not mentioned), three mountain sheep rams, grizzly bear without number, six deer (sexes immaterial), and one bull moose. Elk are absolutely protected.

When on our way out, we stopped in Fernie over night, and President Herchmer called a special meeting of the Fernie District Game Protective Association, at his home. During this meeting we discussed the game law.

We objected to the goat item, on the ground that no man should be permitted to kill more than three goats in a year; and we held that females should not be killed at all. Any man who is unable to distinguish an adult male from a female should not be permitted to hunt goats. We objected to the limit of three mountain sheep rams, on the ground that in view of the scarcity of those animals, one ram in one year is enough for one man. "Six deer" should be changed to "three male deer," and unlimited grizzly bears to one only.

STATEMENT OF LICENSE LAW

Legal to kill in 1905:
5 Caribou (males only),
5 Goats,
3 Mountain Sheep Rams,
5 Deer,
2 Moose (males only),
Unlimited Grizzly Bears,
Unlimited Black Bears,
No elk.

As it should be:
3 male Caribou,
3 male Goats,
1 Sheep ram of each species,
3 Male Deer of each species,
1 Grizzly Bear,
2 Black Bears,
No Moose south of lat. 52° until 1910,
No elk on mainland until 1920.

The present law prohibiting the sale of game heads is admirable, but it needs more rigid enforcement than at this date (1905) prevails. So long as large sheep heads are worth from $25 to $50 each, unmounted, just so long will hunters and taxidermists take risks in selling them.

The big game of British Columbia is a public asset of very considerable value. If rightly protected and exploited, it can be made to yield to the southern districts many thousands of dollars annually—in the hire of guides and horses, the purchase of supplies, and in license fees. At the same time, by carefully protecting *all female animals*, the game can be maintained at a point which does not spell extinction. The Fernie District Game Protective Association was not organized a moment too soon. Its work is cut out for it, and it is to be hoped that it will retain a large membership, together with a large annual income, in order that it may have the power to protect. Game cannot be really protected without the expenditure of some money.

Possibly my American Reader may be tempted to think that all this is of little interest to him; but not so. The perpetual preservation of the grand game of the grand mountain-land just beyond our northern boundary is of interest to every American sportsman; and I hope this seeming digression will be endorsed.

Mr. Phillips and I have strongly recommended to the Fernie Association that immediate steps be taken by the provincial parliament to permanently set aside, as a game preserve, the country between the Bull and Elk Rivers, with Charles L. Smith in charge of it as warden. The reasons for such a step are too many to mention here, but let me say that there are practically no reasons against it. Whoever aids in preserving from extinction the grand game of British Columbia renders good service to two countries.

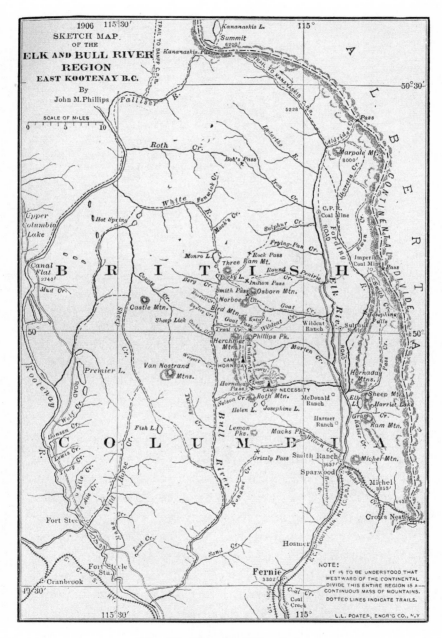

Map of the Elk and Bull River Region
EAST KOOTENAY, B.C.

CHAPTER II

IN THE VALLEY OF ELK RIVER

FERNIE AND MICHEL—MR. CRAHAN AND HIS HOTEL—RETURN
OF PROFESSOR H.F. OSBORN AND HIS FAMILY—THE MEMBERS OF
OUR OUTFIT—THE FIRST WILD ANIMAL—JACK PINE TIMBER—
SHEEP MOUNTAIN—"MY MOUNTAIN," FOR A MONTH—A MARTEN
TRAP—FOOL-HENS.

WE ARE CONSTITUTIONALLY OPPOSED TO long delays
in journeys to hunting-grounds, either on the rails or on paper;
but in the valley of Elk River we found so much of interest it
is impossible to ignore this gateway to our garden of the gods.

I have already said that a spur of the Great Northern
Railway reaches Fernie, the Phoenix City of the great soft-coal
mining district, which incendiaries seem determined to wipe
off the earth by fire, but which refuses to stay burned down. It
is on the Craw's Nest branch of the Canadian Pacific Railway,
which breaks through the main range of the Rockies at Craw's
Nest Pass about one hundred and twenty miles south of Banff
and the main line. At Fernie you feel that you have fully

arrived in British Columbia, for on all sides lofty mountains loom up and frown down in rock-ribbed majesty. One peak of commanding presence, north of the town, is about to be christened Owl's Head; but the name is not satisfactorily apt. The top of the peak looks much like a flying dragon, carved in stone, but little like an owl.

At Fernie any person (with money) can buy almost anything in the outfit line, from a trout-hook to an automobile. The hotels are excellent, and the men of our kind are courteous and hospitable. There are goats on the mountains within ten miles of the town, available for those who have no time to go farther.

We took an east-bound train, ran on north up the Elk River about fourteen miles, then left the Elk Valley and turned abruptly eastward. After four miles more, up Michel Creek, through a timbered valley as level as a dancing-floor and not much wider, we reached the town of Michel, our last stop by rail. Michel is a French name, and in conformity with the one invariable rule in French pronunciation—never pronounce a French word as it is spelled,—it is pronounced Me-shell'. The town is a mile and a quarter long by five hundred feet wide; and along the sides, no suburbs need apply, because there is no room for them. Immediately beyond the outermost houses the mountains rise up and up, steep as a house-roof, and very high. To-day the bare slideways that already lead down the northern slope give grim warning of what can happen hereafter. The town is strung along the bottom of a V-shaped trough in the mountains, and every spring we will dread to hear of its partial burial under a million tons of snow, ice, tree trunks and slide-rock. It reminds one of the fatalistic Italian peasant villages on the slopes of Vesuvius.

All Michel is painted Indian-red. The Crow's Nest Coal Company owns the whole place; red is a good, cheap, durable color, and what more would you have? The coal-mines are in both the northern and southern mountains, the veins are very thick, the coal is good, and the profits are said to be eminently satisfactory to the parties of the first part. The post-office is a freak, no more, no less. Not the slightest attention was paid to "In care of Charles L. Smith" on our letters; and to find the office open one must stalk the postmaster as if he were a mountain lion.

The Hotel Michel is a wonder. In a small mining town, in the heart of a wilderness, one does not expect much of a hotel; but here is every needful luxury, and from bottom to top everything is as clean as a new knife. The food is excellent, and the service away above par.

All this excellence is due to Mr. Thomas Crahan, an American, who is one of the most interesting men in that region. The story of how he tamed the bar-room when he assumed control of the hotel, and has since ruled it with a hand of steel in a velvet glove, is both interesting and instructive as a study in conglomerate human nature Twenty-four nationalities are represented in that little town, and the place is quiet and peaceful to the point of dullness.

Three weeks previous to our arrival, Professor Henry Fairfield Osborn, of New York, took his family up the valley of the Elk to the Sulphur Springs, for an outing under canvas, with plenty of fishing and photography. We found them all on the veranda of the hotel, happy and aglow with the spell of the mountains. They said it was the finest mountain trip they had ever had,—and they have had a-many.

They discovered and christened Josephine Falls, and caught eighteen-inch trout in Fording River until conscience called a halt. On the lofty clay bluffs of Fording River, quite near the Falls, Professor Osborn, with the aid of Charlie Smith, Mack Norboe and Dog Kaiser, cornered a pair of mountain

Michel, British Columbia, Looking West.

PHOTOGRAPH BY THOMAS CRAHAN

goats and photographed them! And after that the guides took the Professor up Goat Creek, and on the peak which we soon made haste to christen Mount Osborn, he photographed more goats. Mr. Phillips and I were among those present when the Professor first met Mrs. Osborn, his son and daughter on his return from the summits, and for the first time told them the story of his remarkable experience with his camera and the goats it caught. It created a profound sensation.

The only store in Michel is a department store, of astonishing size and scope. There we completed our outfit, down to the smallest detail. Mr. Phillips laid in a stock of provisions which fairly made me gasp at the luxuriance—and weight—of the array. I was prepared to fare briefly and to the point, because we were to travel by pack-train; but John believes in living well, and is what old-fashioned folk call "a good provider." For reasons of state, I laid in a special supply of salt, twine, allspice, pepper, oil, doctor's stuff and extra blankets, all of which played their respective parts in due season.

When finally we got into our hunting-clothes and hit the trail, our outfit was absolutely perfect. From my point of view, the supply of canned goods was too heavy; but later on I observed that we made away with nearly the whole of it.

The party consisted of Mr. Phillips and the writer, two guides, a scout, a cook, a dog and eight horses. The guides were Charles L. Smith of the Elk River valley, and R. W. Norboe, of Meyers Falls, Washington. John Norboe was the scout, and G. E. Huddleston was the cook. Kaiser was the official Dog— and a finer hunting-dog I never associated with. Before the hunt ended, I once slept with him in my arms (to keep him warm), and I think I earned his respect and friendship.

From New York to Michel the continent seemed utterly barren of mammalian life, except in the Sioux Reservation, where we saw a few gray-coated Franklin ground-squirrels

(*Citellus franklini*). We saw neither antelope, coyote, swift nor prairie-dog! On the Dakota lakes and ponds there were a few ducks, enjoying immunity until September; but the total number was small.

At Charles L. Smith's ranch, on Elk River, five miles below Michel, we at last saw a Wild Animal! A big pack-rat (*Neotoma*) of sociable habits, calmly climbed into the grub-wagon that was to go as far up as Sulphur Springs, and settled itself for a migration at our expense. The stowaway was discovered, and the alarm sounded. There between two of the boxes, its head in full view under the edge of the tarpaulin, was as droll a face as could be imagined. The big black eyes looked at us inquiringly, but calmly, and even fearlessly. They said: "Well, what's all this noise about? Why don't you drive on? You needn't be afraid of Me; I'm not afraid of You."

How different would have been the action of a domestic rat! One of those villains would have leaped about, and rushed through that load like a murine cyclone, to hide from its just deserts. If cornered it would squeal, and bite, and fight all humanity, and finally be killed in ghoulish glee. But the optimistic attitude of that gray-furred and comfortable rascal instantly disarmed all hostility. At once a cry went up, "Save him for the Zoo!"

Huddleston, the cook, put on his leather gloves, calmly plucked forth Neotoma from amid the boxes, and put him in a cage, to await our return. Around the ranches in the Elk River valley, these handsome and good-natured pack-rats were quite common. During the month we were in the mountains Mrs. Huddleston caught four more for me, alive and unhurt, but two escaped and two died.

I think these creatures could easily be tamed and trained to perform a variety of tricks. They are so steady of nerve, so conscious of their own rectitude, and yet so original and versatile in mind, it seems to me they must be capable of successful training. Who will be the wise party to introduce to the world the first and only Troupe of Trained Rocky Mountain *Neotomas*? When 'tis done, I predict an astonishing display of mental capacity.

On September 3d we "pulled our freight," literally, up the Elk Valley, in a lumber wagon, for one day's easy march of twenty-two miles. A mile above Charlie Smith's ranch a deer was seen bounding away toward the river. At Frank Harmer's ranch, four miles farther on, we found the fresh tracks of a bear, and it was with some difficulty that I checked a digression into the jack pines to look for their maker. To Mr. Phillips it seemed morally wrong to let that bear go unscotched.

Harmer's ranch is enclosed by a fence each panel of which was made of three big jack pine logs, a foot in diameter and about thirty feet long, neatly laid one above another, resting at each end on three logs of the same size about four feet long, laid squarely across the axis of the fence. Both in looks and utility it is a good fence, but rather heavy to build.

At Connor's ranch, fifteen miles from town, we bought a pailful of delicious butter, at thirty-three cents a pound, and continued our northward flight. We forded Elk River, over an awful bed of boulders that seemed certain to break a leg for each horse in the outfit. A mile or so beyond that crossing we forded Fording River and entered a long and beautiful stretch of jack pines, which revealed several interesting pages of natural history.

In British Columbia the jack pine is not merely a tree; it is an institution. (The Western Jack Pine, or Lodge-Pole Pine [*Pinus diviricata*]. Its average height in the good soil of the Elk River valley is very close to one hundred feet, but its diameter is very small. The spread of a one-hundred foot tree is only about eight feet.) At its best it is an arboreal column

Elk River

LOOKING NORTH, FROM A POINT NEAR CONNOR'S RANCH.

from ninety to one hundred and ten feet in height. Its stem is like a gigantic toothpick which rises as straight and flawless as a ship's mast, and gradually tapers up to infinity. The regularity of the taper of the trunk, and the straightness of it, are wonderful. For about fifty feet up the branches are apt to be dead, and gray, and broken; but above that the fine evergreen branches thrust out a little way, most carefully however, in order not to be guilty of provoking a growth outside of the true perpendicular.

Where a tract of timber has been thoroughly burned, in such valleys as that of the Elk, millions of young jack pines spring up. If ever you are tempted to make a short cut on foot through such a natural nursery, shun that lovely snare. Go around it rather than struggle through it. To forge directly through is a very troublesome and tiresome event. A jack pine forest through which fire has recently passed, killing everything, makes one think of an army of skeletons on parade. As the stems lose their hold upon mother earth, and under pressure of winds from all quarters, come sweeping down, they fall across each other, two, three or six deep, and create obstructions to travel of a most serious character. In British Columbia, "down timber" is an oft-recurring curse. Often it is a nuisance of the first magnitude. We saw much of down timber, before we were many days older, and upon one or two members of our little party it rang many changes.

When you have travelled up the Elk Valley about ten miles from the railway, to your right, across two miles of valley there rises a fine mountain mass five miles long and half a mile high. It is called Sheep Mountain, because of the notable rams of *Ovis canadensis* which Mr. Phillips and his boon companions, Smith, Norboe and Jack Lewis, have killed and eaten upon its rock-ribbed sides. John never will forget his first ram, an inexperienced young creature, chased and shot on the central summit, late in October, with the wind blowing cold and strong, when he and Jack Lewis were benighted on the rocky top, without blankets or food. Later on he told me the whole story.

At mid-day we halted for luncheon opposite a mountain which rises directly north of Sheep Mountain, and separated from it only by the narrow rift through which Pass Creek flows westward into the Elk. It is about four miles long, its height is about the same as Sheep Mountain, and by reason of its isolation it is clear-cut and monumental. I asked its name, and the men all admitted, with apologies, that it had none. Then Mr. Phillips announced, with convincing emphasis, that it should be named in my honor; and it was so set down.

This was a very complimentary proposition, but on the official maps of British Columbia, the motion will hardly prevail. The local authorities will not tamely submit to the naming of so fine a mountain after a mythical eastern "tourist." Nevertheless, for the brief month that we were in those wilds, that mountain was always spoken of in our party as my mountain, and I have at least known-for thirty days-how it feels to have a tall namesake of Nature's fashioning for my very own.

Mile after mile, the wagon-trail led us along an evergreen tunnel through a dense forest of jack pines, and on the way through we saw many interesting things. One of the first was two small saplings from which the bark had recently been stripped clean by an elk who wished to rub the velvet off his new antlers. And close beside the two white stems was a third sapling, the size of a walking-stick, which not only had been peeled but also bitten in two about four feet from the ground. It was good to see such fresh proofs of the fact that elk still survive in the valley of the Elk.

The next object of special interest was a marten trap, close beside the trail. It was such as any good axeman can make in about two hours, with an axe and a sapling. It was a very neat piece of work. A spruce sapling about ten inches in diameter was cut off four feet above the ground, so squarely that the top of the stump was practically level. From somewhere or other, three very thin pieces of spruce, like shingles seven inches wide, were split off and driven into three cracks split in the top of the stump, cornering together to form a tight box, open on top and one side. Then a ten-foot length was cut out of the sapling stem, one end placed on the ground, and the other rested in the box with one side out. This was a deadfall. With two sticks a very simple trigger was made, the log was raised, the triggers fixed to hold it up, and a bait adjusted on the end of the long arm of the trigger. The upper end of the log was raised six inches above the edge of the stump. Result: The wandering marten smells the bait. He cannot reach it from above, so he climbs nimbly up the side of the stump, crawls under the deadfall and into the shingle-box, seizes the bait with a greedy growl of exultation, and crash I the log comes down upon his devoted back, at $10 per crash.

There are many advantages about this axe-made marten trap. A wolverine cannot steal it and throw it into the nearest river; it is never stolen by the Bad Man of the Fernie District; it never rusts, it is cheap, and there is no need to "order it from the factory." The only drawback about it is that martens do not always range in timber suitable for deadfall traps.

As we rode ahead of the wagon, Mr. Phillips on "Lady-Bug," Charlie on "Muggins," and I on old "Warrior," Dog Kaiser side-stepped into the jungle and gave tongue. In a deep, rich voice he cried "Oh! Woo! Woo! Woo!" with his nose pointed upward into a low jack pine.

"Fool-Hens," said Charlie, dismounting. About ten feet above Kaiser's nose sat a fine, full-plumaged male Franklin grouse, with a superbly black breast and neck, but no mental

Hornaday Mountain
LOOKING NORTHEAST ACROSS ELK RIVER.

capacity. To all appearances it was a bird of only two ideas: (1) to forage on the ground until disturbed, and (2) when disturbed to fly only ten feet into the nearest tree and wait to be shot. Naturally, a bird with only two ideas is not long for this world. Five birds rose before the dog and perched in five nearby jack pines and spruces. I sat down within ten feet of a particularly intelligent-looking bird, while the others went off, and killed birds for supper. I wished to see how the noise and bustle would affect my bird's nerves.

Using his .22-calibre pistol in a most business-like way Mr. Phillips proceeded to "pop" down the more distant birds, in rotation. At each shot I expected that my bird would either protest, or take wing; but it did neither. It calmly sat there, sodden in stupidity; it looked about in wonder, and waited until the hunters came up, all ready to add it to the bag. But some one interposed with a suggestion that the bag was already large enough, which was readily accepted. At last the bird was fairly driven to flight. With a loud whir of wings it disappeared in the forest, and I presume it is yet in that jungle, breeding fool-hens still more foolish than itself.

With this strange bird, the pendulum seems to have swung the wrong way, and it will hardly survive through a sufficient number of generations to acquire the doctrine of self-preservation. It is a phenomenon. Charlie Smith tells this story of our genial friend, Mr. G.N. Monro, of Pittsburg, who has hunted in this region:

Two years ago a party very much like ours was passing through that same jack pine jungle. Mr. Monro and Mack Norboe were ahead, and as usual, some fool-hens were scared up. One alighted in a tree near the tenderfoot, who very naturally became fired with a desire to possess it.

"Stop, Mack, stop!" said Mr. Monro. "Get my shot-gun out of the wagon, quickly."

"What d'ye want it for?" asked Mack in his sepulchral voice.

"To shoot this grouse! Look there I don't you see it?"

"Yes, I see it. Do you really *want* that bird?"

"*Want* it? Of course I want it! Get my gun, quick, before it flies."

"Oh, well, if you want it, I'll get it for you," said Mack. Dismounting, he picked up a small club, threw it at the bird, at very short range, and hit the mark. The bird fell dead; whereupon Mack calmly picked it up, and handed it up to Mr. Monro, saying indifferently, "Here it is."

"And," said Charlie, "you ought to have seen the disgusted look on Mr. Monro's face as he looked at Mack, and took that bird!"

I skinned the finest male grouse of the bunch that Mr. Phillips shot. It was seventeen inches in total length, tip of beak to end of tail, with a wing-spread of twenty-four and one-half inches. Its crop contained a dessert-spoonful of blueberries, eight blueberry leaves and six needles of the jack pine. The species could not be called plentiful in the region we traversed. From first to last we saw about thirty birds, always in green timber.

About two hours before sunset we came to a level meadow of a hundred acres, heavily set in rank grass, and lying very low. Two hay-stacks towered aloft to a height of about seven feet, and from them it was evident that we were on the "ranch "of Wild-Cat Charlie, at the Sulphur Spring. We pulled up the steep ridge that bounded the meadow on the west, and went into camp on its summit. Elk River flows by the western foot of the ridge, and across the meadow, half a mile eastward, is the already famous Sulphur Spring.

If you don't know about the Spring, and sleep on the ridge with a strange man in your tent, and the wind blowing from the east, you will be horrified by the discovery (as Charlie Smith once was) that the stranger is far on the way toward decomposition.

On our day's journey up, we saw twenty bluebirds, a pigeon-hawk (*Falco columbarius*) and a golden eagle.

CHAPTER III

A GOLDEN DAY ON FORDING RIVER

A BATH IN THE SULPHUR SPRING—A RIDE TO FORDING RIVER—
CUT-THROAT TROUT GALORE—JOSEPHINE FALLS—EVENING
OVER THE ELK VALLEY.

READER, DID YOU EVER HAVE a day of ideal trout-fishing, in a rushing mountain stream? I hope you have, for if so it leaves that much less to desire. It is good to have one fling at a fine thing, even though the day and the hour never return.

In Elk River, below the Sulphur Spring there is no extra-fine fishing, for the reason that the accessibility of the stream has caused the biggest fish to disappear via the short line. So Charlie Smith planned that we should make a trip for trout over to Fording River, partly, as he phrased it, "to break the director in gradually, before we get into the high mountains." In New York I hunted long for rubber-bodied may-flies, and I carried a rod and reel twenty-five hundred miles for one day on Fording River; but that day was worth it!

When we made camp on the ridge, the wind was easterly, and there poured across that meadow, and up over the ridge, a wave of sulphuretted hydrogen that plainly told us we had arrived at the Sulphur Spring.

Forthwith Mr. Phillips bade me prepare to bathe, and follow him. To bathe in that awful hole was the regular thing to do; so we sadly tramped across the meadow to the foot of the mountain-ridge that rises from its eastern side; and there we found the Spring.

At the edge of the grass lay a pale-green pool, eighty feet long, forty feet wide, and in the deepest place about twelve feet deep. The water was very clear, except where a metallic scum floated upon the surface, and the bottom looked like corroded copper. For a bath it was the most uncanny-looking proposition I ever encountered; and I have bathed with alligators, gavials and sharks, more than once. The bottom looked most unsatisfactory; but being unable to make or to mend it, we disrobed—very slowly and reluctantly it seemed to me,—and prepared to take our medicine.

It was necessary to cross one end of the pool, on two villainous saplings which tried hard to throw us down; and the sharp stones on the hinterland cut our bare feet most exquisitely. John bravely led the way into the horrid hole, and when I followed, the warmth of the water proved unexpectedly grateful and comforting. The temperature was about 72 degrees, except where the water streamed up out of the ground, and there it must have been about 90 degrees. In a few minutes we became hardened to the powerful yellow fumes which lay like a blanket on the surface of the pool, and then the bath became really enjoyable—all but the bottom. The slime in which we stood, whenever we ceased to swim, was neither nice nor tidy, and so we swam as much as possible. In the centre of the pool, where the water was dark, and one could not see the bottom, I tried to measure its depth, but found it far over my head.

Already this spring is locally famous for its healing properties as applied to rheumatism. Close beside the pool, on the ridge side, stood a little seven-by-nine log cabin with a yawning fireplace at the farther end. Along the north side of the cabin extended a seven-foot trough, dug out of a big spruce log, with a cavity large enough to contain a man. This was the outfit of an old trapper who had been afflicted with rheumatism, and spent a winter here, treating himself with commendable diligence and hot sulphur water. When it was too cold to bathe in the pool he filled his log bath-tub with sulphur-water, heated it with hot stones from his fire, then got in and loafed and invited his soul at 90 degrees or more. A hundred feet farther south stood another and a better cabin in which my guide, philosopher and friend, Charlie Smith, lived for three months last spring while he cured his rheumatism—at least temporarily.

Some day in the near future, this spot will be ruined forever by the erection on the ridge of a modern Hot Springs Hotel, with electric lights, telephones, lobster salad and starched linen. Therefore I am glad that we have gambolled in the Sulphur Spring in all its primitive rawness, and that Mr. Phillips shot a coyote from the edge of it immediately after our bath. Our men came out from camp to carry in a deer, and had the disappointment been caused by any one else than the patron saint of Elk River, uncanny things might have been said.

Charlie Smith and Mack Norboe assured me that when the wind is easterly, the odor of the Sulphur Spring can plainly be detected at the top of the mountain on the western side of Elk River, fully three miles away.

From our camp in the Elk Valley, Fording River lies eastward, beyond a mountain and miles away. Mr. Phillips and Mack Norboe set out to walk to the fishing place, in order to hunt on the way, for mule deer. We were to meet at noon at

Josephine Falls. Charlie and I rode, in order to have horses on which to carry home the fish.

We entered the meadow, and rode north the entire length of it, to where it terminates in a beautiful park like tract of scattered spruces and pines. Then we climbed the easterly ridge, up through an open growth of more pines and spruces, birch and quaking asp, up and up, for at least a thousand feet. After a long ride on the ridge side and over its northern crest, we entered an awful tangle of fallen timber and brush. We wound to and fro, up and down, to find a practicable route for the horses. That the faithful animals did not break their legs was a source of wonderment, and their skill in getting over tree-trunks without accident was really remarkable.

At last we reached the edge of the plateau we had painfully crossed, and saw below us a deep and narrow valley, with a very steep pitch downward. On its farther side were shaly perpendicular bluffs, rising high. Fortunately the ground was soft, and we were able to ride down with little difficulty. The descent seemed endless, but we zigzagged lower and lower until at last we reached the bushes and cobble-stones which indicated the bottom of the valley.

At its widest, the valley was only about seventy-five feet wide, and about half of it was occupied by the swiftly racing stream. Three hundred yards above our landing place, a cataract, about thirty feet high by fifty feet wide, poured a torrent of foam down a series of ragged steps worn in the edge of a thick bed of decomposing shale. The incline was about 60 degrees, and the volume of water churned itself into froth the moment it made its first plunge. On the south side of the falls the shale steps offer a very good footway to the top.

This picturesque waterfall was discovered by Professor Henry F. Osborn and his family, only three weeks previous to our visit, and named in honor of Miss Josephine Osborn,

Trout Fishing at Josephine Falls

a sweet maid in her teens, who caught the largest trout thus far recorded from that spot. During the two days' stay of the Osborn family in that romantic spot, they had the novel pleasure of feeding bread from their luncheon to a small flock of harlequin ducks that were disporting in the pool at the foot of the falls.

There are two other falls a short distance above Josephine Falls, but we did not take time to visit them.

But the fishing! Do not think, patient Reader, that we lost any time after our arrival in looking at scenery of any kind. It seemed to me, however, that many precious moments were wasted in getting out our fly-books and reels, and in putting things together.

"Try a cast in there," said Charlie, indicating a section of the stream where the swift current was all crowded together at the farther side, and went rushing against the rock wall at the rate of ten miles an hour.

I threw my fly upon the racing water, and let it ride downstream, bobbing up and down on the waves. The first cast went for nothing, but in the next, the fly had not ridden more than half-way down when there was a golden-yellow flash across the current, a rush, and a greedy pull on the line.

"There! You've got one already!" cried Charlie.

"Be careful, and don't let your line slacken!"

The first trout! It was a thrilling moment. My blood seemed to be suddenly set back about twenty years. With every new tug on the end of the rod my fingers tingled as if I held the poles of an electric battery. It was a new thing to hook a big fish and *see* it, every instant.

I was too anxious to land my first fish for any indulgence in exhibition play. The trout rushed in many directions, mostly upstream on the bias, or across, for I gave him no chance to run down. As he turned half over in rushing away from my side of the stream, the sun caught his golden side and lit it up gloriously. How fine he did look!

With as little delay as possible I reeled him in and swung him shoreward until Charlie was able to reach out, and land him fairly upon the clean cobblestones. He was a Cut-Throat Trout (*Salmo clarkii*) better named Black-Spotted Trout, but by people of this region known as "Dolly-Varden" Trout. The upper half of the body is of a pale golden-yellow color, dotted all over from upper lip to tail tip with small elliptical black spots that stand vertically. The lower half of the body is suffused with a warm sunset glow of pinkish color, while the under surface is silvery white. The lower edge of each membrane covering the gills, under the head, looks as if a painter had given each side a stroke with a paintbrush charged with rose-madder, making a red V; and from this "effect," suggesting a cut throat, has come the gruesome English name by which this fish is known to the great majority of its acquaintances. The real Dolly Varden Trout is a char (*Salvelinus parkei*), closely related to the spotted brook-trout, with a much more pointed head, light spots instead of dark, and only one fourth as many of them as the Cut-Throat. Both species, however, inhabit the mountain-streams of the Pacific slope from California and Montana to Alaska.

But all this while we lost no time in moralizing over the exact scientific status and affinities of our first fish. From start to finish it was a wild revel. I soon became so set up with four or five big fish that I refused to engage any small fry. Whenever I saw a small fish dart toward my fly, I snatched it away from him, and angled for his betters. Whenever by any untoward accident a one-pound fish took the hook in spite of me, we landed him without loss of time, took the hook from his lip, and with an admonition never to do so any more until he got big, gently dropped him back home.

The Cut-Throat Trout is, after all, a dainty biter. Although he takes an imitation may-fly swiftly, and even joyously, he does not greedily gulp it far down into his anatomy, and make all kinds of trouble. He seizes with his lips only, not his throat; and almost invariably the hook is found holding feebly in his lip. This scanty hold requires much care in playing the fish, and a line constantly taut, to keep the hook in its place. With the least carelessness, away goes the fish. It also makes it easy to remove a fish that is too small, and put it back in the stream as good as new. One fly lasts a long time, and is good for at least three or four fish of approved size.

While the fun was at its height, and we had five fine fish to the good, Mr. Phillips and Mack Norboe joined us, ready and eager for the fray. John quickly developed his rod, reeved the line home and bent on a fly. With the first cast, above my fishing-place, he hooked and landed a fine fish, and in less than three minutes had landed four more!

Then he paused, turned to his admiring audience with a guilty laugh, and exclaimed, "This is nothing but slaughter!"

Truly it was. The fish struck as fast as he could throw in his line and haul them out. We both paused to consider, for every man in our party believed in the policy of stopping at "enough." We had ten fish, and our limit was forthwith fixed at fifteen for the two days that six men would be trying to consume them.

We scrambled along the rocks up to Josephine Falls, and I determined to have a try in the boiling caldron at the foot of the cataract, to see if trout could see to take a fly in such white water. It was no trouble to get a good position on the shale steps close beside the foot of the torrent, where the facilities for fly-casting were of the best.

I threw into the caldron, many times, reaching every yard of its surface, but got only one really good fish. Then

The Pack-Train Leaving Sulphur Spring Camp

Mr. Phillips yelled to Charlie, and above the roar of the falls, Charlie passed it on to me.

"He wants to take you taking out the fish! Hold on a minute!"

"Tell him to hurry!"

The trout fought gamely, and never gave up for an instant. John worked with his camera, and I with the fish, to hold my game for the desired moment—but all the time fearing that it would get away. At last the expected happened. My line suddenly slackened, and communicated to my nerve-centres the sickening sensation that when written out spells "lost!"

A little later I hooked another and a smaller fish, and John fired when he was ready; but the result is not good to look upon. The fewer snap-shots that are made of a one-hundred-and-eighty-pound man, dressed décolleté who is really fishing or hunting, the better; for they are apt to be the reverse of picturesque, and seldom show the victim to any advantage.

For the Cut-Throat Trout the pool at the foot of Josephine Falls is the head of navigation. Charlie Smith says there are no trout above. I saw individuals trying to leap up the falls, but they did not rise more than four or five feet out of the water. It would take an Atlantic salmon eight feet long, with horse-power to match his size, to overleap that fall.

At one o'clock we camped on the bank, amid clean rocks and bushes, with an abundance of drinking-water close by, and ate our luncheon. Some one suggested broiling a couple of trout; and for appearance's sake I would like to record the fact that we did so. It would have been the regular thing to do; but I must tell the truth. The fact is, we were all too much overcome with the languor of lotus-eaters to do more than think about it. In other words, we were too lazy to clean the fish, and broil them properly. There was plenty of luncheon, the sunshine was gloriously inviting, the river was like a dream, its roar was soothing music—and what more would you have!

After a quiet hour, we sprang up, eager for the remainder of our quota of fish. We tried the stream for "big ones," but from the falls down to the first still water we got not a single rise. The strife between us was not merely to catch fish, and land them, but to catch the biggest ones, only, and avoid hooking the small fry. We became quite expert in snatching our flies away from fish that were too small.

Up to the fourteenth fish, Mr. Phillips was ahead of me on size; but No. 15 came to my fly, and finally was landed in triumph. It measured eighteen inches, beating John's largest by a whole eighth of an inch. Later on, however, I remembered that he did the measuring, and I will always have grave doubts about the actual existence of that eighth. I fear the steel tape slipped in my favor. At all events, that fish weighed two pounds four ounces; and we all joyously guessed far above its weight.

It is needless to say that the flesh of the Cut-Throat Trout, as we found it, is hard, juicy, and delicious. How could it be otherwise? It is a pity, however, that this fish is so easily taken, for gullibility in game always spells early disappearance. It would be better all around if the fish were more shy and persistent, for few men have the iron resolution to halt at the fifteenth or twentieth fish, and take the long trail back.

In returning, there was no such thing as riding our horses up the terrific hill which led to the plateau. We scrambled up on foot, rest by rest, and were fairly glad to reach the top. Only an iron horse could carry a man or woman up that slope.

As we rode home, the view over the valley of the Elk, and into the lofty mountains beyond, was fairly entrancing. The level valley,—it seemed level, from that lofty height,—was laid out in patterns of dense green timber, gray dead timber, and yellow-green meadow, with a silver serpent of river winding gracefully to and fro. Beyond all this a great bank of mountains loomed darkly into the evening sky. A smoky haze, which softened the outlines of both valley and mountain, was pierced at one point by a column of smoke from burning timber. Even while we looked with great enjoyment upon this fascinating and restful picture, we saw under the smoke the bright gleam of fire; and a moment later, a one-hundred foot spruce-tree suddenly became enveloped in flames. The blaze quickly climbed to the top of the leafy spire, burned brightly for a minute,—a veritable pillar of fire,—then died down and glowed dully against the dark shadows that lay beyond.

CHAPTER IV

TRAVEL IN THE MOUNTAINS

"HOUSE-ROOF MOUNTAINS"—MAKING UP PACKS—WHEN
CHARLIE THREW DOWN HIS PACK—VALLEY THOROUGHFARES—
GREEN TIMBER—DOWN TIMBER—TRAIL-CUTTING—BERRIES OF
THE MOUNTAINS.

IN THE MATTER OF MOUNTAIN TRAVEL, be it remembered that there are mountains and mountains. In some of them, valleys of comfortable width and openness are a kind of habit. Others have a bad way of bringing you up against the rocky nose of an overhanging cliff, and taking toll from your nerves or your muscles before your pack-train is safely by. In some, you are eternally fighting with timber, brush, and decaying moss-covered forest *debris*. By reason of its hot-house atmosphere and rains, I believe the mountains of Borneo are to the climber the most exhausting of all on earth.

Some mountains seem morally upright and fair, while others, despite their heights, are actually mean. Some give the hunter a fair reward for much hard labor, but others tantalize him into wearing out his soul for naught. Think of seeing twenty-one bears in twenty days, without being able to get a shot at one! (This by reason of snow-bent willows on the slides.) It is not all of hunting to kill game; and why should one hunt in mean mountains, monotonous forests or water-soaked plains!

In our little corner of British Columbia, the heights are of the kind which may best be described as houseroof mountains. They are cleanly cut, they rise very steeply and have very narrow valleys. Often they terminate at the top in sharp knife-edges, and fairly bristle with peaks and precipices. In them, travel by pack-train means creeping up or down the narrow valleys until a crossable divide is found. Travel on foot, especially in hunting, always means hard climbing, either up or down. In hunting, you climb up a long and steep acclivity, hoping for a restful table-land at .the top, only to find the summit a chisel's edge terminating at either end against a sheer precipice. Usually the other side of every ridge is worse than the first, dropping down into a great basin, so fast and so far that you halt dismayed at the thought of going down to the bottom, and climbing back again before nightfall. With the Columbian Rockies, familiarity breeds anything but contempt.

All the valleys that we saw in the mountains between the Elk and the Bull were very narrow, and difficult to traverse. Take a small postal card, bend it along the middle into a right angle, and you will have, if you set it up on the apex of the angle, a very fair representation in miniature of the mountain-slopes in the goat mountains, and the width of the valleys between them. There are many places where the valleys between high mountains are not over fifty feet wide at the bottom, and above that you work hard for every foot that you win.

In nine miles out of every ten, the mountain-sides are so steep, or so badly enmeshed in down timber, that horses cannot travel along them without exhausting labor. It is therefore a fixed line of action that whenever a laden pack-train is seeking to cover distance it must stick to the bottoms of the valleys; and when it climbs a steep ascent, it is either to surmount a pass, or to avoid an obstruction.

The ascent of Goat Creek to its source may well be taken as an example of travel by pack-train in the mountains of British Columbia.

For farm wagons, the Sulphur Spring is at present the head of navigation, and on the morning after our day on Fording River our pack-train was regularly made up. In rugged mountains, the proper making up of the load for each horse is a matter which no packer can make light of. Charlie, Mack and John spent a long hour in overhauling our freight, weighing sections of it on my game-scales, and parcelling out the loads. They accepted "air-tights" nailed up in their original packages, with a cheerfulness that spoke volumes for their experience. I never before saw such an array of heavy wooden boxes put upon six horses with such supreme indifference. And I never before saw six packs made up and cinched with so little fuss. The work the horses did during the next four weeks in carrying those packs was really very severe, and to the credit of "the boys" I must record the fact that not once did a load cause trouble; not a single breakable object was broken; and above all, no horse was punished by a sore back.

The foundation principle in making up packs is to class things according to their genera and species, and make each load as homogeneous as possible. For instance, they did not load a horse with a bed-roll on one side and canned goods on the other. Dead weight on one side calls for similar weight on the other, and bulk demands bulk. The diamond hitch with its cutting ropes was not employed, every load being provided with broad girths made especially for packs. In making up a packtrain, Charlie Smith is a pack master, but the Norboes also are very skillful at it.

Just above our Sulphur Spring Camp, we passed the cabin of a lame and solitary but cheerful German rancher named Wild-Cat Charlie. When we passed his establishment, he was absent, making hay; and on his cabin door hung a large padlock.

"Well," I said, "this is the first lock I have ever seen on a ranchman's door in the wild West."

"Oh, pshaw! That's all bluff," Charlie Smith hastened to say. "He locks his door, because he is proud of having the only padlock in the Valley; but he tells everybody where he keeps the key. There it is,—on that nail."

It is known that Wild-Cat Charlie is no great reader, and is wellnigh destitute of books and papers. Our men are constantly wondering what he thinks about,—or whether he thinks at all,—during the fearfully long winter evenings, as he sits by his fire and smokes. Although somewhat cranky, he is very hospitable, and many a half-frozen trapper has had occasion to bless the welcoming hand and warm fireside to be found at "Wild-Cat Charlie's."

And this reminds me of the story our Charlie and Mack told me, jointly, of their forced march in the dead of winter, from Bull River, thirty miles over two ranges of mountains, and down Goat Creek through deep snow, all in one day.

"That," said Charlie, "was the only time I ever threw down my pack; but I surely threw it down that night, and only two miles from the Dutchman's cabin. For the last two hours of that tramp I walked just like a wooden machine. I was all the time *afraid I would fall down*; for I knew that as sure as I did, I couldn't get up! Cold? It was forty below zero, and we hadn't had any too much to eat, either. At last I did throw away my pack, and when we finally got to Charlie's cabin, I was the worst played-out I ever was in my whole life. I couldn't have gone another mile, not to have saved my own life."

Fording Elk River
THE TREES ON THE BANK ARE JACK PINES. ONE SPRUCE ON THE EXTREME RIGHT.

For about three miles from Wild-Cat Charlie's cabin, along the west bank of the Elk, we jogged on northward at a rapid. Pace. At last we reached the mouth of a creek that came brawling down from the goat country. It was Goat Creek; and turning into its narrow valley, die climb to the summits began.

In that country it is no uncommon thing for a mountain stream to drop at the rate of three hundred feet to the mile. Often the descent is even more than that. As a rule, you do not realize how much you are climbing until you reach the source of the trouble and start down. You climb up slowly, with constant meanderings, and cannot gauge the elevation gained; but in coming down, with your seven-league boots on, you can better judge of the situation as a whole. Near the end of the trip I was part of a striking illustration of this strange fact.

Our first half-day's travel up that steep mountain groove was spent chiefly on the northern slope. There were long stretches of "green timber,"—which means living coniferous timber, green all the year round. In it the ground was covered with a velvet carpet of brown needles, and ornamented with a setting of thimbleberry bushes bearing bright crimson berries. There were thousands of slender, open-topped currant bushes bearing scattered clusters of jet-black currants, bitter to the taste but good to allay mouth-dryness and thirst. The trees are mostly the Canadian white spruce (*Picea Engelmanni*) and the jack pine, with a sprinkling of balsam, juniper, quaking asp and larch. Throughout that whole region the deciduous trees are so few that they are very inconspicuous, and those which do exist are mostly mere bushes.

In the green timber the soft ground is very restful to feet that are dead tired from the ankle-strain of rugged slide-rock. The aroma of the coniferous foliage is both grateful and comforting, but the best hunting-grounds for large game animals are found elsewhere. No wonder that in past years the Indians occasionally set fire to the forests, and burned out great areas in order to let in the sunlight, grow grass and create good feeding-grounds,—and also hunting-grounds,— for hoofed animals.

But the beautiful and all-embracing "green timber" has its habitants. Its resinous shadows envelop and shelter the agile lynx, the sinister wolverine, the too-confiding marten, the prosy porcupine, the busy red squirrel, and an occasional wolf. The grizzly and the black bear are transient guests, but in times of real trouble, no wild creatures value green timber more than they. The elk and deer also find it a welcome retreat.

One of the most impressive features of those mountains is the sharpness with which everything is delineated. The different elements which make up the face of Nature are not always softly and artistically blended together, as a skillful artist blends the color boundaries on his canvas. Each patch of green timber is as sharply defined at its edges as the grounds of a county fair. In one step you leave the glaring sunlight, and are swallowed up by the dark, restful shadows, just as when one steps from the glare and stress of a stone pavement into the soothing shadows of a cloister. By one step you make your exit, and land full upon the angular agonies of slide-rock, or into the horizontal terrors of "down timber." For a mile or more a creek will go brawling noisily over its bed of stones, and all at once drop entirely out of sight, under a great mass of slide-rock. Down the steep mountain-side, the track of each avalanche is cut as clean as the swath of a mower going through tall grass, Even timber-line itself is not half so long drawn out as one usually sees in other mountains. There is no difficulty in drawing a contour line to mark it out on your sketch.

Throughout our mountains, there was no such thing as travelling by pack-tram without a cut-out trail. The down timber positively forbade it; and even in the evergreen tracts there were so many fallen trees that it was impossible to get on without the axe. Had we at any time lost both our axes, our horses would have been compelled to turn back and retrace their steps.

A loaded pack-horse can step over any log that is not more than twenty-six inches from the ground, but before one exceeding that height, something else must be done. If it is a small log, the trail-cutter chops a three-foot section out of it, or cuts it in two in order that the top section may fall down. If it is a large trunk, the trail must go around it. A good mountain-horse can get over any log that he can step over with his fore-legs, for with his forelegs well placed, he can successfully jump his hindlegs over.

In bad down timber, like that of lower Avalanche Creek, a trail takes a course about like this, beside which chain light-ning is ruler-straight:

If anything will teach a man patience, a bad case of down timber will do so. There is no use in fretting over it; and swear-ing at it is the height of folly. The secret of such navigation lies in a calm determination to give the horse plenty of time, and "stay with it." To hurry your horses is to invite broken legs,—a thought which will promptly cool down the wildest impatience.

Naturally, the laying out of a trail calls for a quick eye and good judgment in choosing the route which demands the least chopping, and that does not tack too often nor too far. As the axe-man proceeds, he must mark the course between log-cuttings by lopping off a bush, or scalping the top of a log with a single sweep of his axe as he walks along, leaving a spot of clean, bright wood.

The Valley of Goat Creek

THE LIGHT STREAKS COMING DOWN FROM THE LEFT ARE SNOW-SLIDES. OUR GUIDES WERE ONCE DETAINED HERE THREE DAYS BECAUSE THEY DARED

NOT ATTEMPT TO PASS THOSE SLIDES.

Where conditions are not too severe, men like our four can chop out a trail with astonishing rapidity; but occasionally they encounter long stretches of down timber that simply "break their hearts." In such places as lower Avalanche Creek, there is nothing to do but to camp and chop.

In several creeks that we opened up to our packtrain, we found old Indian trails, some of which helped us very much. The first sign of such a trail is a large bush or a small sapling that has been cut down by many feeble blows.

"Squaw hatchet!" or "Squaw work!" our guides often exclaimed, pointing to a stem that had been unskillfully hacked down. A white man, with a sharp axe, cuts down with one or two clean blows a sapling that a squaw assaults a dozen times with her dull hatchet before it falls.

A long stretch of slide-rock is always a hard road for a pack-train, unless a good trail has already been made across it. I will have more to say of slide-rock farther on, but in entering the mountains we encountered it, soon and plenty. I know of but one species of rock travel that is worse for a horse, and that is the slippery, rounded boulders, big and little, that so often underlie the fording-places of mountain rivers. They seem specially designed to break horses' legs, and the only way to cheat them of their prey is by permitting the horse to creep along, feeling cautiously for each stepping-place.

On slide-rock, the rocks are horribly angular, sharp-edged and cruel, and occasionally an unshod horse leaves a trail of blood behind him. But the train moves straight forward, even though its progress is slow; and fortunately one does not strike miles and miles of continuous slide-rock.

In travelling by pack-train through rough country, much time is lost by deploying to pass obstructions. On Goat Creek we sometimes climbed from two hundred to four hundred feet up the steep mountain in order to pass above a sheer bluff, and immediately after would lose all our altitude by being forced to drop back to the bottom of the valley. When thoroughly tired, such diversions, in climbing up only to climb down again, seem a sinful waste of horse-power.

Beyond the first half-day's travel up Goat Creek, there was no trail, and Charlie and the Norboes had to cut one the remainder of the way to the summit. Mr. Phillips and I elected to go ahead of the outfit, hunting on foot, and reach the camping-place on Goat Pass about the same time as the others.

At the point where we were to leave Smith and his axe, we halted to rest, and as we looked about for places to sit down, Charlie exclaimed, "Here are some red raspberries, all ripe and ready for ye!"

It was indeed true. Over a space as large as a New York City lot, there grew a scattering cover of bushes a foot high, bearing red raspberries, fully ripe, and delicious. We flung ourselves upon them, and feasted. I like to hunt in a country that contains something in the form of fruit, nuts or berries that a hungry man can eat. In the tropics it is seldom indeed that one finds in a forest any of these wilderness luxuries. The traveller who cannot live by his gun or rod must carry his food with him, or starve. Beside the poverty-stricken tropical forests, the forests of the temperate zone are rich in things edible to man. Now when Charlie and I went on that side hunt and discovered Josephine Lake, we found a whole mountain-side covered with delicious huckleberries, of three species, upon which we gratefully fed. Had there been a grizzly bear "among those present," he would have stood aghast at the havoc we wrought.

CHAPTER V

THE MOUNTAIN GOAT AT HOME

OUR WELCOME TO GOATLAND—THREE GOATS STAMPEDE
THROUGH OUR CAMP—A WILD SPOT—MOUNTAIN COLOR ON
A GRAY DAY—AN EARLY MORNING CALLER—GOATS AT REST—
HOW GOATS CLIMB—STALKING TWO BIG BILLIES—TWO GOATS
KILLED—MEASUREMENTS AND WEIGHT.

JOHN PHILLIPS AND I WERE scrambling along the steep
and rough eastern face of Bald Mountain, a few yards below
timber-line, half-way up 'twixt creek and summit. He was light
of weight, well-seasoned and nimble-footed; I was heavy, ill-
conditioned, and hungry for more air. Between the slide-rock,
down timber and brush, the going had been undeniably bad,
and in spite of numerous rests I was almost fagged.

Far below us, at the bottom of the V-shaped valley, the
horse-bell faintly tinkled, and as Mack and Charlie whacked
out the trail, the pack-train crept forward. We were thankful
that the camping-place, on Goat Pass, was only a mile beyond.

Presently we heard a voice faintly shouting to us
from below.

"Look above you,—at the goats!"

Hastily we moved out of a brush-patch, and looked aloft. At the top of the precipice that rose above our slope, a long, irregular line of living forms perched absurdly on the sky-line, and looked over the edge, at us. Quickly we brought our glasses to bear, and counted fourteen living and wild Rocky Mountain goats.

"All nannies, young billies, and kids," said Mr. Phillips. "They are trying to guess what kind of wild animals we are." I noticed that he was quite calm; but I felt various things which seemed to sum themselves up in the formula,—"the Rocky Mountain goat,—*at last!*"

For fully ten minutes, the entire fourteen white ones steadfastly gazed down upon us, with but few changes of position, and few remarks. Finally, one by one they drew back from the edge of the precipice, and quietly drifted away over the bald crest of the mountain.

For twenty years I had been reading the scanty scraps of mountain-goat literature that at long intervals have appeared in print. I had seen seven specimens alive in captivity, and helped to care for four of them. With a firm belief that the game was worth it, I had travelled twenty-five hundred miles or more in order to meet this strange animal in its own home, and cultivate a close acquaintance with half a dozen wild flocks.

At three o'clock we camped at timber-line, on a high and difficult pass between the Elk River and the Bull. That night we christened the ridge Goat Pass. While the guides and the cook unpacked the outfit and pitched the tents, Mr. Phillips hurried down the western side of the divide. Fifteen minutes later he and Kaiser,—in my opinion the wisest hunting-dog in British Columbia,—had twenty-eight nanny goats and kids at bay on the top of a precipice, and were photographing them at the risk of their lives.

Rifle and glass in hand, I sat down on a little knoll a few yards above the tents, to watch a *lame* billy goat who was quietly grazing and limping along the side of a lofty ridge that came down east of us from Phillips Peak. A lame wild animal in a country wherein a shot had not been fired for five years, was, to all of us, a real novelty; and with my glasses I watched that goat long and well. It was his left foreleg that was lame, and it was the opinion of the party that the old fellow was suffering from an accident received on the rocks. Possibly a stone had been rolled down upon him, by another goat.

Suddenly sharp cries of surprise came up from the camp, and I sprang up to look about. *Three goats were running past the tents at top speed,*—a big billy, and two smaller goats.

"Hi, there! Goats! Goats!" cried Smith and Norboe.

The cook was stooping over the fire, and looking under his right arm he saw the bunch charging straight toward him, at a gallop. A second later, the big billy was almost upon him.

"*Hey! You son-of-a-gun!*" yelled Huddleston, and as the big snow-white animal dashed past him he struck it across the neck with a stick of firewood. The goat's tracks were within six feet of the camp-fire.

The billy ran straight through the camp, then swung sharply to the left, and the last I saw of him, his humpy hindquarters wildly bobbing up and down among the dead jack pines, as he ran for Bald Mountain.

The two smaller goats held their course, and one promptly disappeared. The other leaped across our water-hole, and as it scrambled out of the gully near my position, and paused for a few seconds to look backward, instinctively I covered it with my rifle. But only for an instant. "Come as they may," thought I, "my first goat shall *not* be a small one!" And as the goat turned and raced on up, my .303 Savage came down.

We laughed long at the utter absurdity of three wild

Goats Running Through our Camp

THE MEN WERE POSED AND PHOTOGRAPHED AS THEY STOOD, AND THE THREE GOATS HAVE BEEN DRAWN IN TO SHOW WHERE THEY RAN.

goats actually breaking into the privacy of our camp, on our first afternoon in Goatland. In the Elk Valley Charlie Smith had promised me that we would camp "right among the goats," and he had royally kept his word.

At evening, when we gathered round the camp-fire, and counted up, we found that on our first day in Goatland, we had seen a total of fifty-three goats; and no one had fired a shot. As for myself, I felt quite set up over my presence of mind in *not* firing at the goat which I had "dead to rights" after it had invaded our camp, and which might have been killed as a measure of self defense.

Our camp was pitched in a most commanding and awe-inspiring spot. We were precisely at timber-line, in a grassy hollow on the lowest summit between Bald and Bird Mountains, on the north, and Phillips Peak, on the south. From our tents the ground rose for several hundred feet, like the cables of the Brooklyn Bridge, until it stopped against a rock wall which went on up several hundred feet more. In a notch quite near us was a big bank of eternal ice. In that country, such things are called glaciers; and its melting foot was the starting-point of Goat Creek. Fifty paces taken eastward from our tents brought us to a projecting point from which we looked down a hundred feet to a rope of white water, and on down Goat Creek as it drops five hundred feet to the mile, to the point where it turns a sharp corner to the right, and disappears.

Westward of camp, after climbing up a hundred feet or so, through dead standing timber, the ridge slopes steeply down for a mile and a half to the bottom of a great basin half filled with green timber, that opens toward Bull River. It was on this slope, at a point where a wall of rock cropped out, that Mr. Phillips cornered his flock of goats and photographed them.

At our camp, water and wood were abundant; there was plenty of fine grass for our horses, spruce boughs for our beds, scenery for millions, and what more could we ask?

The day following our arrival on Goat Pass was dull and rainy, with a little snow, and we all remained in camp. At intervals, some one would stroll out to our lookout point above Goat Creek, and eye-search the valley below "to see if an old silver-tip could come a-moochin' up, by accident," as Guide Smith quaintly phrased it.

That gray day taught me something of color values in those mountains. As seen from our lookout point, the long, even stretch of house-roof mountain-slope on the farther side of Goat Creek was a revelation. In the full sunlight of a clear day, its tints were nothing to command particular attention. Strong light seemed to take the colors out of everything. But a cloudy day, with a little rain on the face of nature, was like new varnish on an old oil-painting.

During the forenoon, fleecy white clouds chased each other over the pass and through our camp, and for much of the time the Goat Creek gorge was cloud-filled. At last, however, about noon, they rose and drifted away, and then the mountain opposite revealed a color pattern that was exquisitely beautiful.

For a distance of a thousand yards the ridge-side stretched away down the valley, straight and even; and in that distance it was furrowed from top to bottom by ten or twelve gullies, and ribbed by an equal number of ridges. At the bottom of the gorge was a dense green fringe of tall, obelisk spruces, very much alive. In many places, ghostly processions of dead spruces, limbless and gray, forlornly climbed the ridges, until half-way up the highest stragglers stopped. Intermixed with these tall poles were patches of trailing juniper of a dark olive green color, growing tightly to the steep slope.

The apex of each timbered ridge was covered with a solid mass of great willow-herb or "fireweed" (*Chamaenerion angustifolium*), then in its brightest autumn tints of purple and red. The brilliant patches of color which they painted on the mountain-side would have rejoiced the heart of an artist. This glorious plant colored nearly every mountain-side in that region during our September there.

Below the fireweed, the ridges were dotted with small, cone-shaped spruces, and trailing junipers (*Juniperus prostrata*), of the densest and richest green. The grassy sides of the gullies were all pale yellow-green, softly blended at the edges with the darker colors that framed them in. At the bottom of each washout was a mass of light-gray slide-rock, and above all this rare pattern of soft colors loomed a lofty wall of naked carboniferous limestone rock, gray, grim and forbidding.

It seemed to me that I never elsewhere had seen mountains so rich in colors as the ranges between the Elk and the Bull in that particular September. The rain and the drifting clouds were with us for one day only. Very early on the second morning, while Mr. Phillips and I lay in our sleeping-bags considering the grave question of getting or not getting up, Mack Norboe's voice was heard outside, speaking low but to the point:

"Director, here's an old billy goat, lying right above our camp!"

It was like twelve hundred volts. We tumbled out of our bags, slipped on our shoes, and ran out. Sure enough, a full-grown male goat was lying on the crest of the divide that led up to the summit of Bald Mountain, seventy-five feet above us, and not more than two hundred and fifty yards away. The shooting of him was left to me.

I think I could have bagged that animal as he lay; but what would there have been in that of any interest to a sportsman? I had not asked any goats to come down to our camp, and lie down to be shot!

Not caring greatly whether I got that goat or not, I

The Size of a Mountain Goat

THE AUTHOR'S SPECIMEN, AFTER FALLING 100 FEET, AND ROLLING 200 FEET ON THE SLIDE-ROCK.

attempted a stalk along the western side of the ridge, through the dead timber, and well below him. But the old fellow was not half so sleepy as he looked. When finally I came up to a point that was supposed to command his works, I found that he had winded me. He had vanished from his resting-place, and was already far up the side of Bald Mountain, conducting a masterly retreat.

After a hurried breakfast, we made ready for a day with the goats on the northern mountains. Although there are many things in favor of small parties,—the best consisting of one guide and one hunter,—we all went together—Mr. Phillips, Mack, Charlie and I. Our leader declared a determination to "see the director shoot his first goat"; and I assured the others that the services of all would be needed in carrying home my spoils.

As we turned back toward camp, and took time to look "at the sceneries," the view westward, toward Bull River, disclosed a cloud effect so beautiful that Mr. Phillips insisted upon photographing it, then and there. To give the "touch of life" which he always demanded, I sat in, as usual.

By Mr. Phillips's advice, I put on suspenders and loosened my cartridge-belt, in order to breathe with perfect freedom. We wore no leggings. Our shoes were heavily hobnailed, and while I had thought mine as light as one dared use in that region of ragged rocks, I found that for cliff-climbing they were too heavy, and too stiff in the soles. Of course knee-breeches are the thing, but they should be so well cut that in steep climbing they will not drag on the knees, and waste the climber's horse-power; and there should be a generous opening at the knee.

In those mountains, four things, and only four, are positively indispensable to every party,—rifles, axes, field glasses and blankets. Each member of our hunting party carried a good glass, and never stirred from camp without it. For myself, I tried

an experiment. Two months previously Mrs. Hornaday selected
for me, in Paris, a very good opera-glass, made by Lemaire, with
a field that was delightfully large and clear. While not quite so
powerful a magnifier as the strongest binoculars now on the
market, its field was so much clearer that I thought I would pre-
fer it. It was much smaller than any regulation field-glass, and
I carried it either in a pocket of my trousers, or loose inside my
hunting-shirt, quite forgetful of its weight.

It proved a great success. We found much interest in testing it with binoculars five times as costly, and the universal ver-
dict was that it would reveal an animal as far as a hunter could
go to it, and find it. I mention this because in climbing I found
it well worth while to be free from a dangling leather case that
is always in the way, and often is too large for comfort.

From our camp we went north, along the top of the eastern wall of Bald Mountain. Two miles from home we topped
a sharp rise, and there directly ahead, and only a quarter of
a mile away on an eastern slope lay a band of eleven goats,
basking in the welcome sunshine. The flock was composed of
nannies, yearling billies and kids, with not even one old billy
among those present. Two old chaperons lay with their heads
well up, on the lookout, but all the others lay full length upon
the grass, with their backs uphill. Three of the small kids lay
close against their mothers.

They were on the northerly point of a fine mountain
meadow, with safety rocks on three sides. Just beyond them
lay a ragged hogback of rock, both sides of which were so precipitous that no man save an experienced mountaineer would
venture far upon it. It was to this rugged fortress that the goats
promptly retreated for safety when we left off watching them,
and rose from our concealment. Their sunning-ground looked
like a sheep-yard, and we saw that goats had many times lain
upon that spot.

Near by, behind a living windbreak, was a goat bed, that looked as if goats had lain in it five hundred times. By some curious circumstance, a dozen stunted spruces had woven themselves together, as if for mutual support, until they formed a tight evergreen wall ten feet long and eight feet high. It ranged north and south, forming an excellent hedge-like shield from easterly winds, while the steep mountain partially cut off the winds from the west. On the upper side of that natural windbreak, the turf had been worn into dust, and the droppings were several inches deep. Apparently it was liked because it was a good shelter, in the centre of a fine sky-pasture, and within a few jumps of ideal safety rocks.

From the spot where the goats had lain, looking ahead and to our left, we beheld a new mountain. Later on we christened it Bird Mountain, because of the flocks of ptarmigan we found upon its summit. Near its summit we saw five more goats, all females and kids. At our feet lay a deep, rich-looking basin, then a low ridge, another basin with a lakelet in it, and beyond that another ridge, much higher than the first. Ridge No. 2 had dead timber upon it, but it was very scattering, for it was timber-line; and its upper end snugged up against the eastern wall of Bird Mountain. Later on we found that the northern side of that ridge ended in a wall of rock that was scalable by man in one place only.

"Yonder are two big old billies!" said some one with a glass in action.

"Yes sir; there they are; all alone, and heading this way, too. Those are your goats this time, Director, sure enough."

"Now boys," said I, "if we can stalk those two goats successfully, and bag them both, neatly and in quick time, we can call it genuine goat-hunting!"

They were distant about a mile and a half, jogging along down a rocky hill, through a perfect maze of gullies, ridges, grass-plots and rocks, one of them keeping from forty to fifty feet behind the other.

Even at that distance they looked big, and very, very white. Clearly, they were heading for Bird Mountain. We planned to meet them wherever they struck the precipitous side of the mountain ahead of us, and at once began our stalk.

From the basin which contained the little two-acre tarn, the rocky wall of Bird Mountain rose almost perpendicularly for about eight hundred feet. As we were passing between the lake and the cliff, we heard bits of loose rock clattering down.

"Just look yonder!" said Mr. Phillips, with much fervor.

Close at hand, and well within fair rifle-shot, were four goats climbing the wall; and two more were at the top, looking down as if deeply interested. The climbers had been caught napping, and being afraid to retreat either to right or left, they had elected to seek safety by climbing straight up! It was a glorious opportunity to see goats climb in a difficult place, and forthwith we halted and watched as long as the event lasted, utterly oblivious of our two big billies. Our binoculars brought them down to us wonderfully well, and we saw them as much in detail as if we had been looking a hundred feet with the unaided eye.

The wall was a little rough, but the angle of it seemed not more than 10 degrees from perpendicular. The footholds were merely narrow edges of rock, and knobs the size of a man's fist. Each goat went up in a generally straight course, climbing slowly and carefully all the while. Each one chose its own course, and paid no attention to those that had gone before. The eyes looked ahead to select the route, and the front hoofs skillfully sought for footholds. It seemed as if the powerful front legs performed three-fourths of the work, reaching up until a good foothold was secured, then lifting the heavy body by main strength, while the hindlegs "also ran." It seemed that the chief function of the hind limbs was to keep what the fore-legs won. As an exhibition of strength of limb, combined with surefootedness and nerve, it was marvelous, no less.

Often a goat would reach toward one side for a new foot-hold, find none, then rear up and pivot on its hindfeet, with its neck and stomach pressed against the wall, over to the other side. Occasionally a goat would be obliged to edge off five or ten feet to one side in order to scramble on up. From first to last, no goat slipped and no rocks gave way under their feet, although numerous bits of loose slide-rock were disturbed and sent rattling down.

It was a most inspiring sight, and we watched it with breathless interest. In about ten minutes the four goats had by sheer strength and skill climbed about two hundred feet of the most precipitous portion of the cliff, and reached easy going. After that they went on up twice as rapidly as before, and soon passed over the summit, out of our sight. Then we compared notes.

Mr. Phillips and I are of the opinion that nothing could have induced mountain sheep to have made that appalling climb, either in the presence of danger or otherwise. Since that day we have found that there are many mountain hunters who believe that as a straight-away cliff-climber, the goat does things that are impossible to sheep.

As soon as the goat-climbing exhibition had ended, we hurried on across the basin, and up the side of Ridge No. 2. This ridge bore a thin sprinkling of low spruces, a little fallen timber, much purple fireweed and some good grass. As seen at a little distance, it was a purple ridge. The western end of it snugged up against the mountain, and it was there that we met our two big billy goats. They had climbed nearly to the top of our ridge, close up to the mountain, and when we first sighted them they were beginning to feed upon a lace-leaved

Weighing Mountain Goat No. 1, by Sections

THE TWO GOATS WERE FIRST SEEN ON THE THINLY TIMBERED RIDGE IN THE MIDDLE DISTANCE.

anemone (*Pulsatilla occidentalis*), at the edge of their newly
found pasture. We worked toward them, behind a small clump
of half-dead spruces, and finally halted to wait for them to
come within range.

After years of waiting, Rocky Mountain goats, *at last*!
How amazingly white and soft they look; and how big they
are! The high shoulder hump, the big, round barrel of the
body, and the knee-breeches on the legs make the bulk of the
animal seem enormous. The whiteness of "the driven snow," of
cotton and of paper seem by no means to surpass the incom-
parable white of those soft, fluffy-coated animals as they appear in a setting of hard, gray limestone, rugged slide-rock and
dark-green vegetation. They impressed me as being the whitest
living objects I ever beheld, and far larger than I had expected
to find them. In reality, their color had the effect of magnify-
ing their size; for they looked as big as two-year-old buffaloes.

Of course only Mr. Phillips and I carried rifles; and we
agreed that the left man should take the left animal.

"It's a hundred and fifty yards!" said Mack Norboe, in a
hoarse whisper.

My goat was grazing behind the trunk of a fallen tree,
which shielded his entire body. I waited, and waited; and there
he stood, with his head down, and calmly cropped until I became wildly impatient. I think he stood in one spot for five
minutes, feeding upon *Pulsatilla*.

"Why don't you shoot?" queried Phillips, in wonder. "I
can't! My goat's hiding behind a tree."

"Well, fire when you're ready, Gridley, and I'll shoot
when you do!"

It must have been five minutes, but it seemed like twenty-
five, before that goat began to feel a thrill of life along his keel,
and move forward. The annoying suspense had actually made
me unsteady; besides which, my Savage was a new one, and

unchristened. Later on I found that the sights were not right for me, and that my first shooting was very poor.

At last my goat stood forth, in full view—white, immaculate, high of hump, low of head, big and bulky. I fired for the vitals behind shoulder.

"You've overshot!" exclaimed Norboe, and "Bang!" said Mr. Phillips's Winchester.

Neither of us brought down our goat at the first fire!

I fired again, holding much lower, and the goat reared up a foot. Mr. Phillips fired again, whereupon his goat fell over like a sack of oats, and went rolling down the hill. My goat turned to run, and as he did so I sent two more shots after him. Then he disappeared behind some rocks. Mack, John and I ran forward, to keep him in sight, and fire more shots if necessary. But no goat was to be seen.

"He can't get away!" said Norboe, reassuringly.

"He's *dead*!" said I, by way of an outrageous bluff. "You'll find him down on the slide-rock!" But inwardly I was torn by doubts.

We hurried down the steep incline, and presently came to the top of a naked wall of rock. Below that was a wide expanse of slide-rock.

"Thar he is!" cried Norboe. "Away down yonder, out on the slide-rock, dead as a wedge."

From where he stood when I fired, the goat had run back about two hundred feet, where he fell dead, and then began to roll. We traced him by a copious stream of blood on the rocks. He fell down the rock wall, for a hundred feet, in a slanting direction, and then-to my great astonishment—he rolled two hundred feet farther (by measurement) on that ragged, jagged slide-rock before he fetched up against a particularly large chunk of stone, and stopped. We expected to find his horns broken, but they were quite uninjured. The most damage had been inflicted upon his nose, which was badly cut and bruised. The bullet that ended his life (my second shot) went squarely through the valves of his heart; but I regret to add that one thigh-bone had been broken by another shot, as he ran from me.

Mr. Phillips's goat behaved better than mine. It rolled down the grassy slope, and lodged on a treacherous little shelf of earth that overhung the very brink of the precipice. One step into that innocent-looking fringe of green juniper bushes meant death on the slide-rock below; and it made me nervous to see Mack and Charlie stand there while they skinned the animal.

As soon as possible we found the only practicable route down the rock wall, and scrambled down. The others say that I slid down the last twenty feet; but that is quite immaterial. I reached the goat a few paces in advance of the others, and thought to divert my followers by reciting a celebrated quotation beginning, "To a hunter, the moment of triumph," etc. As I laid my hand upon the goat's hairy side and said my little piece, I heard a deadly "click."

"Got him!" cried Mr. Phillips; and then three men and a dog laughed loud and derisively. Since seeing the picture I have altered that quotation, to this: "To a hunter, the moment of humiliation is when he first sees his idiotic smile on a surreptitious plate." It is inserted solely to oblige Mr. Phillips, as evidence of the occasion when he got ahead of me.

The others declared that the goat was "a big one, though not the very biggest they ever grow." Forthwith we measured him; and in taking his height we shoved his foreleg up until the elbow came to the position it occupies under the standing, living animal. The measurements were as follows:

ROCKY MOUNTAIN GOAT
OREAMNOS MONTANUS

Male, six years old. Killed September 8, 1905, near Bull River, British Columbia.

Standing height at shoulder . . . . 38 *inches.*
Length, nose to root of tail . . . . 59.25 *inches.*
Length of tail vertebrae . . . . 3.50 *inches.*
Girth behind foreleg . . . . 55 *inches.*
Girth around abdomen . . . . 58 *inches.*
Girth of neck behind ears (unskinned) . . . . 18 *inches.*
Circumference of forearm, skinned . . . . 11.25 *inches.*
Width of chest . . . . 14 *inches.*
Length of horn curve . . . . 9.75 *inches.*
Spread of horns at tips . . . . 5 *inches.*
Circumference of horn at base . . . . 5.60 *inches.*
Circumference of front hoof . . . . 10.50 *inches.*
Circumference of rear hoof . . . . 7.75 *inches.*
Base of ear to end of nostrils . . . . 10.50 *inches.*
Front corner of eye to rear corner
　　nostril opening . . . . 7 *inches.*
Widest spread of ears, tip to tip . . . . 15 *inches.*

Total weight of animal by scales, allowing 8 lbs. for blood lost . . . . 258 lbs.

The black and naked glands in the skin behind the horn were on that date small, and inconspicuous; but they stood on edge, with the naked face of each closely pressed against the base of the horn in front of it.

On another occasion I shot a thin old goat that stood forty-two inches high at the shoulders, and Mr. Phillips shot another that weighed two hundred and seventy-six pounds.

After we had thoroughly dissected my goat, weighed it, examined the contents of its stomach, and saved a good sample of its food for close examination at camp, we tied up the hindquarters, head and pelt, and set out for camp.

And thus ended our first day in the actual hunting of mountain goats, in the course of which we saw a total of forty-two animals. The stalking, killing and dissecting of our two goats was very interesting, but the greatest event of the day was our opportunity to watch those five goats climb an almost perpendicular cliff.

"The Moment of Triumph"—Caught Unawares

CHAPTER VI

ON BIRD MOUNTAIN: PHOTOGRAPHING MOUNTAIN SHEEP

A MOUNTAIN CYCLORAMA—THE CONTINENTAL DIVIDE—
PHILLIPS PEAK—A LAND UNMAPPED AND UNMEASURED—
MOUNTAIN ALTITUDES ALONG ELK RIVER—STATEMENT
BY GEOLOGIST MCEVOY—MOUNTAIN SHEEP AFOOT—
PHOTOGRAPHING TWO SHEEP ON THE GOAT ROCKS—SHEEP
AND GOATS SEEN AT THE SAME MOMENT.

WE RESERVED FOR THE FOURTH day of our stay at Goat
Pass a treat which was like dessert after meat. We climbed to a
mountain-top for a general survey of our domain.

Of the region in which we were, Phillips Peak is the highest mountain; but its northern and western faces are unscalable, and its southern slope too far away. Near at hand, and
excellent as a lookout, was the bald crest of Bird Mountain,
and to it we climbed, on a glorious afternoon of alternating
sunshine and cloud.

The top of Bald Mountain, beside our camp, consists of
fine, decomposed shale, and the goat-trail over it is wide and

deep. Stepping from its soft side to the steep slope of Bird Mountain is like going from an ash pile to a hill of hair mattresses. The zone between timber-line and summit is thickly carpeted with a soft, springy, moss-like ground-plant called mountain avens (*Dryas octopetala*), which to tired feet is most soothing and restful. In places the surface of the slope forms a long series of level benches a yard wide and five or six feet long, each one generously cushioned with this odd plant.

Climbing a mountain over such footing as that is like exploring a wilderness in a Pullman car. But mark the contrast. From this zone of living carpet we climbed upon the terminal cap of the mountain, a huge mound of broken, sharp-edged rock, ragged, jagged, and barren of all vegetable life. It was the remains of a prehistoric peak, which foot by foot had remorselessly been torn down by wind and sun, frost and rain, until its last pinnacle had been laid low. The whole mountain-top was a mass of clean rock—carboniferous limestone the color of a postal card,—that looked as if it had just come from a quarry, suitably broken for rubble-masonry foundations.

The view from that rocky summit disclosed a magnificent mountain-cyclorama. In every direction, to the uttermost limit of vision, there rose and fell a bewildering succession of saw-tooth mountains, deep valleys and far-distant peaks. The level mountain-plateau feature was totally absent. Nowhere was there visible a level spot large enough for a foot-ball field. It was mountains, mountains, everywhere, a labyrinth of steeps, a bewildering maze of summits, valleys, precipices, basins and passes.

Looking eastward over the northern spurs of Phillips Peak, across the valley of Elk River and beyond Sheep Mountain, we saw, about thirty miles away, a long line of lofty snow-clad peaks, much higher than any of the intervening summits. They marked the crest of the great Continental

Divide, and the boundary between British Columbia and Alberta. Our distance from the United States boundary was about seventy miles. South-eastward, and very near at hand, rose the sharp cone of Phillips Peak, the culmination and hub of everything in the region round about. From its precipitous sides spring at least five small mountain-chains, which radiate like the spokes of a wheel. Mr. Phillips's fine photograph of his namesake renders a feeble word description quite unnecessary.

Although the northern and western faces of the upper five hundred feet of the peak are so appallingly steep that only a mountain goat could scale them, we found later on that the southern face is apparently accessible. I longed to stand on that summit, and with two months in the mountains I would gladly have made the attempt to do so; but as matters stood, the many interesting things zoological that lay before us quite crowded out the idea of a well-considered attempt to make the climb during that trip. On his next visit Mr. Phillips will un-doubtedly write his name on the top of his peak.

The moral uplift, and the corresponding ego depression, of such a mountain-cyclorama as circles around the summit of Bird Mountain cannot adequately be portrayed by me in words. I never before felt quite so puny or so wholly insignificant as then. I have seen other mountains in plenty, but nowhere else have I felt so overwhelmingly impressed as by that particular two thousand square miles of heaving mountain-billows and deep-plunging valleys in view from Bird Mountain. And think what it must be from the top of Phillips Peak, on a clear day in September!

Down to this date, the region north and north-west of Michel, for a radius of perhaps fifty miles, has never been touched by aneroid or surveyor's chain. We can give no heights nor distances with mechanical accuracy. Above Michel there is not a datum point of any kind. Naturally, however, we were

Phillips Peak, from Bird Mountain

ELEVATION ABOUT 10,000 FEET. OUR CAMP ON GOAT PASS WAS UNDER THE RIGHT SHOULDER OF THE SITTING FIGURE.

much interested in the heights of the mountain summits in the region we visited, between the Elk and Bull Rivers. Our estimates of the height of Phillips Peak, and other points in the mountains surrounding it, were based on the following memoranda which were kindly supplied by Mr. James McEvoy, Geologist of the Crow's Nest Pass Coal Company:—

"I have not the exact figures for the elevation of the Elk River at Wild-Cat Charlie's ranch, but it must be very close to 3,900 feet above sea-level."

"The elevations of the mountains near Fernie on the east side of the river are about 7,000 feet. These mountains are of cretaceous coal-bearing rocks. On the west side of the Elk River at Fernie the mountains are composed of Carboniferous and Devonian limestone, and quartzites, reaching elevations of from 9,000 to 10,000 feet. The average height of the summits would be about 9,200 feet. These summits stand about four miles back from the river. Lower hills and spurs of these come closer to the river, and will average about 7,000 feet elevation."

"Farther up the Elk River, on the east side, in the neighborhood of Sparwood, the elevations are the same as near Fernie. On the west side, however, the mountains reach a higher elevation, probably 10,500 feet above the sea, and the distance of the summits from the Elk River is increased to about ten miles. North of the mouth of Michel Creek I cannot give you any close figures for the elevation. The valley of the river for the most part is occupied by a narrow band of cretaceous rocks, and the mountains on either side, at least the higher ones, are composed of Carboniferous and Devonian. On the west side of the river, from what I could see of the mountains, they seem to increase in elevation as you go northward, and on the east side the lower hills, which are composed of cretaceous rocks, seem to dwindle into insignificance."

Judging from the facts stated above by Mr. McEvoy, we

estimated the height of Phillips Peak at about 10,000 feet, and the average elevation of timber-line at 8,500 feet. We think that the goats we found and shot high up on the south-western side of the peak were feeding at a height of about 9,000 feet.

Even on the rugged and forbidding summit of Bird Mountain, we found bird life. While Mr. Phillips was busily maneuvering for mountain photographs, staggering over the cruel rocks, camera in hand, a flock of willow ptarmigans flew up almost from under his feet, crying "cluck-cluck-cluck-cluck." Their snow-white wings and tails flashed and fluttered for a hundred yards, then dropped among the stones. Instantly the mountain views were forgotten, and there began a long series of maneuvers to photograph the birds. Mack Norboe was detailed to herd the birds, and hold them from stampeding while the camera man worked within close range.

Shot after shot was made, sometimes at fifteen feet, and at least ten times the birds flew because they were too closely pressed. The difficulty lay in the bad light, and the inability of the camera to differentiate the bodies of the birds from the stones. The pictures were not successful, and in lieu of them Mr. Phillips offers a photograph of a single female ptarmigan, in summer plumage, herded by Mr. G.N. Monro, at a distance of about five feet.

PHOTOGRAPHING MOUNTAIN SHEEP

I SHALL ALWAYS REMEMBER THE date,—September 11,—because that date once was the wedding-day of a Lady whom I know.

We had decided to leave Goat Pass on that day, move southward about ten miles, and make a new camp in the picturesque valley of Avalanche Creek. In order to lose no sportsman's opportunity, it was decided that Mr. Phillips, Charlie, and I should go ahead on foot, hunting by the way, and that the others should follow on with the pack-train, as soon as it could be made ready.

For the second time in my hunting experience, a strange coincidence was brought about by the desire of a brother sportsman to show me the exact spot whereon a strange thing had happened to him. As we shouldered our rifles and climbed the hill south of our tents, Mr. Phillips said, "Now, Director, if you will come with me, I will show you where I corralled those goats and photographed them, the day we arrived here." I had previously expressed a desire to examine the spot, in order to see where the goats had stood at bay and unwillingly leaped down.

We soon topped the crest of the ridge, and started down the long and steep western slope which constitutes the Bull River side of the divide. We were just below timber-line, and the mountain-side was thinly covered with stunted white spruces, half of them dead. Far below us lay a deep, round basin, like a gigantic washbowl set between the peaks. The bottom of this basin was half covered with a beautiful growth of dark-green timber, into which the growth upon our mountain-side climbed down and merged.

In going down a mountain, I think the distance always is greater than one expects. Mr. Phillips led us down, down, and still farther down, and steeper all the while, until the slope seemed interminable; and then we reached the top of a rock bluff which cropped out and ran along the mountain-side from south to north.

"There," said he, pausing at last. "It was right here that Kaiser rounded up those goats for me, at the top of this wall. You see, if it hadn't been for that perpendicular drop of eight feet, the band would have gone on down, immediately. Do you see that dead tree? Well, they bunched up behind that, with

A Female Sooty Grouse (left)
Female Ptarmigan, in Summer Plumage (right)

Kaiser on that side, me on this side, and the eight-foot drop below. They didn't like to take that jump—probably because of the kids. Well, Kaiser held them from getting away on his side, and I exposed on them all the films I had, right from this old dead stub. I leaned against it until it cracked, and I feared it might go over with me."

"And what did the goats do, finally?"

"At last the old ones got their courage up, and gingerly jumped off; and the kids had to follow suit. The nannies and yearlings landed on their feet, and their momentum carried them on, slipping and sliding headlong down the rest of the way [about fifty feet]. You see, the rest of it is not quite perpendicular, and they slid down very well, of course holding back with their feet wherever the rock was rough."

"How about the kid that fell?"

"Poor little beggar, he was really hurt. When he jumped from here, he landed on his nose, and gave a bleat of pain. And what was worse, he couldn't recover himself entirely, but went on, half tumbling and half sliding, until he reached the bottom. It made his mouth bleed, and must have hurt him cruelly. I felt awfully sorry for him."

Mr. Phillips had barely finished his story, when Charlie Smith, who had been closely scanning the thick, green timber of the basin, suddenly exclaimed, "Something's coming! Something's coming this way,—on a dead run!"

"What is it, Charlie?"

"I think it's a bunch of deer."

"Or an old silver-tip—eh, Charlie?" cried Mr. Phillips.

"No; it's no silver-tip."

We started in a mad scramble along the mountainside, and before ten paces had been covered each man had thrown a loaded cartridge into the barrel of his rifle. We had not moved more than fifty paces from the goat rocks when we saw two brown-gray animals scurrying nimbly and swiftly along the tree-covered mountain-side, almost on our contour line, and coming straight toward us. Exclamations flew all about.

"Here they come!" "Sheep!" "Mountain sheep!" Mechanically we threw our rifles into position, but Charlie cried out sharply, "Don't shoot, men! Don't shoot! *They're both ewes*!"

On they came, headed straight for us, and the combined nimbleness and strength with which they ran was beautiful to see. They carried their heads well up, ran close together, and their speed was astonishing. They seemed to sweep over the ground as easily as a hawk flies.

They did not see us until they were within about a hundred feet, and then in a graceful curve they swerved off sharply downhill, and flew for safety to the rocky wall below. Then they disappeared. As they passed near us, we saw that the one in the lead was a full-grown ewe, and the other a two-year-old ram.

As soon as we could recover from our astonishment, and get our thoughts once more in motion, we naturally concluded that the sheep had kept on running, and soon would be a mile away. No one dreamed of seeing them again. But suddenly, like a bolt out of the blue, we heard, "Ah, woo! Woo! Woo!"

It was the voice of Kaiser, only a few yards away, coming up from the rocks below.

"By jove! Kaiser has stopped those sheep on the goat rocks!"

"We'll photograph 'em, Charlie! Get out your camera, quick, and come on!" said Mr. Phillips.

In two minutes we were peering over the edge of the precipice, in an effort to locate the subjects.

"They're right down *there*. If one of you go down there, and the other this way, you'll get them right between your two cameras!"

"This is good enough for me!" said Charlie, swinging himself over the edge into a perfectly frightful situation. "I see them! I see them!"

Mr. Phillips scrambled down the other way, in a most reckless fashion.

"Now, boys," said No. 3, "for goodness sake, mind your footing; and don't fall down that wall for a million old pictures!"

Those two dare-devils went down to positions on that precipice that I would not have ventured with a camera for any pictures, heads or horns ever taken, or that ever will be taken. If empty-handed, it would not have been quite so bad; but to see them "monkeying around "on the face of a treacherous precipice, handicapped with cameras, relying solely upon their feet to hold them upon a few bumps and edges of rock, with Sure Death below, was about all that my nerves could endure. I felt like shouting at them constantly, to be careful, and then more careful still—for I have no desire to camp with a Tragedy; but beyond a few mild admonitions, I held my peace.

Leaving my rifle above, I crept down behind Mr. Phillips's position,—at a very easy spot,—until I could see the tableau on the wall.

The sheep occupied a comfortable ledge, and the most of the time were aggravatingly concealed from Mr. Phillips by an angle of the wall. They were many feet below Charlie's best position, and although he saw them very plainly, the images his camera got of them were too small to represent much value.

Mr. Phillips made several exposures, but in reality had not even one fair chance at a sheep in full view. His best pictures were made when the young ram was looking at him around the angle of rock which usually concealed it. The photograph may well be entitled, "On the Alert," for it shows a sheep as wary and wide awake as it is possible for one to be. There were

Young Mountain Sheep Ram
PHOTOGRAPHED SEPTEMBER 11, 1905.

moments when that ram seemed to be all eyes. A number of times he craned his neck around the rock, and stared hard at us to see whether we were coming nearer.

After the lapse of about ten minutes, the sheep decided that they must be going. Without more ado, they lightly sprang from step to step, straight away from Mr. Phillips and me, rapidly descending all the while. The Goat Rocks were soon left far behind, and the last we saw of the photographed mountain sheep was their dull white rump-patches flitting away northward, through the dead timber and up the mountain-side, a mile away.

May they live long, and prosper.

Some one has said, much too easily, that mountain sheep and mountain goats never inhabit the same locality at the same time. As we looked for the last time at the running sheep, and then mechanically glanced at the summit of the mountain-side up which they were bounding fast and free, we saw once more the band of five goats which for days had been loafing on that isolated peak. That was the band which had not received word of our baneful presence.

CHAPTER VII

A GREAT DAY WITH GOATS

GOATS FAR UP—THE CLIMB, AND ITS DIFFICULTIES—AN ELUSIVE
PAIR—TEN BIG BILLIES AT HAND—OBSERVATIONS OF AN HOUR—
FOUR GOATS KILLED, AND UTILIZED—THE TALLEST GOAT, AND
THE HEAVIEST—ROLLING CARCASSES—DOWN AVALANCHE
CREEK TO A BEAUTIFUL CAMP.

THIS DAY, ALSO, WAS THE eleventh of September,—after
the incident of the mountain sheep on the Camera Rocks.

Mr. Phillips, Charlie Smith and I descended the steep
side of Goat Pass, crossed the basin and slowly climbed the
grassy divide that separates it from the source of Avalanche
Creek. When half way down the southern side of that divide,
we looked far up the side of Phillips Peak, and saw two big old
billy goats of shootable size. They were well above timber-line,
lying where a cloud-land meadow was suddenly chopped off at
a ragged precipice. The way up to them was long, and very steep.

"That's a long climb, Director," said Mr. Phillips; "but
there are no bad rocks."

I said that I could make it, in time,—as compared with eternity,—if the goats would wait for me.

"Oh, they'll wait! We'll find 'em there, all right," said Charlie, confidently. So we started.

As nearly as I can estimate, we climbed more than a mile, at an angle that for the upper half of the distance was about 30 degrees—a very steep ascent. At first our way up led through green timber, over smooth ground that was carpeted with needles of spruce and pine. That was comparatively easy,—no more difficult, in fact, than climbing the stairs of four Washington monuments set one upon another.

At climbing steep mountains, Mr. Phillips, Charlie Smith and the two Norboes are perfect fiends. They are thin, tough and long-winded, and being each of them fully forty pounds under my weight, I made no pretense at trying to keep up with them. As it is in an English workshop, the slowest workman set the pace.

In hard climbing, almost every Atlantic-coast man perspires freely, and is very extravagant in the use of air. It frequently happened that when half way up a high mountain, my lungs consumed the air so rapidly that a vacuum was created around me, and I would have to stop and wait for a new supply of oxygen to blow along. My legs behaved much better than my lungs, and to their credit be it said that they never stopped work until my lungs ran out of steam.

As I toiled up that long slope, I thought of a funny little engine that I saw in Borneo, pulling cars over an absurd wooden railway that ran from the bank of the Sadong River to the coal-mines. It would run about a mile at a very good clip, then suddenly cease puffing, and stop. Old Walters, the superintendent, said:

"There's only one thing ails that bally engine. The bloomin' little thing can't make steam fast enough!"

I was like that engine. I couldn't "keep steam"; and whenever my lungs became a perfect vacuum, I had to stop and rest, and collect air. Considering the fact that there was game above us, I thought my comrades were very considerate in permitting me to set the pace. Now had some one glared at me with the look of a hungry cannibal, and hissed between his teeth, "*Step lively!*" it would have made me feel quite at home.

In due time we left the green timber behind us, and started up the last quarter of the climb. There we found stunted spruces growing like scraggy brush, three feet high, gnarled and twisted by the elements, and enfeebled by the stony soil on which they bravely tried to grow. Only the bravest of trees could even rear their heads on that appalling steep,—scorched by the sun, rasped by the wind, drenched by the rains and frozen by the snow. But after a hundred yards or so, even the dwarf spruces gave up the struggle. Beyond them, up to our chosen point, the mountain-roof was smooth and bare, except for a sprinkle of fine, flat slide-rock that was very treacherous stuff to climb over.

"Let me take your rifle, Director!" said Charlie, kindly.

"No, thank you. I'll carry it up, or stay down. But you may keep behind me if you will, and catch me if I start to roll!"

On steep slopes, such as that was, my companions had solemnly warned me not to fall backward and start rolling; for a rolling man gathers no moss. A man bowling helplessly down a mountain-side at an angle of 30 degrees quickly acquires a momentum which spells death. Often have I looked down a horribly steep stretch, and tried to imagine what I would feel, and *think*, were I to overbalance backward, and go bounding down. A few hours later we saw a goat carcass take a frightful roll down a slope not nearly so steep as where we climbed up, and several times it leaped six feet into the air.

To keep out of the sight of the goats it was necessary for

us to bear well toward our left; and this brought us close to the edge of the precipice, where the mountainside was chopped off. In view of the loose stones under foot, I felt like edging more to the right; for the twin chances of a roll down and a fall over began to abrade my nerves. Mr. Phillips and Charlie climbed along so close to the drop that I found myself wondering which of them would be the first to slip and go over.

"Keep well over this way, Director, or the goats may wind you!" said Charlie, anxiously.

"That's all right, Charlie; he's winded now!" said John.

I said we would rest on that; and before I knew the danger, Mr. Phillips had taken a picture of me, resting, and smiling a most idiotic smile.

At last we reached the pinnacle which we had selected when we first sighted our game. As nearly as we could estimate, afterward, by figuring up known elevations, we were at a height of about nine thousand feet, and though not the highest, it was the dizziest point I ever trod. Except when we looked ahead, we seemed to be fairly suspended in mid-air! To look down under one's elbow was to look into miles of dizzy, bottomless space.

The steep slope had led us up to the sharp point of a crag that stuck up like the end of a man's thumb, and terminated in a crest as sharp as the comb of a house roof. Directly in front, and also on the left, was a sheer drop. From the right, the ragged edge of the wall ran on up, to the base of Phillips Peak. Beyond our perch, twelve feet away, there yawned a great basin-abyss, and on beyond that rocky gulf rose a five-hundred-foot wall at the base of the Peak. A little to the right our position another ragged pinnacle thrust its sharp apex a few feet higher than ours, and eventually caused me much trouble in securing my first shot.

We reached the top of our crag, and peered over its highest rocks just in time to see our two goats quietly walk behind a ragged point of rock farther up the wall, and disappear. They were only hundred and fifty yards distant; but they had not learned of our existence, and were not in the least alarmed. Naturally, we expected them to saunter back into view, for we felt quite sure they did not mean to climb down that wall to the bottom of the basin. So we lay flat upon the slope, rifles in hand, and waited, momentarily expecting the finish. They were due to cross a grassy slope between two crags, not more than forty feet wide, and if not fired at within about *ten seconds* of their reappearance, they would be lost behind the rocks! The chance was not nearly so good as it looked.

But minutes passed, and no goats returned. It became evident that the dawdling pair had lain down behind the sheltering crag, for a siesta in the sun. We composed ourselves to await their pleasure, and in our first breath of opportunity, looked off southeasterly, over the meadow whereon the two goats had been feeding. And then we saw a sight of sights.

Rising into view out of a little depression on the farther side of the meadow, lazily sauntering along, there came ten big, snow-white billy goats! They were heading straight toward us, and there was not a nanny, nor a kid, nor even a young billy in the bunch. The air was clear; the sun was shining brightly, the meadow was like dark olive-brown plush,—and how grandly those big, pure-white creatures did loom up! When first seen they were about four hundred yards away, but our glasses made the distance seem only one-third of that.

For more than an hour we lay flat on our pinnacle, and watched those goats. No one thought of time. It was a chance of a lifetime. My companions were profoundly surprised by the size of the collection; for previous to that moment, no member of our party ever had seen more than four big male goats in one bunch.

The band before us was at the very top of a sky meadow
of unusual luxuriance, which climbed up out of the valley on
our right, and ran on up to the comb of rock that came down
from Phillips Peak. In area the meadow was five hundred yards
wide, and half a mile long. Afterward, when we walked over it,
we found it was free from stones, but full of broad steps, and
covered with a dense, greenish-purple matting of ground verdure that was as soft to the foot as the thickest pile carpet. The
main body of this verdure is a moss-like plant called mountain
avens, closely related to cinquefoil, and known botanically as
Dryas octopetala. It has a very pretty leaf measuring about 7/16
by 3/16 inches, with finely serrate edges. In September a mass
of it contains a mixture of harmonious colors,—olive-green,
brown, gray and purple. On this the goats were feeding. This
plant is very common in those mountains above timberline,
especially on southern slopes; but it demands a bit of ground
almost exclusively for itself, and thrives best when alone.

Along with this there grew a moss-like saxifrage
(*Saxifraga austromontana*), which to any one not a botanist
seems to be straight moss. It grows in cheerful little clumps of
bright green, and whenever it is found on a mountain-pasture,
one is pleased to meet it.

I record these notes here, because our ten goats had been
in no hurry. They were more than deliberate; they were almost stagnant. In an hour, the farthest that any one of them
moved was about one hundred yards, and the most of them
accomplished even less than that. They were already so well
fed that they merely minced at the green things around them.
Evidently they had fed to satiety in the morning hours, before
we reached them.

As they straggled forward, they covered about two acres
of ground. Each one seemed steeped and sodden in laziness.
When out grazing, our giant tortoises move faster than they

did on that lazy afternoon. When the leader of this band of weary Willies reached the geographical centre of the sky-meadow, about two hundred yards from us, he decided to take a sun-bath, on the most luxurious basis possible to him. Slowly he focused his mind upon a level bench of earth, about four feet wide. It contained an old goat-bed, of loose earth, and upon this he lay down, with his back uphill.

At this point, however, he took a sudden resolution. After about a minute of reflection, he decided that the head of his bed was too high and too humpy; so, bracing himself back with his right foreleg, like an ancient Roman senator at a feast, he set his left leg in motion and flung out from under his breast a quantity of earth. The loose soil rose in a black shower, two feet high, and the big hoof flung it several feet down the hill. After about a dozen rakes, he settled down to bask in the warm sunshine, and blink at the scenery of Avalanche Valley.

Five minutes later, a little higher up the slope, another goat did the same thing; and eventually two or three others laid down. One, however, deliberately sat down on his haunches, dog-fashion, with his back uphill. For fully a quarter of an hour he sat there in profile, slowly turning his head from side to side, and gazing at the scenery while the wind blew through his whiskers.

So far as I could determine, no sentinel was posted. There was no leader, and no individual seemed particularly on the alert for enemies. One and all, they felt perfectly secure.

In observing those goats one fact became very noticeable. At a little distance, their legs looked very straight and stick-like, devoid of all semblance of gracefulness and of leaping power. The animals were very white and immaculate,—as were all the goats that we saw,—and they stood out with the sharpness of clean snow-patches on dark rock. Nature may have known about the much overworked principle of "protective coloration" when she fashioned the mountain goat, but if so, she was guilty of cruelty to goats in clothing this creature with pelage which, in the most comfortable season for hunting, renders it visible for three miles or more. Even the helpless kidling is as white as cotton, and a grand mark for eagles.

That those goats should look so stiff and genuinely ungraceful on their legs, gave me a distinct feeling of disappointment. From that moment I gave up all hope of ever seeing a goat perform any feats requiring either speed or leaping powers; for we saw that of those short, thick legs,—nearly as straight as four Indian clubs,—nothing is to be expected save power in lifting and sliding, and rocklike steadfastness. In all the two hundred and thirty-nine goats that we saw, we observed nothing to disprove the conclusive evidence of that day regarding the physical powers of the mountain goat.

While we watched the band of mountain loafers, still another old billy goat, making No. 13, appeared across the rock basin far to our left. From the top of the northern ridge, he set out to walk across the wide rock wall that formed the western face of Phillips Peak. From where we were the wall seemed almost smooth, but to the goat it must have looked otherwise. Choosing a narrow, light-gray line of stratification that extended across the entire width of the wall, the solitary animal set out on its promenade. The distance to be traversed to reach the uppermost point of our sky-pasture was about fifteen hundred feet, and the contour line chosen was about four hundred feet above our position. The incident was like a curtain-raiser to a tragic play.

That goat's walk was a very tame performance. The animal plodded steadily along, never faster, never slower, but still with a purposeful air, like a postman delivering mail. For a mountain goat, not pursued or frightened, it was a rapid walk, probably three miles an hour. Its legs swung to and fro with

The Sky Pasture of Thirteen "Billy Goats (top)

ELEVATION, ABOUT 9,000 FEET. THE GOATS OCCUPIED THE CENTER OF THE PICTURE, BUT
APPEAR ONLY AS WHITE SPECKS. THE HUNTERS LAY ON THE TOP OF A PINNACLE LIKE THAT IN
THE FOREGROUND.

Taking the First Shot (bottom)

THE END OF "OLD TWO-TEETH." GUIDE SMITH LIES WITHIN SIX FEET OF THE BRINK OF A
PRECIPICE.

the regularity and steadiness of four pendulums, and I think they never once paused. The animal held to that one line of stratification, until near the end of its promenade. There a great mass of rock had broken away from the face of the cliff, and the goat was forced to climb down about fifty feet, then up again, to regain its chosen route. A few minutes later its ledge ran out upon the apex of the sky-meadow. There Billy paused for a moment, to look about him; then he picked out a soft spot, precisely where the steep slope of the meadow ended against the rocky peak, and lay down to rest.

Up to that time, Mr. Phillips and I had killed only one goat each, and as we lay there we had time to decide upon the future. He resolved to kill one fine goat as a gift to the Carnegie Museum, and I wished two more for my own purposes. We decided that at a total of three goats each,—two less than our lawful right,—we would draw the line, and kill no more.

The first shot at the pair of invisible goats was to be mine; and as already suggested, the circumstances were like those surrounding a brief moving target in a shooting-gallery. Before us were two rocky crag-points, and behind the one on the left, the animals lay hidden for fully an hour. Between the two crags the V-shaped spot of the meadow, across which I knew my goat would walk or run, looked very small. If he moved a yard too far, the right-hand crag would hide him from me until he would be three hundred yards away. I was compelled to keep my rifle constantly ready, and one eye to the front, in order to see my goat in time to get a shot at him while he crossed that forty feet of ground.

And after all, I came ever so near to making a failure of my vigil. I was so absorbed in watching that unprecedented band of billies that before I knew it, the two goats were in the centre of the V-shaped stage, and moving at a good gait across it. Horrors!

Hurriedly I exclaimed to Mr. Phillips, "There they are!" took a hurried aim at the tallest goat, and just as his head was going out of sight, let go. He flinched upward at the shoulders, started forward at a trot, and instantly disappeared from my view.

The instant my rifle cracked, Mr. Phillips said, imperatively,

"Don't move! Don't make a sound, and those goats will stay right where they are."

Instantly we "*froze*." All the goats sprang up, and stood at attention. All looked fixedly in our direction, but the distant eleven were like ourselves,—frozen into statues. In that band not a muscle moved for fully three minutes.

Finally the goats decided that the noise they had heard was nothing at which to be alarmed. One by one their heads began to move, and in five minutes their fright was over. Some went on feeding, but three or four of the band decided that they would saunter down our way and investigate that noise.

But what of my goat?

John slid over to my left, to look as far as possible behind the intercepting crag. Finally he said, "He's done for! He's lying out there, dead."

As soon as possible I looked at him; and sure enough, he lay stretched upon the grass, back uphill, and apparently very dead. The other goat had gone on and joined the ten.

The investigating committee came walking down toward us with a briskness which soon brought them within rifle-shot; and then Mr. Phillips picked out his Carnegie Museum goat and opened fire, at a range of about three hundred yards. The first shot went high, but at the next the goat came down, hit behind the shoulder. This greatly alarmed all the other goats, but they were so confused that three of them came down toward us at a fast trot. At two hundred yards I picked out one, and fired. At my third shot, it fell, but presently scrambled up, ran for the edge of the precipice and dropped over out of sight. It landed, mortally wounded, on some ragged rocks about fifty feet down, and to end its troubles a shot from the edge quickly finished it.

Mr. Phillips killed his first goat, and before the bunch got away, broke the leg of another. This also got over the edge of the precipice, and had to be finished up from the edge.

But a strange thing remains to be told.

By the time Mr. Phillips and I had each fired about two shots of the last round, in the course of which we ran well over to the right in order to command the field, to our blank amazement my first goat,—*the dead one!*—staggered to his feet, and started off toward the edge of the precipice. It was most uncanny to see a dead animal thus come to life!

"Look, Director," cried Charlie Smith, "your first goat's come to life! Kill him again! Kill him again, quick!"

I did so; and after the second killing he remained dead. I regret to say that in my haste to get those goats measured, skinned, and weighed before night, I was so absorbed that I forgot to observe closely where my first shot struck the goat that had to be killed twice. I think however, that it went through his liver and other organs without touching the vital portions of the lungs.

My first goat was the tallest one of the six we killed on that trip, but not the heaviest. He was a real patriarch, and decidedly on the downhill side of life. He was so old that he had but two incisor teeth remaining, and they were so loose they were almost useless. He was thin in flesh, and his pelage was not up to the mark in length. But in height he was tall, for he stood forty-two inches at the shoulders, with the foreleg pushed up where it belongs in a standing animal.

Mr. Phillips's Carnegie Museum goat was the heaviest

A Mountain Goat at Home

TAKEN SEPTEMBER 15, 1905. DISTANCE, TWELVE FEET.

one shot on that trip, its gross weight being two hundred and seventy-six pounds.

Charlie decided to roll the skinned carcass of my goat down the mountain, if possible within rifle-shot of the highest point of green timber, in the hope that a grizzly might find it, and thereby furnish a shot. He cut off the legs at the knees, and started the body rolling on the sky-pasture, end over end. It went like a wheel, whirling down at a terrific rate, sometimes jumping fifty feet. It went fully a quarter of a mile before it reached a small basin, and stopped. The other carcass, also, was rolled down. It went sidewise, like a bag of grain, and did not roll quite as far as the other.

By the time we had finished our work on the goats,—no trifling task,—night was fast approaching, and leaving all the heads, skins and meat for the morrow, we started for our new camp, five miles away.

We went down the meadow (thank goodness!), and soon struck the green timber; and then we went on down, down, and still farther down, always at thirty degrees, until it seemed to me we never would stop going down, never reach the bottom and the trail. But everything earthly has an end. At the end of a very long stretch of plunging and sliding, we reached Avalanche Creek, and drank deeply of the icy-cold water for which we had so long been athirst.

After three miles of travel down the creek, over slide rock, through green timber, yellow willows, more green timber and some down timber, we heard the cheerful whack of Huddleston's axe, and saw on tree-trunk and bough the ruddy glow of the new camp-fire.

The new camp was pitched in one of the most fascinating spots I ever camped within. The three tents stood at the southern edge of a fine, open grove of giant spruces that gave us good shelter on rainy days. Underneath the trees there was no underbrush, and the ground was deeply carpeted with dry needles. Grand mountains rose on either hand, practically from our campfire, and for our front view a fine valley opened southward for six miles, until its lower end was closed by the splendid mass of Roth Mountain and Glacier. Close at hand was a glorious pool of ice-water, and firewood "to burn." Yes, there was one other feature, of great moment,—abundant grass for our horses, in the open meadow in front of the tents.

To crown all these luxuries, Mr. Phillips announced that, according to mountain customs already established, and precedents fully set, that camp would then and there be named in my honor,—"Camp Hornaday." What more could any sportsman possibly desire?

CHAPTER VIII

THE MOUNTAIN GOAT
AS WE SAW HIM

A MOUNTAIN GOAT'S PARADISE—GENERAL CHARACTER OF
THE ANIMAL—ITS PLACE IN NATURE-NOT AN"ANTELOPE"-
DESCRIPTION-DISTRIBUTION-FOOD-SLEEPING-PLACES-
ACCIDENTS IN SNOW-SLIDES-SWIMMING-STUPID OR NOT
STUPID-COURAGE-A PHILOSOPHIC ANIMAL-AFFECTION-
FIGHTING POWERS-A GOAT KILLS A GRIZZLY-BEAR-SHY GOATS-
THE TRAGEDY OF THE SELF-TRAPPED GOATS.

> "On dizzy ledge of mountain wall, above the timber-line,
> I hear the riven slide-rock fall toward the stunted pine.
> Upon the paths I tread secure no foot dares follow me,
> For I am master of the crags, and march above the scree."
>
> —*The Cragmaster.*

OF THE THIRTY DAYS SPENT BY us in the home of the
mountain goat, two only were devoted to hunting goats
to shoot them. Scarcely a day passed without at least one
flock of goats in sight. We saw two hundred and thirty-nine

individuals, challenging all repeaters, and carefully eliminating those seen a second or third time. It was because we shot little that we saw much.

The high country between the Elk and the Bull Rivers is indeed a mountain goat's paradise, and what I there saw of that strange creature gave me an entirely new set of impressions regarding its character and habits. We studied goats alive, we photographed them, shot them, measured, weighed and ate them. Finally, we brought back with us five living specimens; and as I became really acquainted with this creature, its stock gradually rose to par.

In its form, the mountain goat is the most picturesque and droll-looking of all our large game animals. In some respects it is the bravest and hardiest of our hoofed animals, and the only one that is practically devoid of fear.

I am tempted to believe that of the few men who have hunted this strange animal, not many have taken time to become thoroughly acquainted with it, or to formulate a careful estimate of its character as revealed in its native mountains. Many writers have called it stupid, and very few have recognized it as an unrivalled mountaineer.

It is folly to attempt to compare any animal with the Himalayan tahr, the markhor, ibex or chamois until the comparer has seen and studied them in their homes. It is my belief, however, that no animal, hoofed or clawed, can surpass the climbing feats of the mountain goat. Certainly there is no American quadruped, not even the bold and hardy mountain sheep, which will with the utmost indifference climb an eighty-degree precipice, or jog across the face of a five-hundred-foot wall on a footing so narrow and uncertain that the strongest glass cannot detect it. I have never seen a mountain sheep take such desperate chances on the rocks as any goat will essay as serenely as a *boulevardier* promenades along a ten-foot sidewalk.

Once while bear-hunting at Lake Josephine with Charlie Smith, we came to a particularly high, long and smooth precipice. The rock wall was nearly half a mile long, and I think at least six hundred feet high, with a hundred feet of very steep slide-rock at its foot. It curved around a basin, like the wall of a gigantic colosseum. A big and shaggy billy goat elected to walk across the face of that appalling wall, about half-way from bottom to top, and as we slowly marched past far below, we watched him.

He was so high up that he felt no fear of us, and on the dizzy course that he elected to take, he looked like a mechanical toy pegging along. In that clear air, however, our glasses brought him down to us exceedingly well.

As is always the case when upon rocks, the firmness with which each hoof was planted,—to avoid slips, and to detect loose rocks,—gave the animal a very stiff gait. His steps were long, as regular as the tick of a clock, and not for one second did the animal hesitate regarding his course. His gait was as steady as if he were walking along a smooth road, and the directness of his course was remarkable. Occasionally he paused to look down and scrutinize us, but after each inspection he jogged on as indifferently as before. I am sure no mountain sheep, nor any other American animal, ever would attempt to go over that appalling course. It was a sight worth coming far to see.

How could the goat have known that a practicable route lay before him? There must have been a stratum of rock, harder than that above it, which had disintegrated more slowly than the rest of the wall, and left a projecting rim; but if so, our glasses failed to show it. The spectacle we saw was of a big goat briskly promenading on nothing, straight across the face of a bare wall. We watched him with bated breath, as one watches a steeple-jack who is repairing a finial; and for my part, I would not have shot him for a hundred dollars. To have killed him as he traced out that dizzy path would have been murder, no less; and think of the unforgettable horror of his fall through space upon that jagged slide rock!

Among naturalists, a good deal has been said about the inappropriateness of calling this animal a "goat." Some have laid stress upon its antelope-like characters, and some have seriously proposed, and even used, the name "goat antelope." If the mountain goat has about him anything that is particularly like the typical antelopes, it must be very deep down in his anatomy, for thus far it never has been pointed out. Think of an antelope with a form like a pygmy bison, carrying its head lower than its shoulders! Certainly the resemblance alleged is not found in his massive hoofs, his short cannon bone, his six-inch tail, his thick and post-like legs, or his *two* humps. The strange glands behind his horns are absolutely unique. His shoulder hump is like that of the European bison, but the hair-hump on his hindquarters is not reproduced on any other animal. His hairy coat is as unlike that of all antelopes now living as could possibly be imagined. His huge, India-rubber hoof resembles that of an antelope about as much as the hoof of a cow resembles that of a deer, but no more. This creature may not be a twin brother to *Capra hircus*—the first known goat; but at the same time, it is at least a million years from being an "antelope," of any sort. In fact, its build is far heavier than that of the other members of the two subfamilies of goats, to say nothing of the long-necked, slender-limbed and agile antelopes. A real crag-climbing antelope would indeed be a zoological novelty.

It is sometimes said that this animal is not a "goat" because it does not belong to the genus *Capra*, a group of animals restricted to the Old World. But there are a number of goats that do not belong to that genus, just as there are many deer that are not found in the genus *Cervus*. The word "goat" is a family name, the same as "deer." Shall we quarrel with the name "deer" as applied to our mule deer, or white-tailed deer, because they are outside the pale of *Cervus*? And yet, such a departure would be quite as well justified as are the objections to "goat" for the white cragmaster of the Rockies. If there are any writers who wish to call *Oreamnos* an "antelope," let them do so; but the Reader is advised that in adhering to the name "mountain goat" he will be sufficiently correct.

In order to set forth at a glance the mountain goat's place in nature, and also its nearest relatives, this diagram is offered:

				GENUS
ORDER UNGULATA,—THE HOOFED ANIMALS.	FAMILY BOVIDÆ: The Cattle, Sheep, Goats and Antelopes.	Subfamily CAPRINÆ: The Long-horned Goats.	First-known Goats . . . Persia, Greece, Palestine, etc.	*Capra*
			Ibexes . . . . . . Asia, Europe, N–E Africa.	*Capra*
			Turs . . . . . . Spain, Caucasus Mountains.	*Capra*
			Markhors . . . . . Himalayas, north-west of India.	*Capra*
		Subfamily RUPICAPRINÆ: The Short-horned Goats.	Tahrs (usually placed in Caprinæ) . . . . India, north and south; Arabia.	*Hemitragus*
			Serows, or Forest Goats . North-east Asia and Japan.	*Nemorhædus*
			Gorals . . . . . . North India, Tibet and China.	*Cemas*
			Rocky Mountain Goat . North-western North America.	*Oreamnos*
			Chamois . . . . Southern Europe.	*Rupicapra*
			Takin . . . . . Southern China.	*Budorcas*

The classification of both these subfamilies was founded upon the genus *Capra*, as first represented by the goats of Greece, Persia and Asia Minor. Later on, to avoid the multiplication of genera, the ibexes, markhors and others were taken

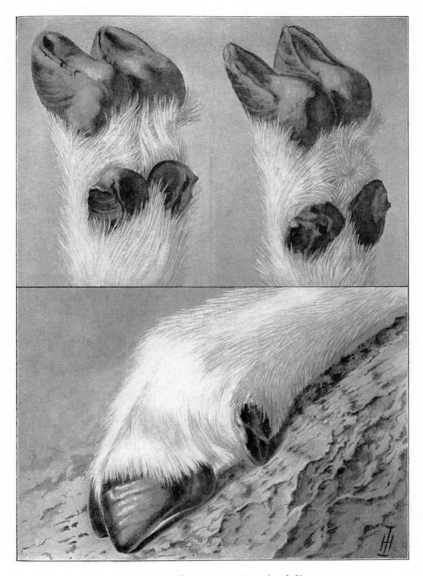

Front Foot of a Mountain Goat (top left)
Hind Foot of a Mountain Goat (top right)
The Function of a Mountain Goat's Rear Dew-Claws
THEY ARE USED AS A BRAKE IN DESCENDING INCLINES THAT ARE VERY STEEP AND SMOOTH.
DRAWN AS SEEN IN USE, IN THE ZOOLOGICAL PARK, NEW YORK.

into that genus. The goats of the Subfamily *Caprinte* are partly distinguished by flattened horns of considerable length, which sometimes curve upward in remarkable lines. From all these forms the Rocky Mountain goat differs materially, just as the prong-horned antelope differs from African antelopes.

The members of the Subfamily *Caprinte* are so much alike that they stand in one group, like a three-peaked island rising out of a sea. In the Subfamily *Rupicaprinte* there are six solitary islets, one each for the tahrs, serows, gorals, mountain goat, chamois and takin—all of them short-horned goats, no more, no less.

In its physical aspect the mountain goat is both striking and peculiar. In September it is brilliantly white, and its coat is as immaculate as a new fur cloak fresh from the hands of the furrier. From nose to tail, it is newly combed, and without spot or stain. It seems as white as newly fallen snow, but in direct comparison with snow there is a faint, cream-like tint. It is the only wild hoofed animal in the world (s.f.a.k.) which is pure white all the year round; for in spring and summer the white mountain sheep stains his coat very badly.

The pelage of the mountain goat is the finest and softest, and also the warmest, to be found on any North American hoofed animal except the musk-ox. To wind, dry cold and snow it is seemingly impervious, but there are times and seasons when the rain-coat is imperfect, and too short to shed rain. In September, the rain-coat is not fully developed, and the fine pelage which covers the sides is almost as soft as down. As winter approaches, the fine hair of the under coat seems to stop growing, but the coarser and straighter hair of he on until it has attained such luxuriant length that the animal takes on a shaggy appearance. Late in November this reaches its full length. Even in September, the beard and knee-breeches are of good length, and these, with the queerly rounded crests, on the shoulders and on the hindquarters, contain the only hair of the whole coat that is coarse and harsh.

About six goats out of every seven are pure white, but the coat of the seventh contains in its tail, and along the pelvic crest, a few scattering, dark-brown hairs. This is noticeable on kids in their first year, as well as on adult animals. Occasionally the tail of a goat contains so many dark hairs that the normal color is really changed; but it should be remembered that these occasional occurrences of brown hairs do not indicate any specific differences.

The goat is very stockily built,—for stability and strength rather than for agility and speed. The long spinal processes of his dorsal vertebrae give him a hump somewhat like that of a bison; and like a bison he carries his head low, and has short, thick legs, terminating in big hoofs. His body is big and full, and his sides stick out with plenty. He can carry his head above the line of his neck and shoulders, but he seldom does so save when frightened, or looking up.

His horns are jet black, round, very smooth for the terminal half, and sharp as skewers. When the goat fights, he gets close up to his assailant's forequarters, and with a powerful thrust diagonally upward, punctures his enemy's abdomen. In attacking, the movements of the goat are exceedingly jerky and spasmodic, advancing and whirling away again with the quick jumps of the modern prize-fighter. The horns are not long, usually ranging in length from 9 to 11 inches by 5-3/4 inches in basal circumference. The longest pair on record is owned by Mr. Clive Phillips-Wolley, of Victoria, B. C., and its length is eleven and one-half inches.

The gland behind the horn of the mountain goat is largest during September and October, and subsides somewhat after the close of the mating season. If it serves any useful purpose, that purpose is as yet unknown. On September 11th, each gland is about the size of a small black-walnut, flattened on the naked surface which touches the horn, and round within the skin. Instead of lying flat upon the skull, as shown by many taxidermists, the naked surface stands *upon its edge*. It is decidedly concave at the centre, black in color, smooth, and practically odorless. It fits up closely against the base of the horn, and of the naked portion only a narrow edge is visible. We found no oil, nor even moisture, exuding. When cut into sections, the interior appears to be calloused flesh, like the palm of the human hand. On the date mentioned above, the naked portion of the gland of a large male goat was one and one-half inches in diameter, and at the centre there was a pronounced depression. Of the six goats killed by us, the horns of none showed evidence of any disintegrating action from these glands. Yet one of my specimens was very old. The female goat possesses these glands, but they are proportionately smaller than those of males of the same age. On the living animal they are not conspicuous.

The eyes of the adult goat are not "jet black." The iris is straw-color, a little darker than Naples yellow, and the pupil is a broad, blunt-ended ellipse. J. Kanofsky, of New York, makes them correctly. The edge of the eyelid, and the naked portions of the nostrils and lips, are black. The eyes of a young kid are so dark they appear to be all black, but when nine months old the iris assumes its true color.

The hoofs are like big, twin masses of India-rubber,—a ball of soft rubber, encased in a strong shell of hard rubber. It is chiefly the soft rubber which enables this strange animal to climb as it does. The shell of hard rubber is thin, and around the front half of the hoof it forms an edge which may be sharp or blunt, according to the wear upon it. On the front hoofs, this edge always is more worn than on the rear hoofs, because the former do the hardest work. The bottom of a goat's hoof is very different from that of a mountain sheep, the former being concave near the toe, and convex at the heel, while that of the sheep is a hollow cup, with sharp edges.

I was rather pleased at finding out the trick by which a goat descends a dangerously steep incline. Over smooth rock that stands at an angle of forty-five degrees,—on which no man can stand, much less move about,—a mountain sheep goes down pell-mell, slipping, sliding and plunging almost helplessly until it reaches some kind of a stopping-place.

Not so the goat. I once induced a captive goat to descend a plank inclined at forty-five degrees, and he tobogganed on his rear hoofs, with his monstrous dewclaws pressed hard upon the wood, and his hindlegs held quite stiff. His hocks were within three inches of the wood and his rubber-like dew-claws acted as first-class brakes. His front hoofs guided his course, and took advantage of every rough spot, but the animal did not slide upon them, as he did upon the posterior pair.

The front feet possess a surprising amount of grasping power. It is natural for a goat leaping high up to hook his front feet over any available edge, and hold fast until his rear hoofs can find a hold, and push up. In the Zoological Park, one of our goats had a great fancy for climbing a tree-box that protected a small red-cedar tree, and perching for minutes upon the tops of the four posts, seven feet from the ground. The posts were covered with wire netting of half-inch mesh. The goat leaped upon the side of this, dug the points of his hoofs against the rough surface, and kept digging until he could reach the top of a post with one foot, and hook it over. After that the rest was easy, and it was always a droll sight to see that creature so poised, calmly surveying the landscape.

The long, straight beard of a male goat always imparts to the animal an uncanny, and even human-like appearance. When he sits down, dog-fashion, and turns his head first one way and then the other while he gazes admiringly upon the scenery before him, his appearance is strongly suggestive of patriarchal humanity.

Although the true abiding-place of the mountain goat is from timber-line to the tops of the summit divides, and the precipices which buttress the peaks, it wanders elsewhere with a degree of erratic freedom that in a cliff-dweller is remarkable. It seems very strange for white goats to range far down into the timber, and remain there, but they often do so. In 1904 a large band of goats, reported at thirty or more, came down to Sparwood station on the railway a few miles below

Michel, to visit a salt-lick. At Skaguay, Alaska, goats have been killed in the suburbs of the town, only a few feet above tide-water. Mr. W. H. Wright says that until very recently goats descended every fall from the main range of the Rocky Mountains in north-western Montana, and crossed the level Flathead Valley, a distance of about fifteen miles, to the Mission Mountains, returning in the spring.

The known range of the mountain goat extends from the Teton Mountains of Wyoming (1892) northward along the main range of the Rockies to the latitude of Ft. Simpson, 62°. Northward of that point, we lack information, but it is very probable that on the main Rocky Mountain range only, but not westward thereof, it will be found much farther north than the sixty-second parallel.

Along the Pacific coast, from Vancouver northward to Cook Inlet, the range of this animal in the coast mountains is almost continuous. From the great interior area of Yukon Territory, from the main chain of the Rockies to the coast mountains, the species is totally absent.

Regarding the eastern limit of the mountain goat, a surprising record has come from Mr. M.P. Dunham, of Ovando, Montana, a guide and hunter of forty years' experience on the

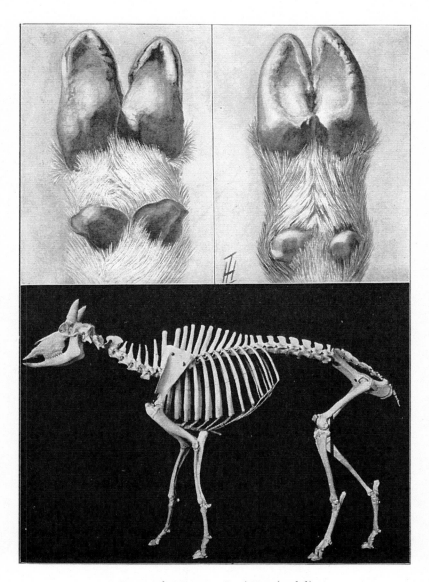

Bottom of a Mountain Goat's Foot (top left)
Bottom of a Sheep's Foot (top right)
Skeleton of an Adult Mail Mountain Goat
By courtesy of the Field Columbian Museum, Chicago. F.J.V. Skiff, Director.

trail, who knows this animal very well. He states that in 1882 or 1883, he killed two mountain goats in the Chalk Buttes on Box Elder Creek, a tributary of the Little Missouri, in western North Dakota. At first the great distance of this locality (about four hundred miles)· from the main range of the Rockies made this report seem almost incredible, but the record comes to me directly from Mr. Dunham, and his standing fairly compels belief. Between the Little Missouri and the Rockies the great plains are broken by only a few small and widely separated groups of mountains, all of which rise like islands out of a sea. Mr. George Bird Grinnell once received a report of goats having been killed by Indians in the Little Snowy mountains, a group well out on the Montana plains.

The map accompanying these notes shows only actual occurrences of *Oreamnos* during the past fifteen years. Along the Coast of British Columbia and Alaska, and the Stickine and Skeena Rivers, the occurrences reported were so numerous that the lines are really continuous. Beyond doubt, the goat occurs in many localities not marked on the map; but it seems best to be exact, and stop short of uncertainties.

We endeavored to learn something regarding the food habits of the goat as displayed on the mountain summits of south-eastern British Columbia. To this end, I took a sample of the contents of the stomach of my first goat, panned it out, and permanently preserved a series of specimens.

First of all, we found that on those mountains, in September, *Oreamnos* is not a grazing animal. Of grass we found only a few blades. It would seem however, that this was due to an autumn caprice, for surely in other seasons, and in other localities, this animal must feed upon grass.

The stomach contained no woody fibre, and nothing to indicate a browsing habit, save a few leaves of the yellow willow, which grows in the sunshine of open valleys, or upon slide-ways. In that locality at least, the goat is not a September browser. During our whole thirty days on his home range, we saw not one twig, nor a piece of bark, that had been bitten off by goat or sheep.

In September, the British Columbian goat is a cropper. He lives by cropping the thick leaves, and stems also, of a number of large weed-like plants which grow abundantly up to timber-line. Our first two goats were shot while feeding upon a lace-leaved anemone or pasque flower, called *Pulsatilla occidentalis*. Its leaves are finely cut and lace-like, and one plant furnishes several good mouthfuls. It was quite abundant, and the goats were fond of it. We found it in fruit, with the peduncle elongated into an upright stalk from eight to ten inches high, crowned by a head of silky achenes, with long, plumose styles, very suggestive of a ripe dandelion.

Here is the whole array of species that we found in my goat's stomach, and matched by plants found growing around our camp. The entire mass would have filled a peck measure, and it was so slightly masticated that we had no great difficulty in recognizing its principal ingredients. My specimens were identified by Dr. D.T. MacDougal, as follows:

Lace-Leaved Anemone . . . *Pulsatilla occidentalis.*
Mountain Sorrel . . . *Otyria digyna.*
Wild Valerian . . . *Valeriana.*
Yellow Willow . . . *Salix.*
Squaw-Weed . . . *Senecio triangularis.*
"Goat-Weed," with flower like candytuft . . . *Unidentified.*
Mountain-Timothy . . . *Phleum alpinum.*
"Wild Pea" . . . *Hedysarum.*
Wild Strawberry . . . *Unidentifiable.*

RANGE OF THE WHITE MOUNTAIN GOAT, AS IT IS IN 1906, EXCEPTING THE TETON MOUNTAINS

UNITED STATES

Wyoming
Teton Mountains, 1892 (W. H. Wright)

Montana
Big Hole Country, 1899 (Samuel C. Pirie)
Granite Country; Mission Range, Flathead
Reservation (W. H. Wright)
St. Mary's Lakes region, 1902 (A. P. Proctor)

Idaho
Bitter Root Mountains (W. H. Wright)

Washington
Silverton, Cascade Mountains, 1892 (A. P. Proctor)
Conconally, 1884; Slocan Mountains and Lake
Chelan (W. H. Wright)

BRITISH COLUMBIA

Fernie: 1904 (H. W. Herchmer)

Elk River: 1905 (John M. Phillips)

Bull River: 1905 (B. T. Van Nostrand)

Spillamachene River: Golden, 1904 (Madison Grant)

Clinton: 1905 (F. Soues)

Quesnel Forks: 1905 (W. Stephenson)

Bakerville (north-east): 1905 (James McKern)

Slocan Lake
East, 1888; Similkameen River, 1888; Coquihalla
River,1888; Harrison Lake; Pitt Lake, north; Princess
Louise Inlet; Bridge River; Wauchope (Brewer Creek);
Yellowhead Pass; Canoe River, 1885; Head of Fraser
River; Peace River, longitude 125°, latitude 56°;
Knight Inlet, latitude 51°; Bute Inlet; Dean Channel;
Gardiner Canal; Kitimat Arm; Skeena River (from
Port Essington 200 miles up); Nass River; Stickine;
Iscoot; McDame Creek (Dease River); Scheslay River;
Francis Lake.

"The Goat is the most widely distributed animal in
British Columbia, and except the black bear is the only
animal found throughout the length and breadth of
the province. Apparently it is equally at home in the
dry belt, and the wet coast belt lying east and west
of the Cascade Mountains."-Letter and map, dated
March 12, 1906. (Warburton Pike)

Big-Horn Hills
Head of Athabasca River, 1902 (Eastern slope of
Rockies.) (G. 0. Shields)

Asbanola
Similkameen; West Kootenay; Bridge River; Empire
Valley; Chilcotin; Knight's Inlet; Stickine River,"and
a dozen other places between Lagan and Wrangel. It
is not found on Vancouver Island. I believe it occurs
almost everywhere else.,"-1906. (Clive Phillips-Wolley)

Tidewater Inlets
Jervis; Bute; Knight's; Kingcome; Khutze and
Gardiner, etc. to 60° north latitude. Not on Vancouver
Island or other islands. (Francis Kermode)

Atlin: 1906 (J. Williams)

South Fork of Stickine River: 1905 (Samuel C. Pirie)

"Skeena and Nass Rivers, for 200 miles up," from
Port Essington. (A. G. Hains)

Goat River Mountains: Isaac's Lake (Barkerville)
(James McKern)

YUKON TERRITORY
Not found north of McMillan River (J. B. Tyrrell)
Not found north of the summit of White Pass, nor
near Lake Bennett . (W. C. McKenzie —Skaguay)

Main range of Rocky Mountains, from Peace River to
latitude of Fort Simpson (W. J. McLean)

**Lake Francis: (eastward; latitude 61° 30', longitude
129°;1906).**
"There are no goats in the Yukon Territory on the
western slopes of the Rocky Mountains, or other
interior ranges. I know nothing about the eastern
slopes. Goats occur on the eastern slopes of the coast
ranges, and some of the spurs. The same statement will
apply to Alaska." (Charles Sheldon)

ALASKA
"Almost anywhere near sea-coast from Washington
to Kenai Peninsula." But "rarely found beyond Coast
Range" (eastward), 1906. (John W. Worden)

Skaguay: Glacier Station (A. L. Andrews and W. C. McKenzie)

Juneau, within 30 miles (I.N. Stephenson)

Chilkat River, 45 miles up, 1905 (R. A. Gunnison)

Kluane Lake, 1905 (W. L. Breeze)

Copper River, 1900, "mountains near mouth" (D. G. Elliot)

Wrangel Mountains, 1900 (Gerdine); Mt. St. Elias range, near Yakutat, 1899; Controller Bay region; between Tanana and White Rivers, 1898. (Alfred H. Brooks)

Knick River, 1901 (J. Alden Loring)

Kenai Peninsula, 1903 (James H. Kidder)

This is the greatest array of species that I ever found in the stomach of one animal. It shows that in choosing his food the goat is a broad-minded creature, with a versatile and vigorous appetite. No wonder his sides are round. It is probable that in spring the goat's bill of fare includes many species of plants not in the above list, and that throughout the year it varies greatly. In spring the flesh of this animal is so strongly flavored by the wild onion, then greedily fed upon, that it is quite unpalatable; but by September that flavor has totally disappeared, and goat's flesh, cooked and seasoned with a modicum of intelligence, is then as good as venison of the same age.

In winter, goats sometimes,—but not frequently— browse upon the twigs of coniferous trees. Mr. Phillips has seen evergreen twigs that have been bitten off for food, when the snow lay deep on the mountains; and he says that in winter the goats go down into the green timber to look for food.

Judging by what we saw in the Elk River mountains, the mountain goat avoids the drifting snows of winter by choosing for its sleeping-places the knife-like edges of high "hogbacks" between mountain peaks. And yet, over those ridges the wind sweeps with a fierceness and frigidity which it seems no living creature could long withstand. It is doubtful if the big-horn ever lies down to rest and to sleep on a hogback over which the wind is blowing seventy miles an hour, with a temperature of forty degrees below zero; but the goat does this very thing. We saw a dozen ridge summits, paved with their droppings, which Norboe and Smith assured us were the winter sleeping-places of goats. In winter goats also seek food upon the bleak ridges from which the snow is continually swept clean by the wind.

Up to the time we left the mountains (September 30) the rutting season had not begun. Our guides say it does not begin until December 1. The old male goats were living quite apart from the herds of females and young males, and there was not the slightest sign of sexual excitement. The herds were quiet, to the point of dullness. The open pastures between timber-line and the naked rocks of the summits were covered with food, and once below his beloved rocks a goat had only to stoop and take. Often we saw goats lie on their pastures, motionless for hours, unable to eat more. They loved to lie on southern slopes, bathing themselves in the glorious sunshine, and blinking away the hours. Whenever a herd was sighted at rest, it was safe to count upon its remaining there for an hour or two, unless disturbed by a hunter.

Everywhere we went, I watched the slides for evidences of accidents to goats through being overwhelmed by spring avalanches, but saw none. I closely questioned Charlie Smith and the Norboe brothers, but none of them could recall a

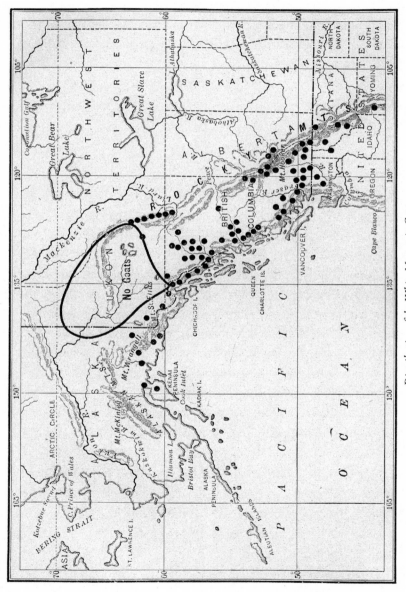

Distribution of the White Mountain Goat

THE BLACK DOTS REPRESENT ACTUAL OCCURRENCES, AS RECORDED.

single instance of a dead goat in a snow-slide. They said the goats are too wary to be caught. But there are exceptions. Mr. W. Stephenson writes me from Quesnel Forks, central British Columbia, of a goat which was killed in a snow slide in May, 1905, in the mountains east of that town. This is the only record of the kind that ever has come to me, but there is one other of a fearfully injured goat, which I fully believe was hurt in an avalanche.

Late in the spring of 1902, when Mr. G. O. Shields was taking photographs in the Rocky Mountains of British Columbia, he found on a small mountain-pasture a goat which for several days remained in one spot. At last his curiosity was aroused, and on procuring a particularly good view of the animal through a powerful field-glass, he found that it had been seriously injured by some accident. "Its face was badly cut and torn," says Mr. Shields, "and a section of its nose some six inches long, extending from about the eyes to the tip of the nose, was an open sore. There was also a wound in one shoulder. I told Mr. Wright, the guide, that I thought it would be best to go up and see what the trouble was with this animal.

"He went, and Coleman with him. They easily got within fifty yards of the goat, and found that the entire upper portion of its face [muzzle] had been torn off, and that the nostrils were exposed and bleeding. They naturally concluded that as soon as warm weather and flies came, the goat would die from the effects of its misfortune. Accordingly they crawled up, made several photographs of the goat in various positions, then killed it, in order to put it out of its misery."

Mr. Shields believes that the carrying away of the goat's face was done in some manner by a snow-slide, in which the goat's head was held very firmly while either a sharp-edged rock of large size, or a log, passed over it, grinding away skin and bone, and laying bare the bottom of the nasal passage.

It seems that when occasion demands it, the mountain goat can swim very well, and does not hesitate to do so. I have already mentioned the spring and fall migrations of goats across the valley of the Flathead, as observed by Mr. W. H. Wright. In making that journey the animals always had to swim the Flathead River. Farther north, in Athabasca, Mr. Wright and Mr. Shields saw the trails of goats that had crossed one of the branches of Athabasca River, by swimming. Beyond doubt it would be possible to learn of many instances of river-swimming by goats.

Many authors have written of the "stupidity" of the mountain goat; and on that subject I may as well record here the conclusions of Mr. Phillips, our guides and the writer.

First, however, let me correct—for British Columbia at least—a trifling error that is rather common in recipes for stalking the mountain goat. Some writers say, "first get above him," etc. We say, spare yourself that trouble; for it is quite unnecessary. While it is possible to scale all sorts of peaks, and climb above the goat, he who does so (in British Columbia) will find his hunting seriously handicapped by impassable slopes of rock that keep him away from the very points from which he would fain look below. The best way to hunt goats is to stalk them on the level, and shoot them on the square. Mr. Phillips says that in all the goat-hunting of which he personally knows, only two goats have been shot from above.

Personally I know not how wary goats are in countries wherein they have been much hunted; for the goats of Elk River actually did not know the significance of the report of fire-arms! This is not necessarily stupidity. Even wolves are "tame "in the far north, where C. J. Jones fought them, and take risks which any southern wolf would regard as suicidal. It takes a little time for a wild species to learn what it is to be shot, and to flee quickly and far from the presence of man.

I regard the primitive mountain goat as an animal to whom fear is almost an unknown sensation. He is serenely indifferent to the dangers of crag-climbing and ledge-walking, and to him a five-hundred-foot precipice is no more than a sidewalk to a domestic goat. So long as he has six inches of rough points on which to plant his rubber-like hoofs, he considers the route practicable. Why, then, he would say, should he be timid about a few strange animals which walk upright, but never dare to meet him face to face on the walls? Why should he jump and tremble because he hears a loud noise, like the bang of a big rock falling a hundred feet and exploding on the slide-rock? Among men, the peacefully minded gentleman naturally assumes that no one will wantonly insult or attack him; therefore he regards his fellows with calmness and serenity, unarmed. The mountain goat has practically no enemies save men and eagles. The grizzly bear knows that *Oreamnos* is not for him, and for good and sufficient reasons the mountain lion and wolf do their hunting far below him.

Truly, the goats we saw at home were unacquainted with fear. They have no nerves! With dogs and men you can corner a goat on a ledge, and hold him there for an hour or two. He will get very angry, and grit his teeth, and perhaps kill several of your dogs, but he will not get " rattled," and he will neither fall off nor leap off to certain death, as any deer surely will do under such circumstances. There are some men, and also some animals, who do not become panic-stricken, even when they are being killed; and of the latter I think the mountain goat is one.

We like a "nervy "man, or a nervy animal—which in common parlance means an individual *without* nerves!

Fifty years ago the grizzly bear was an animal which knew not fear of any living thing; and then he was Great. To-day the grizzly is a quitter. In nine cases out of every ten, the moment

he sees a man, he runs from him, frantically. A cotton-tail rabbit does not turn tail more quickly or more thoroughly than
he. He is wiser than he was; but we don't respect him as much
as we did fifty years ago.

The mountain goat seems to have rather dull visual powers. We think so because he does not seem to see us as soon as
we discover him, or at least does not manifest fear by running
from us. But it may be that he does see us, as quickly as a deer
or sheep, or bear; but having only a fraction of their suspicion
of man, he does not move off until he feels really forced to do
so. Small as its eyes are, a grizzly is very keen-sighted; and I can
see no reason for believing that the goat is of dull vision simply
because he is not ever ready to run at the slightest alarm.

More than once we had positive proof that the mountain goat does not take alarm and run from man the moment
his presence is detected. On the day I killed my grizzly bear,
Charlie Smith and I rode to Goat Pass to inspect our cache
of provisions and other things, half in the hope of finding a
silver-tip in the act of robbing us. Besides ourselves and our
two horses, the dog was with us, and between men, horses and
dog there certainly was a variety of what Mr. Seton aptly calls
"man scent."

When we reached our cache, from which we overlooked
the head gorge of Goat Creek, we saw a billy goat feeding on the
fearfully steep declivity which comes down from Phillips Peak.

"That would be our goat, if we wanted him, Charlie."

"You could surely knock him from here," said Charlie. "I
wonder if he ain't *ever* going to go!"

"Can it be that he don't see us?"

"If he ain't blind he must see us; and unless he's got an
awful cold in his head, he must smell us, too."

For fully five minutes, I should think, that goat kept on
feeding. At last, however, as we were mounting to ride on, he

left off, and started to climb on up the slope,—not exactly in alarm, but in a state of what judges call "reasonable doubt."

As might be expected of an animal that is born and reared amid appalling dangers of many kinds, the mountain goat is a creature of philosophic mind. Through sheer necessity, he is much given to original thinking; and like all thoughtful animals, his mental processes and his moods and tenses are highly interesting. Watch him closely, day after day, and you will soon conclude that the term "stupid "does not apply to him. Let us see whether, with our slight knowledge of him, we can in a small measure put ourselves in his mental place.

In the first place, *Oreamnos* has chosen the rugged crags at and above timber-line as the ground best calculated to enable him to escape from his wild-animal enemies—the bears, pumas and wolves. From these his rugged heights render him measurably secure. When danger threatens, and he climbs up or down to the sheltering arms of the steepest precipice he can find, no wild creature without wings dares to follow him. Unfortunately, however, his evolution did not take into account the necessity of adequate provisions for safety from the modern rifleman. And how could it? There is no such thing as safety for any wild creature, save under man's own laws.

In times of danger the elk, the moose and deer generally stampede wildly over the face of Nature, without much thought. Usually they are able to run straight away from the hunter. To them the great desideratum is *speed for the first mile.* But not so the goat. He must find a retreat accessible to him, but inaccessible to his pursuer. He must disappear as quickly as possible, but he must also avoid getting into a *cul-de-sac* from which he cannot escape.

All these requirements make a goat think. He must look ahead, and plan out his line of retreat, or come to grief. A deer has the quick dash and *elan* of a cavalryman; but the goat figures things out carefully, on scientific principles, like a general of artillery.

Some hunters of wild goats have called the goat a stupid animal, because he does not quickly comprehend the deadliness of man. But is that proof that he really is stupid? Let us see.

No mountain hunter will call the mountain sheep a stupid animal. In regions wherein the sheep have been shot at, and have learned that a "bang "means a rifle, and a rifle means a hunter, the big-horn is a very alert and wary animal. In such regions the successful chase of the mountain sheep demands the qualities that make up a first-class sportsman,—endurance, judgment, and skill with the rifle. But how is it in countries wherein the wild sheep have not been hunted by man, and know nothing of white hunters and fire-arms? Ask Mr. Charles Sheldon, Mr. Carl Rungius, Mr. James H. Kidder and Mr. Thomas D. Leonard about the sheep which they found so abundant in the Kenai Peninsula, in the Yukon Territory and on the Stickine River. They will tell you that the sheep which they hunted did not know the meaning of a rifle-shot; that they only partially realized the deadliness of man; that when a flock was fired at, the sheep threw up their heads, and gazed and hesitated, until often five shots could be fired at a bunch before it finally realized the danger, and ran out of range.

That was not due to dullness of mind, or stupidity. It was due to a *lack of information*,—ignorance of existing facts.

Take the record of our four days on Goat Pass, where we camped literally on the goat's highway between two groups of mountains. The first day we saw forty-seven goats, all of which saw us; and three of them ran through our camp. On the third day we saw forty-two goats, and were seen by all of them. We did not fire a shot on those mountains until the third day, when we killed two goats. On the fourth day it was remarked with surprise that all the goats had "left the country!" This was literally true. Word had been passed around among the ten or twelve flocks originally living there, that there was danger afoot; and as if by magic, one hundred and ten of the one hundred and fifteen goats we had seen simply vanished! The only bunch that remained was a flock of five nannies and kids which were isolated on a rugged mountain that ran off due westward from the main chain of peaks on which we were. Evidently they did not get the word which alarmed all the rest. We had fired our rifles in one spot only, which was at the extreme northern end of that goat-infested area. Our guides remarked, "We've got to get out of here, and look for goats somewhere else, if we want to find any more."

Mr. F. B. Wellman, of Banff, a very observing guide, who has seen much of goat and sheep hunting, does not regard the sheep as any more wary and keen-sighted than the goat. He has seen large herds of goats post sentinels who watched for danger so keenly and intelligently that the approach of a hunter within shooting-distance was quite impossible. The sentries watch in every direction. Mr. Wellman advanced the theory that the goat seems easier to stalk than the sheep because the coat of the former is so conspicuous that the hunter can see it long before it sees him; and it is also easy to keep it in view while stalking. On the other hand, all the colors of the big-horn match so well with his surroundings that he is difficult to locate, and thereby often is enabled to see the hunter before the hunter sees him! I think this conclusion is very reasonable, and entirely correct.

In my opinion, no animal which can live all the year round, and prosper, above timber-line in the British Columbian Rockies, can rightly be called stupid. If the mountain goat were not a good observer, a good reasoner, and at all times cool and level-headed, he would continually be coming to grief. He would be drowned by freshets, or carried down by snow-combs' and avalanches, or blown off precipices, or caught napping by grizzly bears. But none of those unpleasant things happen unto him.

Excepting the musk-ox, the mountain goat is the only North American hoofed animal which does not lose its head when brought to bay by dogs or men. If you round up a deer, elk, moose or caribou on a narrow ledge, or on the edge of a precipice, it will cheerfully leap off into eternity in order to escape the terrors of man and dog. Mr. Wellman says that sometimes a wounded sheep on the edge of a cliff will throw itself over, but that no goat will do this. The latter believes that one goat on a ledge is worth two in mid-air. With marvelous coolness he stands fast, and waits for something favorable to turn up. If he can charge the dogs that annoy him, and gore them to death, or toss them off into space, he will gladly do so; but if he cannot, he "stands pat" on his ledge, grits his teeth and stamps with vexation, and says, "Well, what are you going to do about it?" Among white hunters, it is not considered either fair or sportsman-like to shoot a goat or sheep that has been "cornered "on a ledge, unless it is wounded.

The action of a female goat photographed in August, 1905, on Ptarmigan Mountain, B. C., by Professor Henry F. Osborn, reveals much of goat character, bearing especially upon courage and affection. On the edge of a ragged precipice, which with great care was practicable for goats, the old nanny and her four-months-old kid were overtaken, and brought to bay. The way down to safety was so steep and dangerous that it could be taken only with caution and judgment; but if the mother had disregarded her offspring, she could instantly have found safety for herself by going down where no dog could follow her.

With the dog so close at hand, the mother decided that she could not lead the way down, for fear her offspring would be seized before it left the summit. She therefore faced the dog, with the kid behind her, and several times attempted to charge her tormentor. But the dog was alert, and easily kept out of the way. As long as the dog bayed the pair, the mother goat determinedly but patiently stood her ground. This lasted for some minutes. Finally Professor Osborn called off the dog, whereupon the mother-goat lost no time in climbing down the precipice, with her offspring following close behind. (A full account of this remarkable experience, written by Professor Osborn, and fully illustrated, will be found in the Tenth Annual Report of the New York Zoological Society. The Ninth Annual Report, of the same series, contains an admirable illustrated paper on "The Mountain Goat," by Mr. Madison Grant.)

Excepting the musk-ox and female grizzly bear, what other American animal would have taken such risks for its young, or would have acted so bravely and so sensibly?

Of course it is to be expected that any wild animal will to the best of its ability defend its young against the attacks of other animals. In the spring of 1905, Mr. Charles L. Smith saw a female goat successfully defend her kid from a golden eagle which sought to seize it. The goat stood close beside her young, and whenever the eagle swooped, and sought to seize the kid, the mother reared on her hindlegs, and with her horns made thrust after thrust at the eagle. In a short time the eagle abandoned its attempt.

The mountain goat is not only sublimely courageous in climbing, and in traversing precipices, but as occasion requires, it is also a bold and effective fighter. Those who know the limit of its temper can judge of the risks of life and limb which Mr. Phillips ran when he faced an angry "billy" on a two-foot ledge, at a distance of six feet or less, in taking a series of photographs of the animal. One determined charge, and one fierce upward thrust of those sharp horns, would have thrown the daring photographer off the ledge to instant death.

The fighting qualities of this remarkable animal are best illustrated by the records of actual occurrences. For a number of years Mr. Arthur B. Fenwick has maintained a large ranch about fourteen miles north of Fort Steele, British Columbia. Being an ardent sportsman and nature-lover he has seen much of the mountain goats, sheep, bears and other animals that literally surround him. In response to an inquiry, Mr. Fenwick wrote me as follows:

"As to the fighting capacity of a full-grown billy goat, he will, with a little luck, kill almost anything. The story I told Mr. Van Nostrand related to an occurrence on Joseph's Prairie, where Cranbrook now stands. A full-grown billy goat happened to stray out there, and old Chief Isadore, who was camped there, saw it. He and two other Indians thought that with horses, dogs and ropes they could catch the animal, alive. I think fifteen dogs left the camp for the goat. A little later a squaw saw that they were having a bad mix-up, and ran out to the Indians with a rifle. One of them shot the goat. All but two of the dogs were killed on the spot, or died very shortly. It was with the greatest difficulty that the Indians saved their horses from getting punctured by those terrible little horns.

"I will tell you another fact, which without the explanation you would not believe. A goat will sometimes kill a full-grown silver-tip bear! I once found a big goat, dead, which evidently had been killed by a silver-tip, as there were lots of tracks all around, and the goat's back was broken. I thought it queer that the bear had not taken the goat away and buried it, as usual, so I looked around. I found a large silver-tip bear, dead, and all bloated up; and when I examined him I found that the goat had punched him twice, just back of the heart. He had been able to kill the goat, and had then gone off and died."

In the spring of 1905, when Messrs. Chapman and White, of Fort Steele, caught for us the five goat kids received by me at Fort Steele in October, two of their best dogs were killed by goats. Mr. B.T. Van Nostrand, of Brooklyn, described the occurrence, as follows:

"They started after the goats with ten dogs. The larger dogs ran up to the old goats, and tried to seize them by their heads. Before the dogs could be called off, the first two were instantly gored, and hurled over a precipice. White said the goats stood their ground, and tossed the dogs so quickly they could hardly realize what had happened until they saw the dogs in the air, bleeding from the wounds made by the horns of the goats. When White and Chapman appeared, the goats moved off. The remaining dogs were able to separate the kids from the rest of the band, and finally they caught five."

It seems that sometimes goats kill each other.

"Four years ago," continued Mr. Van Nostrand, "I was shooting in about the same locality as that in which your goats were caught, and there I witnessed the finish of a fight between two large billies. I had shot at a mountain sheep ram on the sky-line, and to find out the effect of my shot I climbed to the summit. At the top I sat down to rest, and look for the ram, and enjoy the grandeur of the view. As I sat there motionless, two goats came around a corner of rock only about fifty yards away from me. They were walking rather fast, and whenever the goat in the rear caught up with the one before him, he gave it a blow with his head. It did not seem to be a vigorous butt, and at first I thought it was play. They were making a low, peculiar sound, such as I cannot describe in words.

"In a very short time, one of the goats lay down behind a large rock, so that I could see only its head. The other goat stood, and looked at the one lying down. Just then they saw me, and this seemed to stop the fight, for the standing goat began to move away. I fired and killed him; but to my surprise the other goat lay still. I could not hit him from where I was without spoiling his head, so I climbed around to get a better shot. Finally I got quite close, and had a good general view of him. Then he stood up, took one or two steps, and stood still. I then saw that he was bleeding around his neck, that one flank was badly torn, and that some of his intestines were hanging out until they almost touched the ground! He was so far gone he could scarcely stand, and to end his troubles quickly, I shot him.

"That was the only fight to the death that I ever saw among wild animals, and it was done quite differently from what I expected. There was no pawing of the ground, and no frenzied charging. One goat quietly walked up to the other, and gave him a fierce thrust. The victorious goat was not even scratched. I presume his first thrust was fatal to the victim."

But there are times when even the icy-nerved goat becomes thoroughly frightened. In questioning Mr. Phillips on this point he related the following incident: "The only time I ever saw a goat really frightened, and show fear, was when Charlie Smith and I were hunting on the head of Wilson Creek. We had sighted a grizzly bear, and were following him up the side of a mountain and over the summit. It took us two hours to climb a distance that he covered in one. Near the summit the bear's trail led us through a little notch, and past the base of a pinnacle of bare rock, about two hundred feet high, that ran up very much like a cathedral spire. "Now it happened that as the bear passed through the little notch he frightened an old, long-bearded billy goat, who immediately started up the pinnacle as hard as he could go, and climbed clear to its summit. And there the old fellow stood, or rather hung, in a most ridiculous attitude. His front feet were hooked over the eastern edge of the point, like a man looking over the peak of a steep house-roof, and holding on by his hands. His body and hindlegs were well down on the other side of the pinnacle, and completely overhung a frightful precipice.

"He was so interested in the bear that he paid no attention to us. We talked to him, and tried to attract his attention, but he would not even look at us. He had the most beautiful set of whiskers that I ever saw on a goat, and as the wind blew through them they waved in the breeze. Evidently, the old fellow could see the bear—below him, and in front. He moved his head in various directions, peering about, twisting his head and squinting like a near-sighted man at a variety show. Four other goats had taken to the high rocks on account of that same bear."

Mr. Phillips has seen goats climb, without being frightened, to the very summits of lofty peaks, and far above their food supply, apparently for amusement only. He has also seen flocks of goats lie on solitary patches of snow in preference to bare earth and rocks.

Among hunters and guides who live in the mountain goat's country, it is a common belief that goats (like men) sometimes lose their lives through going upon precipitous ledges from which they cannot escape. It is difficult to understand how a goat can reach a point on the face of a cliff without carefully climbing to it, either up or down, or how it can become impossible for him to retrace his steps. That such things are possible, however, is proven by a tragedy actually witnessed by Mr. James Brewster, of Banff.

Mr. Brewster relates that quite recently, while out with a hunting-party in the mountains north-west of Banff, they climbed to the top of a rugged mountain, and chased a band of goats around its summit. The goats went down over the edge of a rock wall which overhung so much that the animals could not be seen from above. Later on, when they descended to their camp in the valley, and looked up at the mountain wall, they saw their lost goats, five in number, perched far aloft, on a narrow ledge. When night descended, the goats were still there.

The next morning, the hunters were surprised at finding that during the night the animals had not moved; nor did they move during that entire day. Then Mr. Brewster and his companions became convinced that the goats had trapped themselves, and were unable either to go on or retreat. The band consisted of two adult goats and three young ones. Naturally it was the older animals that led the way into the danger, and it was the belief of the party that the adult goats could not retreat the way they came because the young .ones blocked the way, and were unable to go back. It was thought that the ledge was so narrow the goats could not turn upon it, and the kids were unable to back out. We know that a young goat can easily turn on a twelve-inch ledge, provided the wall does not overhang; but an overhanging wall can make turning impossible.

Mr. Brewster and his party became so interested in the fate of the trapped goats that they remained in that camp long enough to witness the end of the tragedy. One by one, those poor goats fell from their ledge, and were dashed to death on the slide-rock, hundreds of feet below. The hunters saw one of them fall; but the most of them fell at night. The last one fell on the tenth day after they took refuge on the fatal shelf.

CHAPTER IX

TIMBER-LINE AND SUMMIT

ONE-EYED MEN IN THE MOUNTAINS—A MOUNTAIN SAVANT—A
CLIMB IN FALSE NOTCH—FOOT AND NERVE EXHAUSTION—A
DARING GOAT—EXPERIMENTS—THE COMPONENT PARTS OF
MOUNTAIN-SIDES—TEMPERATURE RECORD OF A CLIMBER—A
GREAT BASIN AND A BULL ELK—A TREE SCARRED BY A
MOUNTAIN RAM.

"Here in this workshop of the Sun, Where Nature
hews, and chips recoil,
Note well the work designed, or done ; Behold the
Mountains at their toil!"

—*The Sun's Workshop.*

THE WORLD IS FULL OF one-eyed travellers. One of the
strange things about such mountains as those of British
Columbia is the wide variation between the impressions which
they produce upon different people. I know a miner and pros-
pector to whom the finest mountain-range is merely a place

in which to look for signs of ore. There are sportsmen who see nothing in mountains save what appears over the sights of their rifles. There are photographers who see nature only as it is revealed in their "finder," "stopped down to aperture No. 32, one-twenty-fifth of a second exposure."

Before me at this moment there lies a book about mountains; but it is only a book of heights and depths, scaled or to be scaled. Its author was blind to the glories of mountain vegetation, and to the ever-interesting mammal and bird fauna of the steeps. The works and ways of Nature at timber-line held absolutely nothing of special interest to him, save as they furnished things to climb over. He was interested in forests only as they burned, and their smoke obscured the view of summits to be climbed. In a volume of more than four hundred pages the author devotes half a page to the flora of a magnificent domain of mountains, and three pages to their animal life! Really, is it not strange?

Often when in the tropics I lamented my lack of botanical knowledge, but not half so much as I deplored it in the Columbian Rockies. To pass over twice in one day the uppermost limits of perhaps fifty species of plants and trees, and know of them so very little, was at times really depressing. Each of the few species which I did recognize was as welcome as the face of a friend at a crowded reception.

To me, Charlie Smith was truly a guide, philosopher and friend, and at all times a source of intellectual comfort. He loves the mountains so well that no money consideration can tempt him to leave them. He loves them in storm or in calm, amid the terrors of winter as well as the delights of spring, summer and fall. Once while resting on a lofty summit, with a magnificent panorama spread out at our feet, and stretching away to the Continental Divide, he said to me:

"I have had chances to go into business, and in some of

them I am sure I could have made money. Possibly I could have become moderately rich. But what would all the money of a millionaire be to me if it took me away from the mountains that I love? No amount of money in a business office could make up to me what I would lose in giving up this country. No rich man can get out of his money more satisfaction in life than I find in these mountains; and here I mean to stay until I die."

Charlie is a strange, and even remarkable, combination. He loves steep mountains like another Whymper, and is a very bold and level-headed climber. He loves all animal life, and is not only a keen observer, but his accuracy in observing is grateful and comforting. He loves tree-life and plant-life with the taste of a born botanist. He is a fine hunter and trapper, brave, but sensibly cautious on the trail, and completely free from the boastful and intolerant vein which spoils many a good woodsman. Like most of the mountain men whom I have known intimately, he is clean-minded and high-minded, and as a narrator and describer I have never among frontiersmen known his equal. When he tells a story, he makes you see it as in a moving picture; and he writes with wonderful ease.

I urged Charlie to write out the fascinating stories of adventure and chapters of wild-animal lore that he gradually unfolded to me, and offer them to the magazines which are always on the lookout to discover new and fresh springs of literary refreshment. At first he felt that he "could not write well enough"; but as a matter of conscience and duty, both to him and the public, I urged him until he took courage, and decided to try.

The foregoing "appreciation" is in no sense a digression, for Charlie Smith was far more interesting and noteworthy than any of the mountains up which he led me.

Every sportsman knows that the occasions where four men can profitably hunt together are few and far between. Mr.

Phillips usually went out with Mack Norboe. John Norboe made various special scouting trips for the general welfare, and Charlie Smith and I worked together. After the great day with goats, on Phillips Peak, we devoted our energies to hunting for grizzly bears; and in quest of them we went into all sorts of places. Immediately after camping in Avalanche Valley, our first care was to hunt down the valley, through the ribbon of green timber, six miles or so straight away to the base of Roth Mountain; and although we found about a dozen or fifteen rubbing-trees, where bears had stood up to scratch their backs, we saw no bears.

Continuously we watched the open ground of the "slides" for bears feeding; and as often as we could manage it, we climbed to some new summit, in order to view a new basin, new rock walls, more slides, and more new country far beyond. In such a region as that is, to hunt is to climb; and to climb is usually to go above timber-line before you stop.

I was frequently surprised by the differences between mountain sides and summits that one would naturally ex-pect to find alike. Take False Notch, for instance, about two miles above Camp Hornaday, which came about through my initiative.

One afternoon as Charlie and I were returning from sev-eral hours of climbing to look at the goat remains on Phillips Peak, the trail led across some slide-rock which gave us an open view upward toward the west. In an evil moment, I saw to the westward a ridge that was heavily timbered quite to its sum-mit; and seeing no land higher up, I rashly concluded it was a low pass. So I said, "Charlie, it doesn't look far up to the top of that divide. Suppose we climb up, and take a look over the other side, toward Bull River."

Charlie hesitated two or three seconds, looked at the sun, then quietly answered,

Timber-Line in Winter

MR. PHILLIPS AND GUIDE SMITH ON SNOWSHOES, CARRYING THEIR ENTIRE OUTFIT.

"All right... We'll strike up on the right of this slide, and have easy going."

We struck up, and the climb through the green timber was all right. But when we reached what I had thought was the summit of the divide, behold I we stood at the mouth of a big, bare basin between the two peaks, beyond which there rose a roof of the steepest and most difficult slide-rock that I found on that trip. We were at timber-line, and exactly half-way up to the real summit! I felt as if that notch had deliberately deceived me.

After a brief rest, we crossed the bottom of the basin, chose the best line of ascent, and started up. Never shall I forget that climb. The mountain was frightfully steep, and from basin-bottom to summit, the slope was covered with slide-rock of the best possible size to roll under a climber's foot, and throw him down.

"Be very careful of your footing here," said Charlie, very quietly. "Don't make a misstep. A roll down here might be pretty serious."

There was no doubt about it. A genuine fall on that treacherous stuff, either backward or sidewise, might easily send a man plunging downward so swiftly that there would be no stopping short of the bottom. The slide-rock was mostly in angular chunks about the size of furnace coal, and almost as hard as flint. It reminded me of the inch-and-a-half broken trap-rock that we use in the Zoological Park in surfacing our roads. Imagine the steepest house-roof you ever saw bestrewn with that stuff, ready to roll at the touch of a foot, and you will know what that slope was like as a place to climb.

In taking a step upward, the foot had to win a firm resting-place on the loose rock before the body's weight was thrown upon it; for each step had to be a success. The strain on the ankles was really very severe—and on the mind it was equally so. In a party like ours, no one wants to be a spoil-sport, and get hurt, tie up the whole hunt, and possibly be carried out in a package strapped to a horse's back. Accidents are forbidden luxuries!

I suppose that slope was about six hundred feet long. Charlie kindly offered to carry my rifle for me, and even insisted upon it; but up to that time I had carried my rifle every step of my hunting ways, and I elected to stay with it, up or down.

As we neared the summit, we saw that we were approaching a "knife-edge." It was not a level knife edge, either, but sloped sharply, and at one place broke down very abruptly for several feet. It was then clear that the narrow sky-line was the edge of a precipice, that there was no such thing as hunting beyond, and it looked as if no one could walk on the knife-edge for more than a hundred yards or so.

Feeling that I had been grossly deceived by that notch, I decided to expend no further energy upon it, unless something more than the summit were to be gained by it. Twenty-five years ago I would have followed Charlie to the last gasp; but as it was, I shamelessly allowed him to climb on up to the top, alone. The mental and physical exertion of placing my feet about six hundred times in that loose stuff, each time so carefully that my foot would hold without the possibility of a slide or a roll, had so completely exhausted both my nerves and my ankles that I had neither patience nor strength for another useless fifty feet. I learned that a man who is reasonably fresh can do climbing that is almost impossible to him when his feet and his nerves are equally exhausted. It is very trying to climb for an hour with a feeling that one false step, one turned ankle or one treacherous rock will lead swiftly to a battered body and broken bones.

Charlie climbed on up with the sang-froid of a mountain goat, and soon stood on the sky-line, looking over. "How wide is it up there?"

"Well, in some places it's three feet; but in one place it's nearly twenty."

"Anything to do on the other side?"

"No; I guess not. No good ground, no game in sight. There's no use in your coming up here."

Climbing down seemed quite as dangerous as climbing up. In descending dangerous slopes over loose rock, I always found myself looking forward to a point of altitude low enough that a fall from it would not quite· kill a man; then to the point that meant not more than two broken limbs; then to the one-limb point; to battered knees only, and so on to the bottom. With shoe soles less wooden in their stiffness, and with better nails in the bottom, I would have felt very differently in those mountains.

Perhaps I should note here a few facts regarding the best clothing for a mountain-climber. Naturally, a tenderfoot needs to have all conditions in his favor, but it is likely that few succeed in securing a perfect outfit. The shoes should be high, to protect and support the ankles, but the soles should not be too thick, or inflexible. The soles should yield somewhat to the rocks; and they must be well studded with sharp-pointed hob-nails, screwed into the leather. In rough work and plenty of it, two pairs of good shoes will last but little more than a month.

The trousers should be knickerbockers of gray macki-naw (wool), and the openings at the knee should be six inches long, with buttons, in order that in severe climbing they can be opened wide. With these, woolen stockings are necessary. Suspenders are *absolutely necessary*, for the belt must be worn loose. The outer shirt, of gray flannel, should be of medium weight. The neck demands a large silk handkerchief, of some dark, neutral color.

As we climbed down, a solitary billy goat came over the peak in front of us, beyond the basin, and treated us to a wonderful performance. From the side of the peak a thin shoulder ran out toward the Avalanche Valley. It was about three hundred feet high. The "formation "stood on edge, quite perpendicular, and there was a band of shaly stratification which had weathered a trifle below the general surface of the shoulder. I saw a goat appear on the crest of it, and start down what looked like a pathway of smooth and perpendicular rock.

"Charlie, just see what that goat is doing!"

We settled back against the slide-rock, and adjusted our glasses.

"Well!" exclaimed the guide. "He might as well be standing on his head!"

Coolly and deliberately, without any show either of haste or hesitation, that goat walked down the place that looked perpendicular. Not even once did he make a false step, or hesitate.

Over the worst places he came down two feet at a time. He reached down with his forefeet, planted them far apart, then slid his hindfeet down between them until they too secured a good hold. It looked as if his hindquarters rubbed against the cliff; and beyond question, his rear dew-claws and the lowest joints of his hindlegs did so.

Over the lower third of the descent, where the grade was less steep, and the pathway offered rougher footing, the goat calmly walked down to the bottom, crossed the slide-rock and turned off up the basin, toward a patch of grazing-ground. Very soon it passed behind a point that jutted out from our ridge, and for a moment disappeared.

Cautiously we descended a short distance, and again sighted the animal. It was quietly grazing, and not more than one hundred and fifty yards away. We sat down, and watched him until we were tired; and then I decided to test his ears, his eyesight and his courage. Although we were in plain view of him, he paid no attention to us.

I whistled, faintly at first; but he took no notice. I whistled again, loud enough to have startled any deer feeding at the same distance, and sent it flying; but still no notice. Then I gave three or four very shrill blasts, in a manner specially developed in my boyhood. The goat raised his head, and looked about with an air of curiosity, but stirred not from his position, and manifested no alarm. I presume he thought that a whistling marmot had found out how to whistle with two fingers in his mouth.

So long as we remained motionless, the goat was quite indifferent to our presence. When I left off whistling, he went on feeding. At last we rose quietly, and moved on down; and then he decided to be going. I said "Hello," rather loudly, but he merely went on at a moderately fast walk. When I shouted, he hastened perceptibly; and finally, when I yelled at him, he really took alarm. But even then he did not leap, and stampede in a panicky way, as a deer does. He simply trotted away as fast as he could, climbed the divide before him at its lowest point, and disappeared over its crest.

When Charlie and I reached the bottom of the basin, we examined the goat's pathway, and, as we expected, found it not so nearly perpendicular as it looked from in front. The angle of it seemed to be about forty-five degrees from perpendicular. The wonder was not that the goat managed to descend in safety over a course on which a man could not have travelled ten feet, but that it came down with such contemptuous indifference and ease.

I am tempted to make note of one other climb that Charlie Smith and I enjoyed together, still in quest of new grounds and grizzly bears. To me the wonders of it, and the weirdness of it, never will be forgotten while I live.

Around the head of Avalanche Creek there was a regular nest of "notches" and "divides," and "passes" by courtesy so called. We explored each one of them, always climbing, and

although we found little killable big game, we were so royally entertained by that grand picture-book of Nature that
we felt richly repaid. From first to last I climbed about fifteen
mountains in that country, and next to the grandeur of the
scenery, its most striking feature was the marvelous diversity
of Nature's handiwork. On no two mountains did we find the
vegetation, the ground and the rocks really alike; and this di-
versification continued to the very last hour of the trip.

Bear with me a moment, and I will set down, as in a cata-
logue, the salient features of interest that one passes through,
or over, in the course of one day's climb in that Wonderland. I
take them all from the notes of the day wherein Charlie and I
climbed into the second big notch south of Phillips Peak.

(1) First came the luxuriant, balsamy, sweet-smelling
"green timber "of the valley, which climbed half a mile or more
up the steep slope. In this the rich earth is smooth, and covered deeply with the dry needles of Canadian white spruce,
jack pine, and balsam. The fine-leafed, columnar larches are
turning the color of old gold, and the leaves of the quaking asp
tell their name by their incessant quivering. Just then the frost
was busily painting them Indian red.

(2) Above the heavy green timber comes the dwarf spruces,—which I think must be of a species different from the great
tree,—and the patches of yellow-willow brush.

(3) There are patches of hard, bare earth, usually shaly,
and often so hard and smooth they are not only uncomfortable, but even dangerous. In freezing weather they must be
carefully avoided; for they give no foothold.

(4) The deep gullies that so often score the mountain-
sides, cut down through decomposing shale, are a prominent
feature, and in traversing the side of a steep mountain in freezing weather they must be crossed with the utmost care. At such
times, our guides regard them as decidedly dangerous.

(5) Above the brush-belt, often comes the mossy pasture-grounds, in steps, like great stairs that have been covered with a moss-like carpet of *Dryas octopitala* three inches thick.

(6) The "slides," or avalanche tracks, are everywhere present, sometimes bare of trees and bushes, and nicely set in grass, and again thinly covered with young trees.

(7) In places are found large patches of fine, loose earth, perfectly bare.

(8) Slide-rock is always to be expected, sometimes coming from sources that are visible, and again descended from goodness knows where. High up, it is usually more finely broken than lower down. Near the top of a steep divide, or "pass," it is common to find a wide belt of bad slide-rock (called "scree "by the professional mountain-climbers, and "talus "by geologists), and often the top also is completely capped with it.

(9) Occasionally the climber strikes a stretch of small stones, or, better still, an acre or two of loose shale, which is very safe and comfortable while it lasts. Down a good stretch of this one can plough along fast and fearlessly, as one descends the ashy side of Vesuvius, covering two yards at a stride.

(10) When it comes to snow, and ice,—that is another story, and a long one.

It was through a bewildering succession of such features as the above that Charlie and I made a long and arduous, though nowise dangerous climb, to the top of a pass that looked over into the Elk River water-shed. It was a cold day, and the changes of temperature that a climber experiences in one day were absurdly numerous.

I started up wearing my elk-skin hunting-shirt, a silk muffler around my neck, and two suits of underclothing. At the head of the creek we took our last drink of water, and began to climb upward through the green timber. There being no wind to speak of, the exercise warmed us.

At 500 feet up, my gloves came off, were labeled "not wanted," and stowed away in the hold.

At 700 feet, off came my silk muffler.

At 1,000 feet, my hunting-shirt was voted a superfluous luxury, taken off, and strapped upon my back.

At 1,500 feet, my shirt-sleeves were turned up as high as they could go.

At 1,800 feet, all my shirts were opened wide at the neck, and we had to wait for more air to blow along.

At 2,000 feet an icy-cold wind struck us hard, and the mercury began to fall. Collars were hurriedly closed, and sleeves unreefed and made snug. To take off one's cap to mop away perspiration was like thrusting one's head into a pail of ice-water.

At about 2,300 feet above Avalanche Creek, we reached the summit. It was as cold as Cape Sabine, and the icy wind blew half a gale. The rapid evaporation of the perspiration in my clothing made my body feel like the cylinder of an ice-cream freezer. With all haste, we flung on our outer garments, put on our gloves, and hurried over the sky-line to get out of the wind.

A short distance down the eastern side we found an old goat-bed, in a little depression. In this we crouched, to scan the magnificent landscape below, and if possible to get less cold. The grandeur of what we saw instantly made us forget the icy wind.

The summit behind us was not wider than a city lot, and in one magnificent sweep of half a mile, without a big rock or a tree, it swept down, down, down to the bottom of a huge, green basin in which a grand army could have encamped.

On our right, and close at hand, there rose high above us,—and also dropped far below,—the most awful wall of rock that I saw in British Columbia. From bottom to top its perpendicular face was, I am sure, not less than a thousand feet. From it, there was an almost continuous rattle of falling rock. Even had we seen a sheep on the face of it, we would not have had the heart to shoot the animal and see it fall off.

The impressive height of that grim wall was strongly emphasized by the softer details of the great basin far below. It was fitting that the grandest precipice should rise from the grandest basin in those mountains, and cradle at its foot a tiny lake that was like a big emerald.

The world below us was unrolled like a map. The outlines of the dark-green timber, as yet untouched by fire, and the intervening patches of light yellow-green grass, hemmed in on two sides by frowning walls of dark gray rock and bounded in the distance by a succession of mountains running thirty miles away to the snowy peaks on the Continental Divide, made a grand and impressive picture.

For half an hour we sat with our backs against the mountain-side, absorbing the magnificent panorama into our systems. We spoke little. All at once I saw something new, and looked quickly at Charlie. At the same instant his face lighted up with a gleam of intelligence, and he looked sharply at me.

"An elk, Charlie?"

After a little pause, with his glass at his eyes, he answered, "Yes; a full-grown bull... That's the fellow whose trail we found yesterday in False Notch."

Far down in the bottom of the basin, where the green timber halted at the foot of our slope, an elk had walked out into the middle of a little grass-plat, as if to give us the pleasure of seeing him. He carried a good pair of antlers, and he looked big and beautiful. It was indeed a keen pleasure to see a living, wild, adult bull elk in British Columbia, and to know for fair that even there the species is not yet extinct.

For about five minutes the majestic animal grazed on

A Big-Horn Ram's Signature (top)
Goat Lick, on the Southern Slope of Cyclorama Ridge (bottom)

the grass-plat, then marched to the edge of his little glade, and browsed on some of the green branches that he found there. Finally, like a dissolving view he vanished in the thick green timber, and we saw him no more. It was the only elk that was seen on that trip.

There was no other game visible in the great basin; and we voted unanimously that it was out of the question to descend that long eastward slope, hunt through the basin, and recross the mountain to camp, all in one afternoon.

We decided to hunt back home by skirting the eastern mountain-side of Avalanche Creek, at timber-line, and thereby have a good look for both bear and sheep.

First we went to look at the carcasses of the four goats killed on Phillips Peak, and finding no bear-signs about them, we swung off on our long mountain-side tramp.

By that time, the day had grown stormy. The west wind had borne up a mass of leaden clouds that completely obscured the sun; but fortunately they flew well above us. It was evident that snow was on the wings of the wind. Whenever we crossed a wedge of green timber we went at a swift pace, but at every basin, and every open pathway of an avalanche, we hunted very cautiously.

Before our progress, that mountain-side unrolled like a panorama, in an endless chain of timbered ridges, hollow basins, steep slopes, ridges of slide-rock, and frowning cliffs looming up into the flying clouds.

Once we passed a very curious feature. From the side of a cliff, half way from basin-bottom to summit, there came out a huge mass of slide-rock that looked like an enormous dump from a mountain mine. The level top ran back to the face of the rock wall, and it looked as if cars had run out of the bowels of the mountain, and dumped there ten million tons of broken limestone, in slide-rock sizes. The resemblance was perfect, and

I told Charlie to enter the name of that feature as "The Dump."

That was an awe-inspiring scramble.

Even a sensible dog would have been impressed by the majesty of the rugged rock walls towering heavenward; the rugged terrors of the acres and acres of cruel slide-rock; the weird, squawking cries of the Clark's crows and Canada jays that circled about us, or perched briefly on the tips of the dead and ragged spruces; the whistling of the cold, raw wind through the pines, and over all the dull gray clouds flying swiftly and silently across the tops of the peaks.

We climbed on and on, seeing much but saying little. In a patch of green timber, we found a nut-pine tree that had been butted and badly scarred, by a mountain sheep ram. Its stem was about ten inches in diameter, and about three feet from the ground the horns of a lusty sheep had battered the bark off, quite down to the wood. Two long, elliptical scars were left, with a narrow strip of living bark between them, as a record of the time when a well-fed ram passed that way, and was seized by the boy-like impulse to carve his name in the bark of a tree. This is a favorite pastime of mountain sheep rams during the months of September and October, when they are so full of grass and energy that the mountains seem scarcely big enough to contain them.

To scramble for several hours along a steep mountain-side, going always in the same direction, is very wearing upon the ankles, and tends to make one leg shorter than it really ought to be. At the "psychological moment,"—whatever that may be,—Charlie changed our course, and bore diagonally downward until we struck the bottom of Avalanche Valley close to the circle of light that radiated from the blazing logs of our royal camp-fire.

And then it began to snow.

CHAPTER X

ALONE ON A MOUNTAIN

GETTING NEXT TO NATURE—WATERFALL NOTCH—THE
PIKA AT HOME—GROUND-SQUIRRELS AND GRIZZLY BEARS—
TEMPTATION GOATS—VARIATIONS BETWEEN SUMMITS—FOOL-
HENS AND PTARMIGAN—DWARF SPRUCES—BULL RIVER—MULE-
DEER GROUNDS—BERRIES OF THE MOUNTAINS—CHARLIE
SMITH FINDS GRIZZLY-BEAR SIGNS.

"O, puny Man, wouldst thou atone
For years of swelling ego heart,
Go, tread the mountain-top alone,
And learn how very small thou art!"

—*The Spell of the Mountains.*

IF YOU WOULD GET NEXT the soul of Nature, go to meet
her as you call upon your sweetheart,—alone. There are times
when the presence of one's dearest friend is a distraction. If you
would feel the mystic Spell of the Mountains, go into them as
Moses did when he met God and received The Law—alone. If
you would know what it is to feel so awed by the panorama of
the world that you lose half your desire to find killable game,

and for a few hours cease to be a predatory animal, climb a fine mountain all alone. In that way one sees things and feels things that are veiled by the presence of any other human being. The moral uplift that one feels when alone on a wild prairie is magnified five times on a first-class mountain.

Quite aside from the animal life, the strange vegetation of the mountain heights near timber-line is enough to tempt any one upward. It is far more interesting, yard for yard, than anything one finds in the tropics. On a high mountain, at timber-line one finds only the bravest and the hardiest of Nature's trees, and flowers, and animals. Wherever vegetation climbs up in genuine luxuriance to six thousand feet, and is suddenly and rudely stopped short at seven thousand feet, the finish is as keenly interesting as finishes generally are. It is good to climb up through a living exposition of the survival of the fittest, both in plant life and animal life.

. . . .

Two days after our goat-hunt on Phillips Peak, an incident occurred which caused our little party to scatter, for two days. Just before sunset, we saw far aloft, on the sky-line of the mountain range that ran along the eastern side of Avalanche Creek, a band of twelve mountain sheep, all rams. Naturally this exhibit caused quite a sensation in camp, and eventually it produced several important results. Mr. Phillips wished to kill a big ram for the Carnegie Museum, but having had my chance at sheep, in Wyoming, I had vowed to hunt sheep no more.

Accordingly, on the following morning, Mr. Phillips and the Norboes took packs on their backs, with three days' rations, and departed on a hunt for the rams of the previous day. Charlie Smith went off on a long tramp to look for grizzly-bear signs, for my special benefit. Instead of going with him as usual, on that day I decided to climb to a certain summit west of camp, on which I had noted from Phillips Peak (opposite), some excellent grounds for mule deer. I felt that I would like to explore those summits all alone, and have a good think, game or no game.

As a matter of ordinary precaution, I told Charlie and Huddleston where I intended to go, and asked for any directions that might be helpful. Charlie told me that an old game-trail led around the waterfall I intended to strike, and that if I went hither and yon, and thus and so, I would probably strike it. His directions were clear enough, but somehow I have before now found it difficult to make the ground-plan of a wild western landscape fit the specifications of it. This time, however, I resolved to try to do better in that respect.

Seldom have I seen in any land a finer day. The sun shone bravely, but at intervals it was partly obscured by fleecy white clouds that briskly drifted up from the west, then passed on over. The air was wondrous clear, and just cold enough to be invigorating.

Charlie's one direction which I had so firmly spiked down that it failed to escape, was that I would do well to go as far as possible up the bed of the little creek that came down from my Waterfall Notch. This I did. At first I found it absolutely dry, and the going over the small, smooth dornicks was rather easy. But in a short time, the dense green timber that filled the valley threw so many tree-trunks across the stream's course that I was obliged to scramble out and take to the easier bank.

At that point Charlie's directions were lost in the shuffle, like a creek running under slide-rock; but I hoped they would, stream-like, come to the surface farther on. From moment to moment I chose the least difficult route, as does a wild man or a wild beast in marking out a trail for the first time. On the north side of the creek I scrambled through some very much tangled "down timber" amid the "green timber," always going up, of course, and presently emerged upon a five-acre tract of

Early Morning on Goat Pass

CLOUDS IN THE VALLEY OF BULL RIVER

very coarse and cruelly sharp slide-rock. Over that toilsome stretch I went with the attention which such treacherous and dangerous stuff demands, and finally I reached the upper limit of that also.

Looking ahead, I saw my waterfall, hard at work pouring a collection of two-inch streams over a fifty-foot precipice,— all of which promptly vanished from sight under the slide-rock that had been carried across the stream-bed. At that time, the fall was not very impressive, because the volume of water was too small for grandeur. Still, a natural waterfall in a mountain landscape is always grateful to the eye, and companionable.

As I picked my way upward over the slide-rock, the plaintive, whistling cry of the pika, or little chief "hare," came to me from a chaos of large rocks piled near the edge of a half-acre of weeds. The cry sounds like the word *cheap*, pitched very high and much prolonged. The cry of this creature is so elusive one seldom can locate it with precision, so making as good a guess as possible, I sat down to wait for the little brother of the rocks to appear.

I sat motionless for perhaps ten minutes, and then my small neighbor appeared. Like a modest little gray shadow it seemed to slide out from nowhere to the level top of a chunk of stone, and there halted to observe the world. Except for his short round ears, he looked like a half-grown gray rabbit. I waited for him to go to work at cutting his winter's supply of hay, but he was too deliberate, and before he began his day's work I was obliged to move on.

Let it be remembered at this point that this little creature, so long called the little chief "hare," or crying "hare," is not a hare, nor is it even a member of the Hare and Rabbit Family (*Leporidae*). It is so odd that it stands alone, in a Family limited to its own small self, containing only the pikas. But, small and lonesome though he be, the pika is wise. Neither marten, wolverine nor grizzly can dig him out of his slide-rock, and we never once saw a place where a bear had even tried to do so. But the nearest neighbor of the pika has far less wisdom.

In many localities around Phillips Peak we found big holes in the ground that had been dug by grizzly bears in quest of Columbia River ground-squirrels (*Citellus columbianus*). Indeed, we saw more holes than ground-squirrels. This animal looks like a long-bodied Carolina gray squirrel with a half-sized tail. Usually it is found in the mountain basins, and in other open situations below timberline where the earth is right for burrowing.

We saw between forty and fifty holes, from two to three feet deep, and usually three feet in surface diameter, each of which marked a tragedy. Unfortunately, the silly ground-squirrel has not yet learned, either by inheritance or in the "school of the woods"(!), that a three-foot burrow is the same as a pantry shelf to a hungry grizzly, and that no *Citellus* is safe who stops his burrow anywhere above a vertical depth of six feet. With plenty of time, and no end of earth, the foolish ground-squirrel (here called the "gopher"), rests from his digging just under the frost-line. In October the grizzly joyously rips out half a cubic yard of earth, thrusts his deadly hooks on down to the end of the burrow, and *Citellus* quickly is converted into half an ounce of bear-oil.

Between the grizzlies underground, and the greedy marten above ground, the mountains of British Columbia will not be overrun by ground-squirrels, other small mammals until the fangs and claws decrease.

But this is a digression.

I soon saw that the way around the north side of the fall was very rugged and precipitous, and far too difficult to be chosen voluntarily. Accordingly I crossed the dry stream-bed, and started to climb, by hand and foot, up the extremely steep southern side, which happened to be covered with a good growth of green timber. I had not gone more than a hundred yards when I struck the old trail that Charlie had mentioned. Feeling very complacent over the finding of the right course by plain animal instinct, I blithely swung on up, and soon stood on level ground above the falls.

And then I noted how very different the ground beyond the fall really was from what it had looked to be, as I saw it from the other side of Avalanche Valley. At a distance of two miles, and a higher elevation, it had seemed that from the waterfall a long, gently sloping ridge ran back for a considerable distance. In actuality, behind the waterfall, I found an eight-acre meadow, nearly level, and covered with rank grass. Beyond that, a steep mountain divide climbs on up. On the north rose an easy peak, and on the south, close at hand, there towered aloft a massive dome of naked rock. On getting clear of that, one looks far southward into another big basin, half encircled by a lofty wall of rock that rises sheer to the sky-line. Upon a ledge of that wall, about four hundred yards distant, I saw two billy goats of shootable size, basking in the glorious beams of the morning sun.

When I realized how comparatively easy it would be to climb up, south-westerly, swing around under the skyline and fetch up within easy range of those goats, it gave me a disturbed and anxious feeling. I knew I ought not kill any more goats, having three;—but a head is a head, and my friends are many. Would I be strong enough to resist that temptation throughout a whole sunny day, with twenty cartridges grinning in my belt like the teeth of a wild animal, and those two old billies mine by act of parliament, if I chose to take them?

After a long survey of the animals, I said, "Get thee behind me, Satan!" Resolutely I turned my back upon them, and decided to climb to the summit by way of the gulch that came

The Little Haymaker of the Slide-Rock (top)
The Grizzly's Lawful Prey—The Columbia River Ground-Squirrel (bottom)
EVERY YEAR THOUSANDS OF THESE ARE DUG OUT OF THEIR BURROWS AND
EATEN BY THE GRIZZLIES.

down farthest away from them, northerly. By walking rapidly I would soon be so far away that it would be too much of a task to return for just one or two old goats.

My little gulch came down very steeply, in a course that was almost due south. In each direction from its bed there stretched upward, at the comfortable angle of about thirty degrees, a wide, smooth sweep of ridge-side that suggested Dream Mountains. The hand of Nature had smoothed those slopes, and planted them, to afford a soothing and restful contrast with all the mountains surrounding them. Think of the horrible rock-pile, a mile farther north, which Charlie and I climbed two days previously, in False Notch. Here there were no stretches of grinning slide-rock, no rock walls, no timber, either down or green, no neck-breakers of any kind. All was balmy peace. To save the face of the slopes from having an air of desolation, each was planted very evenly with stunted spruces and junipers, set eight feet apart. They grew with wonderful regularity, and so nicely scattered that walking was not at all impeded by them.

I chose the slope of the western hill, because the sun shone full upon it, and went up on a line about a hundred feet above the bottom of the little naked gulch. The opposite mountain side was so queer, and so beautiful in the nursery-like regularity of its planting, that I frequently sat down to rest and enjoy the sight of it. It looked for all the world like an immense relief-map, such as I have made before now, set with toy evergreens, and tilted up on edge to enable one to look down upon it. I never before saw so odd a picture of mountain verdure. I could have counted every one of the toy trees on that whole mountain side without moving from my seat. It represented timber-line, for fair.

But even there, in the Dream Mountains, the serpent reared its head. When I sat down to enjoy the sceneries, I saw those goats, ever so plainly; and the tempter whispered, "It would be quite a feat to kill those goats, alone and guideless, and carry in the heads of both.... Perhaps one of them is larger than any one of the dead six!...You have come far to reach this country, and without a grizzly bear—which assuredly you will not get, you will have only goats to show. A successful stalk, under the rim of that mountain, would be very interesting; and it would properly round out a glorious day."

I listened to such as this until the iteration of it became irritating, then I sprang up and climbed on in the opposite direction. And then Vishnu, the goddess of Preservation, brought me to a bunch of sooty grouse. When the first bird exploded into the air, close beside me, I was well startled. The bird flew about fifty feet and alighted near its mates, thus giving me a good opportunity to see them on the ground, and note their actions.

The story of a flock of fool-hens is like the annals of the poor,—short and simple. Each bird stalks about stiffly, with head well up, gazing and gazing at the intruder, in stupid wonder that is wondrously stupid. With a shot-gun, there would be about as much excitement in shooting one as there would be in killing a sloth on the run. To a marksman who wants the birds for food, there is some interest in shooting them through the head with a .22-calibre pistol; but with a good rifle or shot-gun, it is plain murder in the first degree. In flight this bird strongly resembles the pinnated grouse, or prairie-chicken, except that the flight of the latter is stronger.

On the summit of the divide, and beyond the last of the stunted spruces, I found some willow ptarmigan. Their snow-white wings and tails, in full winter plumage, contrasted sharply with the brown summer plumage which still clothed their bodies. As usual, these birds slowly stalked about over the sky meadow, quite willing that I should approach within ten feet of them. At last, however, they rose, saying "cluck-cluck-cluck," and flew down the mountain a quarter of a mile.

Above the point where my friendly little gulch starts down, a view from the summit reveals a sudden drop toward Bull River, and a great basin below. Turning southward, I followed the sky-line of the summit in such a manner as to thoroughly inspect every outcrop of sheep rocks, and every patch of open timber. The former might contain mule deer, and either might harbor a band of sheep.

At one point on the summit I found a very interesting growth of stunted spruces. They grew in family clumps, about as far apart as the trees in an orchard, and the curious thing about them was that they were so stunted by the warfare of the elements that they were really pygmy trees. Their large trunks, low stature,—seldom exceeding five feet,—and dwarfed limbs remind me of the strange dwarf trees produced by the tie-back process of the Japanese. On a commanding point, I found a clump which was crescent-shaped, with its convex side toward the west wind, and in its embrace I halted for half an hour to gaze over the top of the evergreen barricade. The encircled ground had been tramped bare, and it was evident that many a goat and sheep had recently sheltered there.

The mountain slope that swept down to Bull River was a gray and melancholy waste. From a short distance below the summit, fire had devastated the mountain side, killing every tree, and exposing all the outcroppings of rugged rock and cliff. Near by, the tall gray tree trunks, shorn of their branches, were like untrimmed telegraph-poles; farther on, we saw what seemed to be a forest of hop-poles, and beyond that appeared a thin mantle of gray quills, like the covering of a hedgehog.

Two miles away, the east fork of Bull River meandered through a narrow valley of dead timber, and on its farther side, narrow valleys climbed up westward, until they stopped abruptly in regulation rock basins, bounded by precipitous cliffs. And even as I looked across, and wondered what big game might be therein, I heard the unmistakable "Ser-*lam*!" of a hunter's rifle. Some one was hunting in the rugged valley directly opposite my eyrie, and had found game. Who could it be, in that wild place? Surely it was no one from the Elk River Valley.

In the course of an hour, I heard about twelve shots; but two months elapsed ere I learned that the hunters were from Fort Steele, and were in quest of mule deer.

The western side of my slope seemed specially favorable for mule deer, and in the hope of finding either deer in the green timber or sheep near the cliffs, I hunted far down. It was good to get on ground that was not rocky, and to hunt through real "mule-deer country." Find it where you may, in bad-lands, foot-hills or mountains, the home of the mule deer is always a beautiful hunting-ground.

But I found no big game; and at one o'clock I selected a lovely spot, in a clump of sturdy spruces, chose a soft resting-place on a bed of dry needles, and sat down to rest and eat my luncheon of Fry's sweet chocolate.

As I settled myself, I noticed that I was on the border of an extensive bed of tiny huckleberry bushes. The shrubs were only about six inches high, but were hanging thick with very small, pink huckleberries, the size of No. 6 shot. That species is very common throughout those mountains. Usually the bushes grow so thinly it does not pay to pick such small berries; but these bore so abundantly that I combed the fruit off the almost leafless stems, by the handful, winnowed it to clear away the *debris*, and ate until my fruit-hunger cried, "Enough!"

An appreciable supply of wild fruit or nuts gives one a very friendly feeling toward the land that produces it. In the tropics, you can starve, at almost any time or place, with rank vegetation all about you, because there is so very little that is edible. After nearly five years spent in tropical jungles, I can count on the fingers of one hand the occasion wherein I was able to satisfy my hunger with wild fruits found in the forest; and as for nuts, I never found one.

But in the temperate zone,—dear me! Think of the delicious plums, the berries of a dozen kinds, the wild grapes, paw paws, persimmons, crab-apples, haws red and haws black, and nuts without end!

Here in these mountains, we found in September the following berries, ripe and edible:

Huckleberries; *five species, widely scattered; abundant in places.*

Black Currants; *very common, dead ripe; quite bitter, but good to quench thirst.*

Saskatoon, or Service-Berry; *favorite food for grizzly bears in September.*

Elderberry; *in clumps in many valleys; plentiful.*

Soap-Berry; *two species, red and yellow; like currants, very bitter.*

Red Raspberry; *but we found only one patch.*
Thimbleberry; *grows solitary, in green timber only.*

Strawberry; *a few found, high on the mountains.*

In addition to the above, which we saw, there is the Sarsaparilla-Berry, of the large river valleys; the Red Cahoosh; and the Bear-Berry, which is a strong cathartic.

The very desirable bull-berry of Montana and Wyoming does not grow in the mountains of British Columbia. In the green timber we found a beautiful scarlet berry, shaped like a long, thin, Boston baked bean, which no one could name or vouch for.

When my mid-day rest was finished, I went on hunting. Striking a much-used game-trail on the summit, I followed it southward until it ran up the southern peak far above timber-line, and led me quite near those temptation goats. Always those goats! I felt quite put out with them because they had fed toward me instead of away from me.

For half an hour I amused myself with watching them, and testing their senses by whistling to them, saying, "Ah!" in various tones, and mystifying them generally, until at last they took alarm on general principles, and concluded to leave. Then in some haste they climbed over the summit. As they disappeared I turned and strode down the eastern slope, campward, after as soul-filling a day as I ever spent in the lap of Nature, but without having fired a shot. I reached camp about half an hour before sunset, and found that the reward for my abstemiousness on those temptation goats was all ready. Charlie Smith had just arrived, after a wearisome tramp of twenty-four miles, and reported that he had visited all the goat carcasses. At those of our first two goats he found two wolverines, and took a long shot at one of them. *There were fresh grizzly-bear signs all about!*

"And to-morrow, Director," said Charlie in conclusion, "you're going to have a chance at a silver-tip!"

Outwardly, I received this assurance with brisk appreciation, but inwardly I felt that the chances against me were as nine to one.

CHAPTER XI

MY GRIZZLY-BEAR DAY

RUBBING-TREES OF BEARS—FRESH GRIZZLY "SIGNS"
REPORTED—A TRIP TO THE GOAT REMAINS—A SILVER-TIP AT
WORK—HER DEATH—THE AUTOPSY—AMATEUR PHOTOGRAPHY
AND ITS RESULTS—THE BEAR'S CACHE—WOLVERINES
OBSERVED—A JOLLIFICATION IN CAMP.

WHEN ONE CAN START OUT from camp, and in a walk
of two hours find at least a dozen rubbing-trees of grizzly
bears, each one with bear hair clinging to its bark, then may
one say, "This is bear country!" That was what we found in
the green timber of Avalanche Valley, between our camp and
Roth Mountain, six miles below. All the rubbing-trees we saw
were from eight to twelve inches in diameter, as if small ones
had been specially chosen. I suppose this is because there are
no large spur roots to interfere with the standing bear; besides
which, a small tree offers a sharper edge.

On those trees we saw where several of the rubbing bears
had bitten the trunk, high up, tearing the bark open crosswise.
We also found, on some, raking claw marks across the bark.
Charlie Smith said that the tooth-marks are always made by

grizzlies and the claw marks by black bears.

As before remarked, Mr. Phillips and Charlie Smith were very desirous that I should find and kill a grizzly, but for several reasons I had little hope that it would come to pass. September is not a good month in which to find a bear of any species on those summits; nor is a short hunting-trip conducive to the development of bear episodes, anywhere. In spite of Charlie's hopefulness, I did not take the prospect seriously, even though in the Michel store Mack had called for twine with which to stretch bear-hides! But in bear-hunting, "it is better to be born lucky than rich."

When Charlie came in on the evening of the 19th of September and reported a bear at the carcass of my first goat, it really seemed time to hope for at least a distant view of Old Ephraim. Believing that one good way to reveal certain phases of wild-animal life is in showing how animals are actually found in their haunts, I am tempted to set forth a statement of the events of September 20th. It may be that others wonder, as I often have, just how it *feels* to hunt a grizzly bear—the most dangerous American animal—and find him, at timberline. The really bold hunters may scoff at the courage and ferocity of the grizzly as he is to-day; but Charlie Smith openly declares that the one particular thing which he never does, and never will do, is to fire his last cartridge when away from camp.

It was the third day of Mr. Phillips's hunt for mountain sheep, and he was still absent. Charlie and I took two saddle-horses and set out before sunrise, intending to visit all the goat carcasses before returning. We pushed briskly up to the head of Avalanche Creek, climbed to the top of the pass, then dropped down into the basin on the north. I dreaded a long climb on foot from that point up to our old camp on Goat Pass, but was happily disappointed. Thanks to the good engineering of some Indian trail-maker, the trail led from the head of the basin, on an easy gradient, up through the green timber of the mountain side, quite to our old camp.

We found fresh grizzly-bear tracks within fifty feet of the ashes of our camp-fire; but our goat-skins in the big spruce, and our cache of provisions near it, had not been touched. It was here that we saw a solitary goat feeding on the precipitous slope beneath the glacier on Phillips Peak, as noted elsewhere. And here we were reminded of Mr. Phillips's uneasiness about the dead trees that stood near our tents, and which he had feared might blow down upon us. A large dead tree *had* fallen upon our camp-ground, *squarely across the green bed of spruce boughs on which Charlie and Mack Norboe had slept four nights!* Had it fallen upon them as they slept, both would have been instantly killed.

With only a few minutes delay, we mounted once more and rode on northward toward the scene of the first goat-kill. As we rode up the ridge of Bald Mountain, a biting cold wind, blowing sixty miles an hour, struck us with its full force. It went through our clothing like cold water, and penetrated to the marrow in our bones. At one point it seemed determined to blow the hair off Kaiser's back. While struggling to hold myself together, I saw the dog suddenly whirl head on to the fierce blast, crouch low, and fiercely grip the turf with his claws, to keep from being blown away. It was all that our horses could do to hold a straight course, and keep from drifting down to the very edge of the precipice that yawned only twenty-five feet to leeward. We were glad to get under the lee of Bald Mountain, where the fierce blast that concentrated on that bleak pass could not strike us with its full force.

At last we reached the lake we named in honor of Kaiser. Dismounting in a grassy hollow that was sheltered from the wind, we quickly stripped the saddles from our horses and picketed the animals so that they could graze. Then, catching up our rifles, cameras, and a very slim parcel of luncheon, we set out past the lake for the ridge that rises beyond it.

The timber on the ridge was very thin, and we could see through it for a hundred yards or more. As we climbed, we looked sharply all about, for it seemed very probable that a grizzly might be lying beside a log in the fitful sunshine that struck the southern face of the hill. Of course, as prudent hunters, we were prepared to see a grizzly that was above us, and big, and dangerous,—three conditions that guarantee an interesting session whenever they come together.

Dog Kaiser was peremptorily ordered to follow us, which he did with a degree of intelligent obedience that would have shamed many a man. He is what is called a" slow trailer," which means that in following big game he either keeps close behind his master, or else goes ahead so slowly that it is possible for the latter to keep up with him, and see the game before the dog disturbs it.

We reached the crest of the ridge, without having seen a bear, and with the utmost caution stalked on down the northern side, toward the spot where the two goat carcasses lay on the slide-rock. The noise we made was reduced to an irreducible minimum.

We trod and straddled like men burglarizing Nature's sky-parlor. We broke no dead twigs, we scraped against no dead branches, we slid over no fallen logs. Step by step we stole down the hillside, as cautiously as if we had known that a bear was really at the foot of it. At no time would it have surprised us to have seen Old Ephraim spring up from behind a bush or a fallen log, within twenty feet of us.

At last the gray slide-rock began to rise into view. At last we paused, breathing softly and seldom, behind a little clump of spruces. Charlie, who was a step in advance, stretched his neck to its limit, and looked on beyond the edge of the hill, to the very spot where lay the remains of my first mountain goat. My view was cut off by green branches and Charlie.

He turned to me, and whispered in a perfectly colorless way, "He's lying right on the carcass!"

"What? Do you mean to say that a *bear is really there?*" I asked, in astonishment.

"Yes! Stand here, and you can see him,—just over the edge."

I stepped forward and looked. Far down, fully one hundred and fifty yards from where we were, there lay a silvery-gray animal, head up, front paws outstretched. It was indeed a silver-tip; but it looked awfully small and far away. He was out on the clean, light-gray stipple of slide-rock, beside the scanty remains of my goat.

Even as I took my first look, the animal rose on his haunches, and for a moment looked intently toward the north, away from us. The wind waved his long hair, one wave after another. It was a fine chance for a line shot at the spinal column; and at once I made ready to fire.

"Do you think you can kill him from here?" asked Charlie, anxiously. "You can get nearer to him if you like."

"Yes; I think I can hit him from here all right."

(I had carefully fixed the sights of my rifle, several days previously.)

"Well, if you don't hit him, I'll kick you down this ridge!" said Charlie, solemn as a church owl, with an on-your-head-be-it air. To me, it was clearly a moment of great peril.

I greatly desired to watch that animal for half an hour; but when a bear-hunter finds a grizzly bear, the thing for him to do is to kill it first, and watch it afterward. I realized that no amount of bear observations ever could explain to John Phillips the loss of that bear.

As I raised my .303 Savage, the grizzly rose in a

business-like way, and started to walk up the slide-rock, due south, and a little quartering from us. This was not half so good for me as when he was sitting down. Aiming to hit his heart and lungs, close behind his foreleg, and allowing a foot for his walking, I let go.

A second or two after the "whang" the bear reared slightly, and sharply wheeled toward his right, away from us; and just then Charlie's rifle roared,—close beside my ear! Without losing an instant, the grizzly started on a mad gallop, down the slide-rock and down the canyon, running squarely across our front.

"*Heavens!*" I thought, aghast. "*Have I missed him?*"

Quickly I threw in another cartridge, and fired again; and "whang" went Charlie, as before. The bear fairly flew, reaching far out with its front feet, its long hair rolling in great waves from head to tail. Even at that distance, its silver-tipped fur proclaimed the species.

Bushes now hid my view, and I ran down a few yards, to get a fair show. At last my chance came. As the bear raced across an opening in my view, I aimed three feet ahead of his nose, and fired my third shot.

Instantly the animal pitched forward on his head, like a stricken rabbit, and lay very still.

"Ye fetched him that time!" yelled Charlie, triumphantly. "He's down! He's down! Go for him, Kaiser! Go for him!"

The dog was ready to burst with superheated eagerness. With two or three whining yelps he dashed away down the ridge, and out of sight. By this time Charlie was well below me, and I ran down to where he stood, beaming up.

"You've fixed him, Director! He's down for keeps."

"Where is he?"

"Lying right on that patch of yellow grass, and dead as a wedge. *Shake!*"

We shook. It would have been conceited folly to have done otherwise. To come twelve miles, find our long-lost silver-tip, and down him by eleven o'clock, made us feel that we were each of us entitled to a few gloats over the result.

"Woo, yow-yow!" said Kaiser far below,—about ten seconds after he had disappeared; and there he was, looking very small, and joyously biting the hams of the dead grizzly. Instead of sitting astride a killed animal, and being photographed with one hand upon it, Kaiser gloats over his dead game by biting its hams.

As quickly as possible, we descended the slope and soon stood beside the dead grizzly. Then, as often happens, its sex changed very suddenly. Every grizzly is a "he," until shot! This one was a fat young female, not as big as we had hoped, but in beautiful pelage for September. In remarking upon the length and immaculateness of the furry coat, which still waved in the wind, Charlie remarked, that at this season the female grizzlies have longer hair than the males. I was sorry we could not weigh the animal, but at that moment my scales were twenty miles away, with the sheep-hunters.

The next thing was to photograph the game; and in view of the wild and romantic scenery that hemmed us in, and stretched away before us, plunging down Goat Creek, I sincerely regretted the absence of Mr. Phillips and his splendid stereo camera. But Charlie Smith had his small camera and four "fillims," and surely he could do something to save the situation. In these kodak days, a grizzly-bear hunter might as well return without the hide of his grizzly as without a photograph of the dead animal.

I said to Charlie that we must take the case seriously, and do our best as long as the films held out.

Now, on the trail and in camp the writer is neither photographer nor cook. He has troubles enough in the departments of taxidermy and osteology. This time, however, I had a borrowed pocket-kodak and three rolls of films, but no skill in the taking of pictures. While I knew how to "compose" a picture, I knew nothing about time-exposures; and besides this, I had great difficulty in finding things in a small finder.

But that bear had to be photographed, and we went at it seriously. Charlie used up his films, and then I took my turn, as if, like Winkelreid, on my sole arm hung victory.

In the middle distance, behind the bear, I found a very tall, columnar spruce that rose like a monument high above its neighbors; and that I adopted as the key to the situation. I photographed with bright light, and again with gray, as solemnly as if valuable results were about to be secured; but it was a great strain on Faith.

A month later, when Mr. E.F. Keller developed my films, and sent me some prints from them, I laughed long. So did Mr. Phillips when I showed him one of the best of my results. Then he was mystified.

"How on earth did a photographic incompetent like *you* ever make such a picture as *that*?" he demanded.

I replied that in photography an ideal picture is solely a matter of technical knowledge and artistic skill! My best picture is reproduced herewith.

We made a careful autopsy of the bear, and were able to determine to a certainty the details of our shooting, and its results. By good luck, my first shot went true to the mark aimed for—the heart region, immediately behind the foreleg. But it did not go through the heart. The animal was quartering to me, sufficiently that my ball passed close behind the heart, tore the lungs and liver to bits, and passed out at the middle of the right side, low down. We thrust a small stick through, in the track of the ball, and left it there.

Charlie Smith fired as the bear was turning to the right.

His bullet entered the left thigh, tore a great hole through the flesh between the skin and the femur, passed through the entrails, and lodged against the skin of the right side, well back. His bullets were of a larger calibre than mine, and this one was fully identified. We marked the course of that bullet, also, with a stick. After receiving those two bullets, the bear ran as if unharmed for about a hundred yards, when my third shot broke its neck, and brought it down in a heap, too dead to struggle. It was not touched by any other bullets than the three described. The distance, as nearly as we could estimate, was one hundred and fifty yards, good measure.

My first shot was of course absolutely fatal, and had I but known it, I need not have fired again. It was marvelous that the animal did not fall at the first fire, and equally so that with its lungs torn to pieces, it was able to run a hundred yards at top speed. How much farther could it have gone, had no other shots been fired? Not far, surely, for as it ran, it spattered the clean gray rocks with an awful outpouring of blood.

After our photographic labors we ate our frugal luncheon, rested, then skinned the bear. That accomplished we set out to examine the work done by our animal, with and unto the carcasses of the two goats. The result proved most interesting.

First we sought the carcass of Mr. Phillips's goat, which was rolled over the cliff, and fell immediately above the spot where our silver-tip gave up her ghost. On seeking it, we found a grizzly-bear's cache of a most elaborate and artistic character. On the steep hillside a shallow hole had been dug, the whole carcass rolled into it, and then upon it had been piled nearly a wagon-load of fresh earth, moss and green plants that had been torn up by the roots. Over the highest point of the carcass the mass was twenty-four inches deep. On the ground the cache was elliptical in shape, about seven by nine feet. On the lower side it was four feet high, and on the upper side two feet.

The Author's Grizzly Bear

PHOTOGRAPH BY W.T. HORNADAY.

The pyramid was built around two small larch saplings, as if to secure their support.

On the uphill side of the cache, the ground was torn up in a space shaped like a half-moon, twenty-eight feet long by nineteen feet wide. From this space every green thing had been torn up, and piled on the pyramid. The outer surface of the cone was a mass of curly, fibrous roots and fresh earth.

In her own clumsy way, the bear had done her best to provide for a rainy day. Her labors would indeed have protected her prize from the eagles, but at that two feet of soft stuff a wolverine would have laughed in ghoulish glee while he laid bare the contents of that cache with about six rakes of his rascally paws.

As already mentioned, on the previous day, Charlie Smith did see two wolverines in the vicinity of these goat remains, and fired at one of them, without effect. Both ran away across the slide-rock, often halting and defiantly looking backward, with short, stubby tail-wisp held stiffly erect.

The bear had been feeding on the body of my goat, which lay far out on the slide-rock, and she had eaten all that her stomach could contain. There being still a good quantity of pickings remaining, she had decided to bury it, but from much feeding was very lazy in carrying out this intention. She had, however, torn up and carried out about twenty mouthfuls of moss, earth and plant-roots, and dropped them, together with half a dozen sticks, upon the remains. It was in an interval of rest from this arduous labor that we first sighted the animal; and she was starting up to fetch down more material when I first fired at her. I photographed the bear's cache, but on the films the cache failed to appear.

At last we finished our work, packed the bear-skin and some of the best of the meat upon one of our horses, and started for camp, riding turn about. We rolled in just before

The Scene of Two Actions — Goats and Grizzly

1. Where we fired from, at the goats.

2. What Mr. Phillip's goat did.

3. What the author's goat did.

4. Where the grizzly was.

5. Where we were.

6. Where the grizzly died.

7. The grizzly's cache.

sunset, tired, but puffed up. Mr. Phillips was there; and when he was finally convinced that we really had seen a silver-tip, and shot at it, and brought back its skin and skull, his surprise and delight were not to be restrained. We danced around the camp-fire, and "Ki-yi-yied," in a wild-Indian fashion that in grown men is most undignified and reprehensible, anywhere east of the Missouri River.

The bear was not our only cause for singing a warsong. Mr. Phillips had shot,—but why spoil a good story?

CHAPTER XII

NOTES ON THE GRIZZLY BEAR

RARITY OF THE GRIZZLY IN THE UNITED STATES—SEASONS—
THE GRIZZLY BEAR'S CALENDAR—SOLITARY HABITS—FOOD
OF GRIZZLIES—A CARRION FEEDER—WEIGHT OF GRIZZLIES—
"GRIZZLY" OR "SILVER-TIP"—RESTRICTIONS IN KILLING.

IN THE UNITED STATES, OUTSIDE the Yellowstone Park and the Bitter Root Mountains, grizzly bears are now so very rare that it is almost impossible for a sportsman to go out and kill one, no matter where he hunts, and no matter how much money he spends. One of our best known writers on hunting matters, who has hunted in the West at frequent intervals during the past fifteen years, recently announced that he has now given up all hope of killing a grizzly in our own country, and has turned to British Columbia.

In British Columbia you can find grizzlies, provided you know when to go, and with whom to go. But the autumn is not the best season for finding bears in that country. If you would see the wild and untamed silver-tip, in the high altitudes, go in the spring, for that is the real season for hunting this grand species. Even then, you may hunt, as did Mr. Phillips's brother Robert, "for forty days, straight," without a sight of a silver-tip, or a shot; but if you are lucky, you may bag two in a month.

In the course of our camp-fire talk about bears and other animals, we had a symposium on the habits of the grizzly at the various seasons of the year. To this all the old grizzly hunters—Charlie Smith, Mr. Phillips, and the two Norboes,—contributed; and I pieced together their individual statements, and made up this

GRIZZLY BEAR'S CALENDAR

January.—About January 20th the cubs are born, in the winter den. Usually they are two in number, crudely formed, and almost hairless. They are about ten inches long, weigh about eighteen ounces, and are blind, and extremely helpless. The mother coils herself around them, moves not for many days, and the helpless little creatures are almost as much enfolded as if they were in an abdominal pouch. In the New York Zoological Park the period of gestation of the Colorado grizzly is two hundred and sixty-six days, or from April 22d to January 13th.

May.—In British Columbia a few grizzlies come out as early as May 1, but the majority appear about the 20th. Their first spring food is the roots of the snowlily, which is found growing on the snow slides. Besides this the grizzly eats other plants, of a dozen or more species, and also grass that is young and tender.

As soon as they emerge from their winter den they begin to rub their backs against trees, to scratch themselves, and they keep it up until the old hair is all off. Shedding begins early in June, and lasts until August 1.

June and July.—During these months the bears range

far and wide, the cubs following at the heels of the mother, searching for edible grubs and roots. In their search for edible insects, they overturn stones and tear old logs to pieces. Under every third stone (in suitable situations), a nest of ants is found; and these are greatly relished. To a bear, those sour and acidulous insects are much the same as pickles are to the human palate. The grizzly hunts up and devours all animals killed by snowslides. Mr. Phillips once knew a dead pack-rat to be eaten. In the Bush River country, Charlie Smith saw the remains of a grizzly that had been killed by a snow slide, and afterward had been dug out and eaten by another grizzly!

By the end of July the shedding of the old coat of hair is completed, and the silver-tip stands forth clad in a glossy new suit of dark brown, several shades darker than the old coat. It is very short, however, even in comparison with the September coat.

August.—In the valleys of the large rivers, berries begin to ripen, and the bears at once begin to feed upon them. Naturally the berries of the lowest and warmest valleys are the first to mature; and as the season advances, the boundary-line of the ripening fruit extends higher and higher up the mountains. In the highest valleys and mountains the berries do not ripen until September, just before the first heavy fall of snow. Strawberries come first, but they are so thinly scattered the total amount of food they furnish is small. Next comes the saskatoon, or service-berry, which is an important item of food, and whenever ripe is much sought by bears. They last so late into September that they detain the bears in the valleys of the large rivers when otherwise the animals would go up into the mountains to feed on huckleberries, and be shot.

September.—It is in this month that the bears take on the greatest amount of fat, for winter use. By September 15 the pelage is quite long, faultless in texture, and very richly colored.

Of the five species of huckleberries and blueberries that grow in the mountains, two are large and fine, and furnish an excellent supply of bear food. This is the month of bear migration, from the lower valleys upward, feeding on berries all the way. The earlier the coming of the first heavy snowfall, the earlier the migration. When the bears cannot get huckleberries, they eat black currants, but not with great relish, because they are rather bitter. The root of a "wild-pea vine" (*Hedysarum*) is eaten with great relish. It tastes precisely like green-pea pods, and is really very palatable. When the root is chewed, its residuum is tough and woody, but the outside is gelatinous, like slippery-elm bark.

October.—After the berries are gone, the grizzlies dig for "gophers" (*Citellus columbianus*), and for *Hedysarum* roots, until the ground freezes to such a depth that they cannot break through it. When digging becomes impossible, the bears seek their winter dens, and hibernate.

At most seasons of the year the male grizzly bear is a solitary creature. As a rule, the only individuals found living together are the mother and cubs. Occasionally it happens that the yearling cubs remain with their mother for some months after the birth of their successors, but the eighteen-months-old cub usually is found quite alone.

It often happens, however, that in the height of the berry season, six or seven bears may be found together in the same berry-patch; but this does not mean that all those individuals had been living together. Mr. W.H. Wright, a very successful bear-hunter, once killed seven bears in one day; and Prof. L.L. Dyche once saw on the head of the Pecos River, in New Mexico, seven grizzlies travelling together. But such occurrences are very rare exceptions, and the rule is exactly the reverse. Mr. Phillips once found two sets of tracks showing how one bear had chased another out of his territory.

Mr. Phillips's Grizzly

Like the wolves of the Northwest, the grizzly bears of to-day know well that a deadly rifle is the natural corollary to a man. Nine grizzlies out of every ten will run the moment a man is discovered, no matter what the distance may be from bear to man. The tenth will charge you, fearlessly, especially if you make your attack from below. It is said that a wounded grizzly always runs down hill; and this may account for some charges toward hunters below, which might not have taken place had the hunter been off to one side.

It must be borne in mind that the grizzly feeds according to the bill of fare available in his locality at a given time. In some localities he feeds upon salmon, the bulbs of various plants, and even upon grass; but wherever found, he is fond of berries.

He is not a proud feeder. He turns up his nose at nothing that he can chew and assimilate, except skunks and porcupines. According to the needs of the hour, he feeds upon the best or the worst. Beyond doubt, he prefers an elk, fat, fresh and filling; but when hunger plucks vulture-like at his vitals, he will not disdain to pick a dead and bloated pack-rat out of a snow slide and put it where he thinks it will do the most good.

The carrion state does not bother him in the least, if he is hungry. Most impartially he cleans up the carcasses of big game left by the hunter. He has been known to eat the flesh of his own kind, which surely is in very bad taste, ethically, but otherwise it is not so bad in him as in the hunters who sometimes devour his hams, regardless of their origin.

Occasionally a grizzly will feed on a carcass in the day-time, but the majority wisely defer their visits until nightfall, and retire before dawn. Many a hunter has tried to kill a grizzly over the remains of a horse specially slaughtered as a bait, but none of my bear-hunting friends ever have succeeded in killing a grizzly by that plan. Usually the bear comes only in the darkness, or else remains away altogether.

I believe that nearly every time the weight of a grizzly bear is estimated, it is greatly over-estimated. The size of a stretched skin, and the length of the pelage in the winter season, always suggests an animal larger and heavier than the reality. Trim down every "estimate" fully one-third, and you will have something near the proper figure. In bear-guessing errors, the writer is no exception. Bears always have seemed to me much larger than the cold and unimaginative scales show them to be.

Both in the United States and British Columbia, the grizzly bears of to-day are not extremely large. I think the bears that do mature are killed by hunters before they have lived the seven years that are necessary to the production of specimens of the largest size. To-day, any grizzly that will weigh seven hundred and fifty pounds may fairly be called a very large one. Those which will weigh a thousand pounds are now as rare as white buffaloes. I never have seen, and never expect to see, a one-thousand-pound grizzly. The largest individual that I ever knew to be weighed was one that died in Lincoln Park, Chicago, and which was found, by Mr. G.O. Shields, to weigh eleven hundred and fifty-three pounds. By old hunters it was "estimated" at eighteen hundred pounds. So far as I can learn, the Rocky Mountains have not produced during the past ten years a wild grizzly *actually weighing*, on scales, over seven hundred and fifty pounds. The great majority of the largest specimens killed and weighed during the last twenty years have weighed between five hundred and six hundred pounds; but records of actual weights, on scales, are very, very rare.

In the Zoological Park at New York, we have had grizzly bears coming from Chihuahua, Mexico, from Colorado, Wyoming and White Horse, Yukon Territory. Between all these there can be discerned no external differences. I believe they all belong to the same species, straight *Ursus horribilis*. Just where the grizzlies of the far north are met by the Alaskan brown bears, no one is as yet able to say. Mr. J.W. Tyrrell found the Barren Ground grizzly about one hundred miles east of the eastern end of Great Bear Lake.

There has been much talk in the Colorado mountains, and in a few other localities, about the "silver-tip "and the "grizzly," and several times I have been asked to state the characters of each. Like the continuous and ever-tiresome "ibex,"—which will not down—there is nothing in this question. A "silver-tip "is a Rocky Mountain grizzly, no more, no less. The two are one and indivisible, but the coat of the animal varies all the way from the gray-washed "bald-faced" grizzly to the darkest of the dark-brown individuals, which in November are sometimes of a dark chocolate-brown color.

I have tried in vain to find constant characters in the claws of grizzly bears, but each time I have concluded that I had found out something that was constant, immediately the old material has been discredited by new, and I now am as far as ever from a permanent conclusion. Some grizzlies have very long claws, that are strongly curved, and again others have claws that are rather short and blunt. They vary greatly, according to conditions, and the uses to which they have been put.

To-day there is in the United States only one locality wherein wild grizzlies exist in any number, and that is the remote fastnesses of the Bitter Root Mountains of Idaho, known as the Clearwater country. Mr. W.H. Wright knows where there are bears, but the mountains are so steep, and the brush so thick, it is not every sportsman who can get a shot, even when grizzlies are seen. Of course every one knows of the tame grizzlies of the Yellowstone Park, and the very few wild ones immediately around that reservation.

For several reasons, I am totally opposed to the trapping of grizzlies for their skins, to poisoning them, and to permitting any hunter to kill more than one grizzly per year. In other words, I think the time has come to protect this animal, at least everywhere south of latitude 54°. As a state asset, every live, wild grizzly of adult size is worth from $300 to $500, and as a hunter's grand object, it is worth much more. The trapping and poisoning of this noble animal should be prohibited, at once, throughout the whole United States and southern British Columbia; and this prohibition should stand forever. It is folly for Idaho, Colorado, Wyoming or New Mexico, to permit the killing of a five-hundred dollar silver-tip for a twenty-dollar skin; and every guide should know this without being told. Moreover, the slaughter of half a dozen grizzlies by one man in a single season is far worse for the big-game interests of America than the killing of that number of bull elk.

Eliminate the bears from the Canadian Rockies, and a considerable percentage of the romance and wild charm which now surrounds them like a halo, will be gone. So long as grizzlies remain to make awesome tracks and dig "gophers," just so long will brain-weary men take the long trail to find them, climb mountains until they are half-dead of precious physical fatigue, and whether they kill grizzlies or not, they will return like new men, vowing that they have had the grandest of all outings.

CHAPTER XIII

PHOTOGRAPHING A MOUNTAIN GOAT AT SIX FEET

WILD-ANIMAL PHOTOGRAPHY—A SUBJECT ON THE CRAGS—AT
THE HEAD OF THE GRAND SLIDE—THE BILLY GOAT AT BAY—
EXPOSURES AT SIX FEET—THE GLARING EYES OF THE CAMERA
STOPS A CHARGE—AT LAST THE SUBJECT STANDS CALMLY AND
LOOKS PLEASANT—IN PERIL FROM A "DEAD "KNEE—A SLEEPLESS
NIGHT FROM THE PERILS OF THE DAY.

AT LAST THE CAMERA HAS fully and fairly captured the elusive, crag-defying Rocky Mountain goat. *Oreamnos* has stood for his picture, at short range, looking pleasant and otherwise, and the pictures call for neither an "if" nor an apology. They are all that the most ambitious wild-animal photographer could reasonably desire.

In photographing rare wild animals in their haunts, the camera always begins at long range and reduces the focal distance by slow, and sometimes painful degrees. To the difficulties always present in photographing a large wild animal in its haunts must be added the dangerous crag-climbing necessary in securing fine pictures of the mountein goat.

So far as I know, the first photographs ever made of *Oreamnos* in his native haunts were taken by the late E.A. Stanfield, on the rock walls of the Stickine River, northern British Columbia, in 1898, not far from where he afterward lost his life in that dangerous stream. This was a single negative showing two goats in the middle distance, and three others, far away, sticking against the side of what appeared to be a perfectly smooth wall of rock several hundred feet high.

After that came three or four pictures of goats taken in timber, on level ground, and amid surroundings that seemed more suitable for white-tailed deer than crag-climbing goats. The distance was so great that it was only when the negatives were much enlarged that the goats became interesting.

On both sides of our ideally beautiful camp in the head of Avalanche Valley, the mountains rose steeply and far. First came the roof slopes, a mile from bottom to top, their faces seamed with parallel "slides "and ribbed with the ridges of rock and points of moss-green timber that climbed up between them. Above all that rose the long stretches of crag and rock wall, crowned by peak, "dome," and "saddle."

From bottom to top we scanned the slide-ways for grizzly bears feeding on berries, or digging roots. We watched the grassy belt just below the cliff-foot for mountain sheep. Goats we saw up there, daily, in little groups of three to five; but we had resolutely drawn our firing-line at three goats each.

But there was one old billy who fascinated us all. When we looked out of our tents on our first morning in that camp, he was calmly lying upon a ledge at the foot of the cliff immediately above us, near a bank of perpetual snow. For two days he remained there, at the same elevation, moving neither north nor south more than three hundred yards. When hungry, he came down to the foot of the cliff and fed on the tender plants that grew at timber-line, then climbed back to his favorite contour line, to lie and doze away the hours.

That goat seemed so sociable that finally we began to regard him as one of us, and we scrutinized him and apostrophize him to our heart's content. On the fourth morning, the beautifully clear sky and faultless atmosphere revealed a rare opportunity. While the cook was putting the finishing touches to an inspiring breakfast of fried mule-deer steaks and other luxuries, those of us who had most quickly succeeded in finding the clean spots on the camp towels took our usual early-morning gaze at "that old goat." (Ye gods! How glorious was the crisp air, the spruce-woods odor, the crackle and snap of the camp-fire, and the golden glow of sunrise on the western peaks and precipices! *That* was life,—without a flaw.)

As we gathered around our standing-lunch breakfast table, I remarked to Mr. Phillips that it would be a glorious feat to secure some really fine photographs of that billy goat in his natural environment. Turning to his side partner, Mr. Phillips said very positively,

"Mack, it is up to the unscientific section to get those pictures!"

"I dunno about them environments," answered Mack slowly, while he steered a long line of condensed cream into his coffee-cup, "but we can shore git a boxful of scenery up thar. We never yet shot a full-grown billy with a camery; and they're mighty onsartin critters. If we corral him too close, he'll like as not go vicious, and knock us clean off the mountain."

We soon saw that an attempt would be made to round up that goat somewhere, somehow, and take a picture of him at short range. In a few minutes we invented a wigwag code of signals by which the cook was to signal at intervals, with a clean towel on the end of a fossil tepee-pole, the position of the goat. Mr. Phillips and Mack Norboe made ready for the event,

The Haunt of the Camera Goat

THE GOAT WAS PHOTOGRAPHED ON THE STEEP ROCKS SHOWN ON THE LEFT, AT THE POINT
INDICATED. TAKEN AT A DISTANCE OF TWO MILES ACROSS AVALANCHE VALLEY.

and with Kaiser to assist in manipulating the goat, presently set out.

Mr. Phillips dislikes writing about his adventures, but in view of the fact that he alone is able to relate the occurrences of that day, I prevailed upon him to write out the following account of that daring and dangerous episode. Had I known on that morning the risks that he would run on those cliffs, hanging by one hand on a knife-edge of rotten rock with an angry goat at a nearness of six feet and threatening to knock him off into midair, I would not for any number of photographs have encouraged the enterprise. It was only the merciful Providence which sometimes guards insane camera enthusiasts which prevented a frightful tragedy; for it is well known throughout the goat country that an old male goat cornered on a ledge will fight dog or man.

In order to assist the photographers to the utmost, Charlie Smith and I considerately went bear-hunting; and this is Mr. Phillips's were obtained:

"Shortly after twelve o'clock, Mack and I started for the goat that had been hanging out above our camp. We took my stereoscopic camera, Charlie Smith's four-by-five camera, the dog, and my big gun in order to kill the goat if he attacked me.

"After crossing the narrow flat of Avalanche Creek, we struck up the long, grassy slide directly opposite our camp. At first its slope was about twenty degrees, but this gradually increased until finally, where it struck the slide-rock, it almost stood on end. We reached the slide rock about 2 P.M., after which the going was harder than ever. Gradually we worked our way out of the slide on to a high, rocky point which rose toward the south.

"Although lightly clad, we were by that time very warm. I had taken off my hunting shirt, and hung it upon my back, and opened the sides of my knickerbockers. Inside and out, we

The Face of the Precipice from Below, with Goat in situ

needed all the air we could get. I wore that day a pair of light golf shoes with rubber soles, tipped at the toes and heels with leather in which were fixed some small steel nails. These soles were very flexible, and adjusted themselves so well to the inequalities of the rocks that I could jump, and stick where I lit. Mack said: ' With them foot-riggin's, you shore kin go whar a bar kin!' Mack was not so well equipped as to footgear, having on an old pair of shoes with turned-up toes, set with nails that were much worn. This handicapped him on the bare rocks.

"'It's about time Cookie wiggled that rag, to show us whar that goat is,' said Mack as we seated ourselves to rest, and took out our glasses.

"Sure enough. In a few minutes we saw Huddleston out on the green flat in front of the tents, waving vigorously; and from his signals we knew that the goat was still there, toward the south, and above us. We decided that the Director's semaphore system was a good thing." We knew that our best chance for success lay in getting above the goat, to prevent his escape to the peaks, then in cornering him, somewhere. After a long diagonal climb we found ourselves under the wall of the snow-capped mountain, which rose sheer up two hundred feet or more, then rounded off into a dome going about three hundred feet higher. Now, just here we found a very strange feature of mountain work. A great rock buttress stretched along the foot of the mountain wall, originally continuous, and several hundred feet long. But somehow a big section had been riven out of the middle of that ridge, going quite down to the general face of that mountain-side, like a railway cut standing almost on end. This central cut-out section is now the head of a big slide, five hundred feet wide at the cliff, from which it descends at a fearful pitch.

"This slide is now bounded at the top by two ridges of rock, each with a steep wall facing the gap. The space lying between these walls is filled with masses of frost-riven rock, from the peak above, varying in size from dust to rocks the size of a freight car. The weight and momentum of the larger rocks had carried them well down the mountain, and some of them were so evenly balanced that it seemed as if a touch would be sufficient to send them thundering on.

"We stood on the top of the northern ridge, close under the foot of the cliff, and looked down the rock wall which dropped almost perpendicularly to the slide-way far below. On the south side of the slide rose a ridge very similar to the one on which we stood.

"From the signals Huddleston made at that time, we knew that the goat was below us. 'Thar he is, now!' exclaimed Mack, pointing down our ridge, and looking as he pointed I saw the animal about one hundred and fifty yards below us on a point of rock overhanging the slide. He was staring down toward our camp, as if he saw Huddleston and his signals, but I doubt if he did see our cook, for without glasses the distance was too great.

"Up to that moment, our dog Kaiser had been obediently following at our heels. Then we showed him the goat, and explained to him what we desired. He seemed to quite understand what we wished him to do. Leaving us at once, he silently worked his way down over the rocks, and in three or four minutes jumped the goat. And then pandemonium broke loose. Kaiser barked excitedly, Mack rolled stones, and I yelled.

"The goat was very much surprised by all this noise, and the sudden assault of the dog. Seeing that his retreat to the upper sanctuary of the cliffs was effectually cut off, he bounded like a great ball of cotton down the almost perpendicular wall of the cliff, into the slide-way two hundred feet below. To get down safely after his game, Kaiser had to hunt for stairs, and before he reached the bottom the goat was well across the slide.

"In the meantime I had scrambled down the rocks into the head of the slide, and found that although it pitched at a frightful angle, I could get footing close under the sheer mountain wall, so I ran and scrambled across, jumping over some water-worn fissures. When I reached the opposite wall, I saw the goat below me coming up the ridge. Owing to the shape of the slide, I had travelled only one-third the distance covered by the goat. "Seeing me above him, the goat thought he was again cut off from the mountain, and so sought safety on the face of the wall that overhung the slide. He did not realize that he could easily have passed me by going up the ridge before I could head him off.

"Seeing that the goat was safe for the moment, I thought of Mack, and fearing that he had fallen, went back. I found him at the bottom of one of the water-worn fissures. It was too wide for him to jump, so he had gone down into the rock crevasse, and when I found him he was on his hands and knees; and no wonder. The bottom was worn quite smooth, and pitched down at an angle of about sixty degrees. When he heard me he looked up, and said: 'I wisht I had some of the legs them octopuses had that the Professor was tellin' us about! I'd shore rope myself over this ditch!'

"When finally Mack crawled out of his trouble, we went over and looked at the goat. I took a picture of him from the slide, then leaving Mack in the slide with my gun, I worked my way with the cameras out up on the ridge, and finally secured a position above the goat. "I found him standing on a ledge about eighteen inches wide, backed against a slight projection on the face of the cliff, which cut the ledge off. The ledge rose at rather a steep incline for about twenty feet up to the level on which I stood. The goat was about eight feet below me, while below him was a sheer drop of a hundred and fifty feet or more, down to the slide-rock.

The Goat on the Stratified Rock
LOOKING TOWARD AVALANCHE CREEK.

"He was a very large goat, weighing, I should say, fully three hundred pounds. He had a magnificent pair of horns, fully ten inches long. I was surprised to note that he did not show the least sign of panic, or even fear. He looked up at me quite calmly, and then, ignoring me entirely, solemnly and serenely gazed out over the crags below.

"After a few trials from above I found it impossible to get a good picture of him without getting much nearer; so I yelled down to Mack: 'I'm going down to him. If he charges me, you must kill him, in a hurry.' "Setting the focus of my stereo camera for six feet, and placing the bulb in my mouth, I gradually worked my way down the ledge, carrying my camera in one hand and holding to the wall with the other. When I was within about twelve feet of him, Mack yelled to me:

"'Look out thar! He's a-raisin' his tail, like a buffalo bull! He's goin' to knock you off!'

"Mack was raised in Texas, with the buffalo, and diagnosed the case correctly. The very next instant, so it seemed to me, the goat came at me, head and tail up, ears drooped forward and eyes blazing green. He came with a bouncing rush, hammering the stones with his front feet so that the loose ones flew like broken ice. I was taken completely by surprise, for I did not think that on a ledge so narrow an animal could or would charge me.

"I was perfectly helpless, for I could not step aside, and it was impossible for me to back quickly up that steep and narrow shelf. The goat was too quick for Mack, for I heard him yell, in great alarm, 'I can't shoot, or I'll hit ye both!'

"Mack told me afterward that he dared not shoot from where he was, for fear the heavy ball would go through the goat, glance against the rock, and either kill me or throw me off the ledge. I was terribly frightened, but mechanically snapped the camera when the goat was about six feet away. There was really

The Goat at Ease

DISTANCE EIGHT FEET. ALL THESE PHOTOGRAPHS OF A LIVING MOUNTAIN GOAT WERE TAKEN SEPTEMBER 15, 1905, WITH STEREO HAWK-EYE CAMERA, No. 1. NO TELEPHOTO LENS USED.

nothing that I could do except to hold the camera at him, and snap it. "He charged up to within a yard of me, but with his eyes fixed on the two lenses. Then he appeared to conclude that any animal that could stand that much without winking was too much for him, so shaking his head and gritting his teeth he stopped, and to my great relief slowly backed into his niche.

"Believing that he would not charge the camera, I followed him down, and secured a picture of him at six feet. Then Mack began to see more symptoms of trouble, and since I had exposed my last film I backed out. Then I remembered the four-by-five camera, and started down with it, but Mack yelled angrily:

"'Hold on there! That goat's plumb dangerous, and if you start down there again, I'll shorely kill him! What's the use o' bein' locoed an' gettin' killed fer a few picters?'

"Mack was so wrought up that to save the goat I abandoned my intention; and when he finally joined me, we slipped another roll of films into the stereo camera.

"Just as we finished our reloading operation, Kaiser took a look down at the goat, at very close range, when all of a sudden, like a Jack-in-the-box, the old billy was up from the ledge and after him. Kaiser ran to us for protection, the goat charging after him, most determinedly. Mack and I yelled, and waved our arms, and finally turned the goat down over the point, this time with Kaiser chasing him.

"They were soon out of our sight, but we could hear the rocks rolling below, and knew that they were going back across the slide. So we slid off the crags into the head of the slide, and running across at some risk to our necks, finally turned the goat on to a small pinnacle, about where we first jumped him.

"It was here that I secured some of my best pictures. Mack, perched on the top of the crag, attracted the goat's attention and tantalized him by waving his hat, while I made pictures

An Angry Mountain Goat at Close Quarters

DISTANCE FOUR FEET; INSIDE THE FOCUS. AFTER CHARGING SO NEAR HE CONCLUDED TO
HALT AND BACK UP TO HIS FIRST POSITION.

as fast as possible. We had to keep Kaiser in the background, for apparently the goat blamed him for all his troubles, and I believe Billy was mad enough at that time to charge the dog through fire.

"My footing was very insecure, and being obliged to hold on with one hand and watch the goat in fear that he would charge me, I could not use the finder of my camera. Once as the goat charged up the rock at Mack I got in close to him, when he suddenly turned on me, gritting his teeth as he did so. His lip protruded like the lower lip of a charging bear, and with his front feet he stamped on the rocks until the small, loose fragments flew in every direction.

"It was just then that I got my best snapshot from in front, although the picture fails to show his ugly temper as I saw it. As I rolled in another film he charged me. Unfortunately I was so scared that I did not have presence of mind to press the bulb at the right distance. He bounced up to within four feet of me, when again the two big, glaring eyes of the camera fascinated and checked him. Just as he turned his head from the unwinking eyes of my stereo, I snapped it, but he was inside the focus.

"At that instant Kaiser, who had escaped from Mack's surveillance, appeared below me, and the goat immediately charged down upon him. Kaiser cleverly eluded him, and then the goat went on down into the slide, running diagonally across it to a rocky point beyond, where we again rounded him up. And then I discovered that my stereo camera was out of films!

"Regardless of the severity of the climb down to camp and back again, Mack insisted upon making the trip and bringing me more films, and immediately started.

"It was my duty to hold the goat at bay as best I could during the two hours' interval that I knew must elapse. The animal was then standing on the side of what seemed to me a sheer cliff, and when I slowly climbed down to look at him, he quite ignored me. Finding a sheltered niche in the cliff a hundred feet above him, I donned my hunting shirt and sat down to watch and wait.

"It was then about 3 P.M., and there followed a long, cold interval. Once Kaiser created a diversion by zigzaging down and taking another peep at his enemy, who immediately scrambled up the rocks at him, as fast as he could come. Kaiser retreated in good order, but soon turned and barked defiantly at the goat. After this futile charge, the goat backed away until his hindquarters hung over the cliff; then he charged a second time. Apparently he was determined to kill the dog, and rushed after him again and again. The goat would raise his tail, throw his ears forward, and without lowering his head go bounding stiff-legged after the dog like a bucking broncho. At times it seemed as if his object was to trample the dog rather than horn him, but Kaiser was quick enough, and easily dodged his rush-es. Then the old goat would stand and glare at him, gritting his teeth and sometimes sticking his tongue out, the personifica-tion of anger. It was a most interesting performance, and in spite of being very cold I was fascinated by it.

"About six o'clock I heard rocks rolling in the slide far below me, and knew that Mack was coming. Then I decided to get a better view of the trouble between the goat and the dog, and crawled down to the point on which the fight was tak-ing place. I worked down within twenty feet of the goat, when suddenly he whirled and came at me. I pointed my rifle at him and yelled, hoping to frighten him. He came within six feet of me, and I was about to fire when Kaiser barked close behind him. The goat turned so quickly he almost trampled the dog, who dodged under him and ran to me!

"Fortunately I was above the goat, and finding that the odds were against him he bounded off the point, and once more fled for the slide. This was the maddest race of all, for it called for quick work to get across the top of the slide in time to head off the goat. On that frightful pitch every jump I made loosened stones which dislodged others, and they went rolling and rumbling down the slide. The dog and goat also started their full quota of rocks, and for a time it seemed as if the whole mountain-side were moving. But I succeeded in heading off the goat, and clambered up on the wall above him.

"A few minutes later Mack joined me, and as he wiped the beads of perspiration from his shiny bald head, I said to him: 'Did you see the beautiful race we had across the slide?' 'Didn't see nothin',' he answered with an air of irritation. 'I thought everything had broken loose up here, and I was too busy dodgin' rocks to care who won any race. You-alls shore tore up the scenery!'

"After placing a new roll in the camera I crawled around on the hanging wall, and secured a very good picture of the goat. As I closed in he started to retreat, but by following him up I secured a picture as he was getting away. Then Mack headed him once more, on the farther side of the cliff, when he took refuge in a niche near the top of the wall.

"As we approached him from above, he again got his eyes on Kaiser, and charged up through the group which we three made. Fortunately Kaiser engaged his attention, which enabled Mack and me to head him and drive him back. For a time we lost him on the crags below. Presently, however, I found him standing on a wall which jutted out of the cliff on the north side of the great slide. At that point, the cliff towered up perpendicularly a hundred feet above the slide, and the goat was about twenty feet from the top, standing on a small projecting edge of rock that looked like a peg driven in the wall.

"At first it seemed utterly impossible to get a picture there, but on studying the rocks a little, I thought I saw a way. Leaving

The Goat Climbing Down and Away

Mack above to watch, I crawled down to a point almost over the goat, where I found that the mountain-side pitched down at an angle of at least thirty degrees, increasing to sixty, and ending in a sheer drop of a hundred feet or more. The rock was stratified, dipping toward the valley, like the slates on a roof. The layers varied from the thickness of ordinary roofslates to three or four inches. Much of this was loose, and had to be removed before I could get a footing.

"As I worked down, I started quite an avalanche of stone, and held my breath while I heard it go rumbling into the depths below. Just as I was thinking of going back, Mack called out, loudly and anxiously: 'Say, Jack! Is that you?' 'No,' I said, 'it's only rock.' 'I thought you had shore ruined the mountain that time.' He tried to appear unconcerned, but by his voice I could tell how he felt.

"At last I succeeded in working over to the edge of the cliff, and found myself on a level with the goat, and only eight feet away. It was as if he stood on a window sill on the gable end of a house, while I hung upon the corner of the slate roof. By reaching far down with my left foot I succeeded in getting one good foot-hold, but I had to double my other leg under me and lean forward upon my knee. After considerable work I broke off pieces of rotten rock, and built up a fair sort of a camera rest, supporting half of it upon my knee. The top slab of my stone-pile projected beyond the face of the cliff, so that between goat and camera there was no obstruction whatever.

"To my amazement and joy, during all this time the goat paid no attention to me, but stood there as calm and cool as an icicle. He really seemed to be enjoying his view of the scenery.

"After I had my camera set, I took a picture of him with his head slightly turned away, then I began to talk to him in a soothing voice, calling to him, 'Hey, Billy!' when he deigned to turn his head and look at me. Mack heard me talking to him,

Mr. Phillips's Most Dangerous Position
DRAWN BY CHARLES B. HUDSON.

and called down,—as evidence that he was near,—'He don't know his name! You might as well call him Mike!'

"This was the best chance I had with that animal; but by that time it was late and the light was not very favorable. However, I gave him time exposures, and got some very fair results. Every now and then the old fellow would stick out his tongue at me, and once I took a snapshot expressly to show that, but the result was not very good.

"After using up the six films in the camera, I swung it on my back and attempted to edge back from the face of the precipice. Then to my dismay I discovered that the bent knee on which I had been resting was as dead as if permanently paralyzed. It was stiff, and worse than useless. I had been frightened two or three times during that afternoon, but this was the climax. I called to Mack, and told him of the fix I was in, but owing to his bad shoes he could not come down to help me. Then I was sorry we had not brought a rope.

"Seeing that I must work out my own salvation I began to punch and beat my leg, and kept it up until at last the circulation started, and feeling returned. Finally I managed to crawl back very slowly to where Mack could reach me, and he soon landed me safely upon a level spot.

"While this was going on, the goat got tired of inaction, jumped up over the wall and started for the peak. For some reason, however, he changed his course and climbed down into the slide, with the dog after him. Expecting to see a good race we stopped to watch it; but poor Kaiser's feet were now very sore and the goat outran him. And then a queer thing happened.

"The goat stopped on the farther edge of the slide, and finding that his human tormentors were nowhere near, he decided to get square with that dog! When Kaiser reached him, the goat charged furiously. Seeing his danger, the dog turned and started back the way he came, with the goat in hot pursuit. The goat pursued by a series of short rushes, and not by the steady, straightaway run that a bear makes. He followed the dog almost to the ridge on which we were, but finally desisted, and retreated southward.

"It was then so late that we started at once for camp in order to get off the crags before dark. It grew dark before we reached camp, but at last we were guided in by the camp-fire, thoroughly exhausted, and half famished for water. I never knew Kaiser to drink so long as then, and his feet were so raw and sore that he scarcely could bear to have them doctored."

Mr. Phillips's narrative, as he records it, does not half adequately portray the frightful risks that he ran on that memorable afternoon. That night, I think he was awake all night, save once. Then he threshed around in his sleeping-bag, and clutched wildly at the silk tent-roof over his head.

"Hey, John!" I called out sharply, to waken him.

"What's the matter? Are you having a nightmare?"

"Oh!" he groaned. "I thought I was falling off those rocks,—clear down to the tents!"

Just before breakfast the next morning Mr. Phillips said to Mack in a quiet aside, "How did you sleep, Mack?"

"I didn't sleep none!" said Mack, solemnly.

"Whenever I dozed off I dreamt that old Oramus was buttin' us off them rocks. Every time I lit I shore made it lively for Charlie."

They were not the first men whose sleep had been destroyed by the recrudescence of the horrors of the rocks.

The next day men and dog rested quietly in camp, too tired and sore to move out.

CHAPTER XIV

A RAINY DAY IN CAMP

THE FINEST OF ALL CAMPS—A RECORD-BREAKING COOK—
FEARFUL SLAUGHTER OF COMESTIBLES—DRYING MEAT FROM
BIG GAME—A GOOD METHOD DESCRIBED—THE NORBOE
BROTHERS—TRAPPING ON BULL RIVER—THE TRAPPERS' BILL OF
FARE—MACK NORBOE'S BIGGEST BEAR—THE BIG BEAR THAT GOT
AWAY.

THE AFTERNOON OF SEPTEMBER 16TH was dominated by
misty rain. It was too wet for hunting, but under the giant
Canadian white-spruce trees which encircled one side of our
camp, we sat, and spat into the camp-fire, and yarned away the
hours most comfortably. Big, fleecy white clouds from Bull
River floated into our valley, dragged softly along the side of the
eastern mountains, and left the green timber and yellow grass
of the slides looking like a freshly varnished oil-painting. Our
horses grazed on the rich meadow in front of the tents, snorted
with satisfaction, tinkled their bell, and fed until they could
feed no more. Dog Kaiser appointed himself special camp-
guard, and whenever a horse crossed his dead-line, there was an
indignant bark, a bitten pastern, a vicious kick in mid-air at a
dog that was always six inches the other way, and a quick retreat.

It was a busy day for Huddleston, the cook; for in camp, the hunter's fancy lightly turns to thoughts of grub. When Charlie and I tramped in at one o'clock, on account of the rain, the others were all there, and for the remainder of the afternoon we snugged down under the three big spruces that formed a triangle around our camp-fire, and loafed, and invited our souls.

Were I to hunt a thousand years longer, I think it would be impossible to find a more ideal camping-spot than that which Mr. Phillips named in my honor. The shelter of the beautiful grove of spruces, the magnificent mountains within a stone's throw on either hand, the long-distance view down the valley to Roth Mountain and Glacier, the slides, the vegetation of timberline, the water, the wild life, and last but not least, the grass for our faithful, never-running-away horses made a combination of conditions rarely, found in this world.

To me, the pace set by our *chef* was highly amusing. Never before have I camped with a cook who took his job as seriously as did Huddleston. To begin with, he was young and vigorous, accustomed to hard work, and there was not a shirking bone in his body. He rose in the morning, he cooked meals, he washed things, hewed wood and drew water as if his life depended upon the perfect doing of each section of his daily work. The amount of food that he cooked on his folding stove, and the quantity of bread that he baked before our campfire in his jolly little reflector-oven, was simply appalling. I used to think that my band of rustlers on the 1886 buffalo hunt ate the most of any human beings I ever camped with; but on this last trip, the crowd ate more. No doubt it was because we had a greater variety, and the temptation was stronger. It will be many a year ere I cease to hear Huddleston saying briskly, "Grub's ready, gentlemen. Now, which will you have? Coffee, tea or chocolate? I've got 'em all!"

We all believed in having luxurious camp-fires; and wood was plentiful and cheap. Each night and morning it was a white man's camp-fire, for fair. You know the familiar Indian saying current in the West,—"White man make heap-big fire, get way off!" It was against the rules to cut logs shorter than six feet—save when away from home, and camping on a trail.

From the very first, I began to dry wild meat, after a very good fashion which I had learned of my old friend L.A. Huffman, away back in the bad-lands of Montana. Strange to say, none of the other members of our party knew any good method of drying meat, and they watched my work with keen interest, and an eye to the future.

The process is so simple a child can use it, and the ingredients can be purchased in any frontier store, for a few cents. In Michel, I bought half a pound of black pepper, an equal quantity of ground allspice, and four three-pound bags of fine table-salt. The proportions of the mixture I use are: Salt, three pounds; allspice, four table-spoonfuls, and black pepper five table-spoonfuls, all thoroughly mixed.

Take a ham of deer, elk, or mountain sheep, or fall-killed mountain goat, and as soon as possible after killing, dissect the thigh, muscle by muscle. Any one can learn to do this by following up with the knife the natural divisions between the muscles. With big game like elk, some of the muscles of the thigh are so thick they require to be split in two. A piece of meat should not exceed five inches in thickness. Skin off all enveloping membranes, so that the curative powder will come in direct contact with the raw, moist flesh. The flesh must be sufficiently fresh and moist that the preservative will readily adhere to it. The best size for pieces of meat to be cured by this process is not over a foot long, by six or eight inches wide and four inches thick.

When each piece has been neatly and skillfully prepared rub the powder upon every part of the surface, and let the mixture adhere as much as it will. Then hang up each piece of meat, by a string through a hole made in the smaller end, and let it dry in the wind. If the sun is hot, keep the meat in the shade; but in the north, the sun helps the process. Never let the meat get wet. If the weather is rainy for a long period, hang your meat-rack where it will get mild heat from the camp-fire, but no more smoke than is unavoidable, and cover it at night with a piece of canvas.

Meat thus prepared is not at its best for eating until it is about a month old; then slice it thin. After that no sportsman, or hunter, or trapper can get enough of it. Wives and sweet-hearts who love out-doors dote upon it. To men who write about nature and animals, each chew is a fresh inspiration.

No; this is *not* "jerked" meat. It is many times better. It is always eaten uncooked, and as a concentrated, stimulating food for men in the wilds, it is valuable. Charlie Smith and the Norboes were emphatic in their expressions of regret that they never before had known of that process. Said Charlie, ruefully, "Think of the good meat, Mack, that we could have saved for months on Bull River, that long winter, if we had only known about this scheme! We would never have gone meat-hungry!"

There is no question about it. The American trapper has for a century been horribly wasteful of wild life, because he did not know how to dry wild meat, easily and cheaply. Pemmican is all right; but the making of it, on a good, palatable basis, is neither simple nor easy.

While on this trip I cured for Mr. Phillips and myself about forty pounds (when dry) of the meat of mountain goat, mule deer, mountain sheep and grizzly bear. The mountain goat meat was good, but slightly tough in comparison with the other meats. It had not the slightest disagreeable flavor, but in spring it is spoiled by the flavor of wild onions. All the meat of mountain sheep and mule deer was tender and delicious, but that of the grizzly bear, when dried, had a queer fishy taste that made it unpalatable. The flesh of the mountain sheep (*Ovis canadensis*) and mule deer are so nearly identical, both in fibre and in flavor, that in the fall months no human palate can distinguish one from the other.

In our small party there were some good story-tellers,— "raconteurs" they call them, east of Altoona; besides which, my companions were men who had seen and done many things in the late Wild West. Of Charlie Smith, I have already written. The stories he told us of "the Bush River country," and of the wilds of Oregon and Washington, to say nothing of the Elk River region, would make a fascinating book.

Mack and John Norboe, of Norwegian parentage, were born on the plains of Texas, grew up as buffalo hunters, cowboys and Indian fighters, and finally "settled down" as guides and trappers. Both participated in the mad and reckless buffalo slaughter of the early seventies, and killed buffaloes of which they cannot now be induced to tell. In the days of Apache and Comanche Indian troubles, when the murder of settlers' families often called for punitive expeditions gathered on short notice, they rode and fought Indians with other white men who believed in the survival of the fittest. Later on, Mack became foreman of a large cattle-ranch, after which he fell in with Charlie Smith, and settled down permanently as his partner. For six years or more they have guided, trapped and hunted together, drawing in John Norboe as a special partner whenever circumstances tempted him to come in.

As a talker, Mack is more reserved than Charlie and John, and rarely relates a long story, especially when it is possible to put that labor upon his partner. He is a bold and successful hunter, and a hardy mountaineer, but on dangerous rocks, his nerves are not quite so cold as those of his partners. When he is afraid, he does not hesitate to say so; which many a pretty gentleman finds it very hard to do.

John R. Norboe is an almost tireless climber, and bold on the cliffs, beyond the limit of safety. In the telling of stories he is both graphic and picturesque, and the manner in which he unconsciously acts out his stories is always irresistibly amusing. He is a reasonably ready talker, and invariably interesting. In both John and Mack the vernacular of the southern cattle-plains was strongly in evidence, and it made them all the more interesting.

I mention these three men thus particularly because they are to-day successful trappers of fur-bearing animals. Even amid the present scarcity of such wild life, they are sufficiently wise in wood-craft to make at least half their living by trapping marten, wolverine, ermine, mink, lynx, and (I regret to say it) bear. In the United States the fur-trapper is almost extinct, because there are no longer enough fur-bearing animals to make the pursuit interesting.

I am tempted to add the record of one winter's catch, made on Bull River, by the two Norboes alone. From September 15th until the middle of the following June, they caught 96 marten, 7 wolverines, 4 grizzly bears, 6 beavers, 10 mink and 1 lynx. During this period they consumed the following food: 3 bull elk, 7 goats, 700 pounds of flour, 200 pounds of sugar, 50 pounds of dried fruit, 15 gallons of berries, 30 pounds of coffee and 20 pounds of rice.

Let it not be supposed, however, that even in the country in which we then were, it is always possible for hunters and trappers to supply themselves with wild meat on short notice. In the spring of 1904 when three members of our party, Mr. Phillips, Charlie Smith and Mack Norboe, were bear-hunting in the Bull River country, they ran out of meat, and became so hungry for that very necessary item they flung appearances to the winds, and sent Charlie Smith on snow-shoes over two ranges of mountains, thirty miles in and thirty miles back, for a ham! That was sufficiently absurd, but the sequel was even more so. In order to travel rapidly, and be burdened with nothing save the ham and his revolver, Charlie left his rifle behind. On the return journey he was followed up by a grizzly bear which also needed a sugar-cured ham I But Charlie was "dead game "and even when face to face with the grizzly and with no rifle, he refused to jettison his cargo. He finally bluffed and eluded the bear, and steered his precious freight safely into port, having made that severe round trip in two days.

Mack Norboe has had hundreds of interesting adventures, but it is difficult to induce him to tell of one. There are men who talk more of their one bear than Mack does of his hundred. Only the most skillful stalking at the camp-fire ever rounds up an extended narrative by him.

But every man makes exceptions. When the talk turned on the charging habits of grizzlies, amount of silent treatment, backed up by a few well-aimed questions, finally brought forth this incident:

MACK NORBOE'S BIGGEST BEAR

"YES, I'VE HUNTED GRIZZLY B'AR and black b'ar in Colorado, Wyoming, Montana and British Columbia. All told, I think I must have shot up and trapped purty nigh on to a hundred; but out of all the grizzlies I've shot, and shot at, only one ever really charged me. But I don't believe even that one would a-charged me if it hadn't been for my dogs.

"That was in Routt County, Colorado, between the White and the B'ar Rivers, in the spring of '91. I think there's a family of big b'ar in that country, just as there's an outfit of

A Rainy Day in Camp

specially big black b'ar here on Elk River. In this Colorado country that I'm a-tellin' ye about, there was a whalin' big grizzly that they called 'old Jumbo,' and he'd been killin' cattle for five or six years. From the size of his tracks, everybody knew that he was a shore big 'un, but I don't know of any one who had seen or shot at him. Sam Ware, who had a cattle-ranch on B'ar River, tracked him one day down Crooked-Wash Creek, and had Sam run onto him he shore would have rounded old Jumbo up, for he was a good shot, and full o' sand.

"Early in the spring I was out with my two foxhounds, runnin' a mountain-lion, but the track was so old we didn't jump him. There was considerable snow on the ground, and in making a circuit we struck on old lumbo's tracks. Gee! but they were big! He had just come out of his winter quarters in the White River range, and was pintin' out toward B'ar River. The trail was good and fresh, and I put the dogs right on to it. Before they had gone more'n a quarter of a mile, a thunderin' racket broke loose, and I was shore that they had jumped the b'ar.

"It was rollin', hilly ground, covered with cedars, and the branches hung so low it made it very bad for seeing any distance I pulled my freight toward the place where the row was goin' on, but had hardly got fairly started when one of the dogs rushed a-past me makin' for the rear, with his tail between his legs, and his ears a-flappin' up and down like a pair o' bird's wings. The b'ar had plumb stampeded him, and I didn't see him no more until the next day.

"I hurried on as fast as I could go, and just as I reached the top of a hill that lay ahead of me, here comes old Jumbo, just a-tearin' along after my Ponto dog; and Ponto was hikin' along in front, barkin' at every jump. That old dog shore had plenty o' sand. First thing I knew, old Jumbo was right there within twenty yards of me; and when he saw me, he rushed straight at me.

"I had a .45-90 Winchester, and it was all right. Quick as I could, I sent in two shots, one in the centre of the breast, the other in the shoulder. My Ponto dog had jumped from the trail behind a cedar, and he was between me and the b'ar. My first two shots dropped old Jumbo, all right, but while I was throwin' in the third cartridge, he jumps up and starts for me again, full pelt.

"I s'pose my dog thought the b'ar was getting too close to me. Anyway, he jumps from behind that cedar, plumb at the b'ar's throat,—just as I fired! I didn't see the dog till he filled the sight, just as I pulled the trigger; but when the gun cracked, I knew I'd killed him. The ball went clean through his shoulders, killin' him stone dead; but it also hit the b'ar in a front leg, and when he grabbed his leg between his teeth and bit it, it gave me a chance to put a ball into his neck, which finished him.

"The death of my dog made me so mad and locoed I just emptied my Winchester into that b'ar, after he was down for keeps. I felt as I couldn't ever stop shootin' him. He was shore scorched by my last five shots.

"That was the only b'ar that ever charged me. Although he had only just come out of his winter den, he was very fat. We got out of him over a hundred pounds of grease. He hadn't eaten anything since he holed up in the fall. His stomach was about the size of my two fists, and there was nothing in it but wrinkles. He was a dark silver-tip, and his hair was rather short and thin. We got only twelve-fifty out of him, bounty and hide. The bounty was $10. He was the biggest b'ar I ever saw. No, we didn't weigh him, nor measure him. We had no way to do either; but his dry hide was over ten feet long."

THE BIG BEAR THAT GOT AWAY

SOME ONE SAID SOMETHING ABOUT the difficulty of

judging distances in the mountains, particularly over snow; and that led to a remark from Mack Norboe

"Say, Mr. Phillips, how about Big Ben?"

"It is always the biggest fish and the biggest bucks that get away," said Mr. Phillips, reflectively; and on being encouraged to "out with it" he outed with it, as follows:—

"The bear that Mack refers to with that twinkle in his eye was, in one way, the most remarkable bear I ever saw on foot. We were hunting on the head of Wilson Creek, and it was the 12th of May. In many places the snow was deep on the mountains, but there were a few bare spots on the slides, where it had melted off. In those places, wild onions were springing up, and Mack and I started up a slide to look for a salad. But instead of finding small onions, we found big game.

"Mack looked half a mile up a big slide, and said,

"'Oh, my! What a big silver-tip!'

"It was a bear all right, and while he looked very dark, he seemed entirely too big for a black bear. When we looked at him with our glasses, however, we saw that although he was a black bear, he was a whaling big one. He was out on a snow-covered slide, walking slowly about among some low bushes, whose tops rose only a few inches above the snow.

"As soon as we had taken a good look at him, we prepared for a run and a big fight.

"'He's a shore big 'un I' said Mack."

(At that point, Mack laughed.)

"We kept in the edge of the green timber, and ploughed up through the snow at a great rate, shedding clothing at intervals all the way. In a very short time we got up nearly opposite the bear, but a little below him. The distance was only one hundred and seventy-five yards, and the bear looked as big as ever. Without losing a minute I stepped out, knelt down, and just as the bear looked at me, fired at the centre of him.

My bullet flew a foot too high, and the bear started to run. I opened up and fired four more shots at him, and every shot went high, just like so many steps in a ladder.

"The bear plunged into the green timber on the opposite side of the slide, and disappeared. I looked at Mack, and said, '*I missed him!*'

"'Ye *shore*-ly did!' said Mack.

"We went out upon the slide, and looked at the bear's tracks. Then we both burst out laughing.

"That bear was nothing but a measly little *cub*, fifteen months old! He was only two sizes bigger than a full-grown woodchuck, and his tracks were simply ridiculous, they were so small...You see, the little brute was out there on the snow, and there was absolutely nothing to indicate its size. Instead of being one hundred and seventy-five yards away it was only seventy-five, and each time I fired at the bear I shot clean over it. I never touched a hair of it."

"That was the only bear that ever got away from Mr. Phillips!" said Mack.

"Yes," said Charlie Smith, "and to cap the climax of that great big bear-fight, I heard the firing, and rushed up from camp with knives and whetstones and things, to help skin a big bear. But it just shows ye how sometimes the mountains fool a man com-*pletely!*"

CHAPTER XV

CAMP-FIRE TALES

CHARLIE SMITH'S STORY—AN OUTLAW IN CAMP—A SILENT
DEATH SENTENCE—THE PURSUERS OF TOM SAVAGE FIND HIM—
HIS FATE—JOHN NORBOE INTRODUCES OLD JOHN CAMPBELL—
TRYING TO BE CHASED BY A GRIZZLY—THE BEAR THAT FELL
INTO THE FIRE.

WHO IS THERE WHO DOES not love a good story, told to
eager and sympathetic listeners beside a generous camp-fire!
Show me a man who does not, and I will show you a man
whose heart is not right, whose red corpuscles are green, and
whose milk of human-kindness has turned to whey.

There are chums and chums; and guides and guides. I
have camped with several kinds of men—white, red, yellow,
brown and black. In the lot there have been some of the best of
men, and some bad ones. One was a murderer, out of a job; and
another was a donkey with a human head, freshly retired from
a great army for being a fool.

I have already insinuated, however, that the composition
of our party of seven,—counting Kaiser,—left me absolutely
nothing to desire. And it was in our ideal camp, in the head of

Avalanche Valley, that the spirit moved most upon the company, and the best stories were told. The surroundings were so satisfactory that as we sat by the blazing logs and loafed away the hours of storm and ante-bedtime, each camper brought forth his share of story contributions, and told them in his best style. The good stories told around that camp-fire would easily fill a volume; and I would be more than human if I could refrain from reporting here a few of them, as samples of the whole. One of the best was told by Charlie Smith, precisely as follows, concerning.

AN OUTLAW IN CAMP

"I SPENT THE WINTER OF 1878 at Fort Klamath, in southern Oregon, and in January I had some business at the government land-office, which then was at Lake View, ninety miles away. The trip had to be made by team, so early one morning I left Fort Klamath with a span of good horses and a light wagon. The ground was covered with snow, and as the country was sparsely settled it was necessary to haul supplies for myself and my horses, and camp on the trail.

"Late in the afternoon of the second day, I reached the lower end of Drew's valley, and camped for the night. After unhitching my horses and feeding them, I rolled three pitch-pine logs together, and soon had a roaring fire going, over which I boiled a pot of coffee. After supper I spread some hay on the snow, and made my bed for the night.

"When it became dark, I laid down on my blankets, to enjoy a real old camp-out smoke, and watch the flicker of my camp-fire on the pine boughs overhead.

"I had lain there for some time, and was beginning to feel sleepy, when I heard horses coming down the mountain from the west, their hoofs beating a regular tattoo on the frozen road. A few moments later, an Indian rode up to my fire. That didn't surprise me much, for in those days, one was liable to meet an Indian at any turn in the road.

"He reined in his horse, and sprang to the ground, giving a grunt by way of salutation. He had two horses, and had been riding one and leading the other. They were both dripping with perspiration, and seemed just ready to fall in their tracks. After giving me and my outfit a sharp look, he led his ponies to one side, and tied them to a small tree. Then he came and stood by my fire, and asked me for some grass for his horses. I told him I didn't have any grass to spare. It wouldn't have done them any good, even if I had had a ton to give them, for they were just completely run to death. They stood up only a few minutes, and before daylight one of them was dead.

"The Indian was dressed in a buckskin shirt and leggings, and a heavy red blanket was belted around his waist. I was sitting on my blanket, and my rifle, which I always kept near me, was tucked under the edge of my bed, by my side. A cold, raw wind was blowing, and as the Indian turned about to warm himself before the fire, the wind caught the corner of his red blanket and blew it up to one side. To my perfect horror, I saw a woman's scalp hanging from his inside belt, a white woman's scalp, with light-colored hair over a foot long!

"I can't begin to tell you what a feeling that sight sent through me. It was like a current of electricity; and I felt it clean down to the ends of my toes. Like a flash, I knew that that Indian was a murderer, that he had killed some settler's wife,—and probably the whole family,—stolen their horses, and was being followed by somebody. Even an Indian won't run a good pair of horses to death for just nothing.

"Without stopping for an instant to think what I was doing, I grabbed my rifle, cocked it, and brought it to bear on that Indian.

"The Lunch Counter" at Camp Hornaday

W.T. Hornaday – Mr. Phillips – Mack Norboe – John Norboe – Charlie Smith.

"'Lay down, or I'll shoot you!' I fairly yelled at him.

"I'll never forget the look he gave me, it was such a horrible mixture of ferocity and fear. He didn't obey the order at once, but glancing over his shoulder he said, 'You know me?'

"I said, 'No I don't and I don't want to, either.'

"'Me Tom Savage.'

"'Well,' I said, 'I don't give a cuss how savage you are. If you don't do as I say, I'll fill your hide so full of holes it won't hold baled hay; and you'd better not argue the point.'

"Seeing that I had my gun leveled square at his heart, he dropped to the ground.

"'Now,' I said, 'turn your back to me, and if you attempt to get up, or turn over, or look at me to-night, I'll kill you right where you lay.'

"After the first shock of my surprise and horror had worn off, I did some very hard thinking. I was reasonably sure some one was after him, or he would not have run his horses to death. I reasoned that he knew his mounts were done for, and his object in stopping at my camp was to raise my hair, and with my comparatively fresh horses, hit the trail again.

"I was in a mighty uncomfortable position. My better feelings naturally turned against the idea of shooting him, but all the time I was fully resolved he should not escape me. The main cause of immediate uneasiness was that those pine logs might burn out before morning, and that darkness might force me to act.

"And so I spent that long, bitter cold night,—one of the longest I ever spent. Once during the night the logs fell apart, and one of them came near rolling on the Indian. He turned over and made as if to spring to his feet. I yelled at him not to get up, but to kick the log back again; so he put his feet against it and shoved it back against the other. When the fire blazed up again I laid my gun down, and put my hands under the blankets, for the wind was sharp and my bed was too far from the fire for comfort outside of blankets.

"As the night wore away, I began to grow nervous. My business was urgent, and I could not go on without doing something with that fellow. The more I thought over the matter, the more determined I was that he should not escape me. I thought of all sorts of things. "Along about five o'clock in the morning, as I sat there watching and thinking, I noticed the Indian give a slight start, and then appear to be intently listening. I, too, strained my ears for some sound, hoping against hope that some settler would come along; for by that time I had resolved that if assistance did not come soon, I would put a ball through that murderer's head, affix my brand, and leave him in the road.

"To my great relief I soon detected the sound of hoof-beats, coming at a sharp gallop down the hillside, from the west. As they came nearer and nearer, the Indian began to beg of me to let him go. It was the first time he had spoken to me after telling me his name in the evening; but I ordered him to lie still. In a few minutes a lieutenant and four soldiers of the regular army trotted up to my smouldering fire.

"As the officer in command dismounted, his glance fixed upon the blanketed party in front of the fire, and he took in the whole situation. He went up and poked the Indian with his foot, and as the savage turned his head and looked at him, he said to me, very cheerfully, 'Well, stranger, you've got our bird here! We've been wanting this fellow.'

"'Very likely, officer,' I said, 'and if you hadn't showed up for another hour, a hearse would have been of more use to him than handcuffs.'

"'Would you have executed him?'

"'He's got a white woman's scalp under his blanket, and I shorely would have branded him so well that he wouldn't have been taken for a maverick. But I'm mighty glad you've come, just the same; and now I release all claims on him.'

"They soon had the brute in irons, and I soon had a pot of coffee boiling. While we drank our coffee, we talked. The lieutenant told me that this Indian was a Bannock, who had been ranging about Stein's Mountain, and he was an outlaw. He had made a sneak on an isolated settler, and had murdered the whole family,—man, woman and child.

"He hid in the locality for some time, but it soon got too warm for him, and he skipped out and went to the Klamath Reservation. There he hid himself among the numerous tribes living there, until one day while gambling with a Klamath Indian, he stabbed and killed him. This enraged the Indians on the Reservation, and they reported him to the agent, who sent a squad of troopers after him. In some way he got wind of it, and with two stolen ponies he undertook to get back to his old range again.

"He was taken to Fort Klamath, tried far murder, and hanged."

Charlie Smith is no braggart; and when he told of his deliberate resolve to execute Tom Savage for the murder of a white woman, every one of his auditors felt sure that but for the arrival of the outlaw's pursuers, the grim death sentence that Charlie silently pronounced by the embers of his smouldering camp-fire would resolutely have been carried out.

For about the forty-fifth time, the talk and storytelling turned once more to bears. One remark led to another until John Norboe said: "The funniest thing I ever heard of in bear-huntin' was about old Jack Campbell, and...

THE GRIZZLY THAT FELL INTO THE FIRE

"Campbell was a bald-headed old fellow who lived a few

miles above Meeker, Colorado. He was great on killin' grizzlies, and he killed so many of 'em that finally he wasn't ever afraid of one, nohow. One time a feller was drivin' along a trail, and he saw old Jack come a-runnin' out of a thick patch o' young jack pines, with an axe in his hand, lookin' behind him. No, he didn't have no gun. Bimeby he stopped, went back into the jack pines, but soon come a-runnin' out again, just as before. Then he stopped, and blamed if he didn't do it all over again.

"Then the feller on the trail got off his wagon, hitched his horses, and went up to see what it all meant. And what d'ye s'pose that old cuss was up to?"

Everybody gave it up.

"Well, sir, there was a grizzly bear in the middle of them jack pines, eatin' on a dead horse; and blamed if old Jack wasn't a-tryin' to tease that bear into chasin' him out into the open, where he could swing his axe, so that he could kill him,—with his axe! The bear would chase him part way out, then go back to the horse."

"Well, did he get him?"

"No. About the third trip the bear got scared, and ran off the other way. But that wasn't what I started in to tell ye. One time old man Campbell and another feller was out in the mountains huntin'; and one night they camped right at the foot of a rock cliff about,—well, I don't know just *how* high it was. In the morning old Jack got up first, built up a big log fire, and put on the coffee-pot. He had just begun to cook break-fast, when a little bit of rock fell down, and made him look up. Blamed if there wasn't a good big grizzly standin' on the top of the rock wall, lookin' down over the edge, at old John cookin' his breakfast.

"Quick as lightnin' the old man grabs his gun, and sends a ball into the bear; and blamed if the bear didn't come tum-blin' down, and fall plumb into the camp-fire. The coffee, an' ashes, an' fire jest *flew*; and the grizzly jest raised Cain. All that old man Campbell thought about was that good bear-skin,—*on the bear*,—about to get burnt up! He dropped his gun, rushed up, and begun a-grabbin' at the bear, to drag him out of the fire I The bear was only half dead, and he grabbed, and clawed, and bit at the old man, all the time the old man was grabbin' at him, and fightin' with him to get him drug outen the fire before his pelt got burnt. The old man never stopped to think that without his gun in his hands the bear might up and maul him. He thought he must get the bear out first, and then finish a-killin' him afterward." As John reached the point of his story, all unconsciously he acted out, in thrilling style, the frantic manner in which old John Campbell grabbed at a live grizzly, to pluck him as a brand from the burning, and save his vested rights in a twenty-dollar hide. It sent the audience off into roars, the meaning of which John mistook, for he hastened to add,

"Oh, that happened, all right! Mack and me saw that bear's hide, with a burnt patch on the back, didn't we Mack!"

CHAPTER XVI

MORE CAMP-FIRE YARNS

THE CHARGE OF THE DUCHESS—THE DEATH OF THE DUKE OF
WELLINGTON—THE HORROR OF THE ROCKS—THE SHEEP THAT
COULDN'T BE CAUGHT—THE MATCHES THAT WOULDN'T LIGHT.

ON SEVERAL OCCASIONS I HAD heard mention of a
narrow escape that Mr. Phillips enjoyed from the claws of a
wounded grizzly bear; and in the leisure hours of that rainy
day in camp, it occurred to me to draw out all the facts regarding the affair. So I said:

"John, it seems to me that in spite of all the bear killing
that has been done in these mountains, there have been no real
bear scrapes, such as some men are always stirring up."

"He has always shot so well there hain't been any room
for argument," said Mack, with emphasis, "at least not more
than that one time with the Duchess."

"Did the Duchess charge, regularly? "

"She surely did," said Mr. Phillips, quietly, "and I was
properly scared, too."

"How did it happen that she got a chance at you? "

"It was all on account of Charlie's dog, the great and only
Kaiser."

"Aw, *shucks*!" broke in Charlie, warmly. "It was all on ac-count o' yer bloomin' old *camera*, that you made me go after!"

"Well, I know the picture-machine did enter in, in a way, even though it wasn't there at the finish. It was like this:

THE CHARGE OF THE DUCHESS

"IN THE LAST WEEK OF MAY, last year, we were hunting bear on the head of Wilson Creek, some miles below here. We located a grizzly that we named the Duke of Wellington; and being unable to get up to him, in the regular way, Charlie was commissioned to go out to the nearest settlement, buy an old horse, bring him in, and kill him for bait. I started out to go part way with Charlie, and hunt back alone.

"About the middle of the afternoon we saw a silvertip, across Wilson Creek up on a snow slide, about four hundred yards away. The whole mountain-side was covered with snow, and it was easy to make a silent stalk, provided the ascent was not—too steep. Under cover of some green timber I crawled to within three hundred yards of the bear, and let go a shot. It went too low; but with a quick second shot I rolled her over, and she came down the slide tumbling over and over, snow and bear-paws fairly flying through the air, for about fifty yards. There she stopped, and scrambled to her feet, but seemed un-able to go farther on foot.

"'Now,' thought I, 'here is a chance to get pictures of a wounded grizzly.' So I yelled to Charlie to bring up my camera, and started to climb up close to the bear.

"Half-way up, Kaiser, sent on by Charlie, passed me and rushed for the bear. Charlie yelled to me, 'Shoot! Shoot, or she will get away!'

"When the row began, Charlie was three hundred yards below me, and lost time in getting the camera, but as soon as he secured it, he started up as fast as the snow would let him come.

"Up to that time the bear had not seen us, and seemingly paid no special attention to the sound of the gun. She was shot too low,—through the brisket and fleshy part of the forelegs,—and while the shock had knocked her down, the only special result was to throw off her safety clutch, and start her machinery working. She evidently thought a big bug had bitten her; and with her head turned under her breast she was looking for it. "Kaiser boldly went right up to her, and when he came within ten feet she saw him, accepted him as the author of her trouble, and went for him like a runaway car on an incline of forty-five. The dog immediately lost all interest in having his picture taken with the dead game, turned tail, and fled down the slide. He came straight for me, possibly assuming that I ought to protect him; and the bear came plunging after him. She plunged and slid on the snow so far that with every jump she covered about twelve feet, and threw up snow like a snow-plough.

"All this time, the dog ran straight toward me, and I couldn't fire at the bear for fear of killing the dog. It's against the rules to kill Kaiser, ain't it, Charlie! There wasn't the slightest chance for me to fire, and here came the dog, leading that wounded bear right down upon me, as fast as they could plunge. For a time I was scared stiff, with nothing in the world to do but stand and wait for a chance to shoot. I remember thinking that 'no matter how it turns out, it's *great* to see that bear come tearing down that snow-slide!'

"Kaiser ran for his life, looking back once in a while, and by her sliding as she did, the grizzly gained upon him. Finally, when within twenty-five yards of me, Kaiser saw that in one more jump the bear would grab him; so he dove off to one side, head first, into a clump of bushes, and cleared the track. Then the grizzly saw me, and came on at me, straight as a bullet. As quick as I could I aimed just below her left eye and let go. It was my one chance, and I knew that if I missed there would be a bad mix-up.

"My trap-shooting practice stood me in good stead, for that bear's head certainly was a flying target. But the ball struck her right, exploded in her head, and she pitched forward almost upon me, so dead she scarcely kicked.

"Charlie was still far below, making frantic efforts to get up and into the scrape with his new six-shooter. He ran like a fairy across a cracked snow-bridge over the creek, and it made me laugh to see the holes he punched in the snow as he came up the slide. He arrived with a face like an angry father. First he lectured me, severely; then he laughed; then he thanked me formally and politely, for not shooting the bear through Kaiser! The grizzly was a female, and we named her the Duchess. She was not as big as the Duke of Wellington."

"Now, Mack," said Charlie Smith, as Mr. Phillips finished his narrative, "tell 'em about the Duke o' Wellington and old Blucher."

DEATH OF THE DUKE OF WELLINGTON

"WELL," SAID MACK, SLOWLY AND bashfully, "we shore hunted that old Duke for a long time, and we didn't get him at all as we expected. As Mr. Phillips said, we were powerful anxious to bust old Duke, for he was the biggest b'ar we ever got track of up here."

"Did you bait him with an old horse, as first planned?"

"Yes; and it never took a trick. The b'ars never went nigh it. Could they smell it? Well, I should say they could. *We* could smell it a mile; and finally we had to move camp on account of it. Somehow a b'ar never means to do what you want him to do."

A long pause.

"And how did you finally outwit the Duke?"

"Oh, just by huntin' for him,—climbin' and huntin', early and late. Late one afternoon Mr. Phillips and myself happened to spy a couple of old-timers up on a mountain-side, eatin' their supper of roots, in a small, grassy spot in a bushy slide. They were across Wilson Creek from us, and half a mile up a steep mountain. I told John we'd shore have to pull our freight quick to get them b'ars before dark, and we went right at it."

"The first trouble was in gettin' across the creek, where we got badly mixed up in a willow muskeg, and nearly bogged down. After fightin' the brush and mud for an awful long time, and gettin' mighty hot about it, we finally got over, and started for the slide. When we reached an opening we looked up, but the b'ars were gone.

"After considerable loud talk, and plenty o' plannin', we started on up. We hadn't gone far when we found from the noise that the old gents had winded us, and rolled their tails off into the brush at one side of the slide. But they had stopped, and although we could hear 'em snortin' and snappin' their teeth, we just couldn't see hide nor hair of 'em, and couldn't get any sort of a shot. At last I did manage to glimpse 'em two or three times, but soon after that they hauled off into heavy timber.

"The b'ars started climbin' up, and having nothing else to do, we climbed after them. Finally we all got plumb tired, and concluded it would pay just as well to sit down easy like, and watch. Unfortunately, darkness was almost onto us. It wasn't long before old Blucher poked his head outen the edge of the timber, where I could see him. I says to Mr. Phillips, 'Don't you see him?' He says, 'No, I can't. It's too dark.' I was plumb anxious for the ball to open, so I says, 'John, may I shoot?' 'Yes! Bust him!' says John. *Bang!*

"Down went old man Blucher, hollerin' and bawlin', 'I'm shot!' And then Mr. Phillips caught sight of the Duke, and passed *him* one. He hollered, 'So am I!' and away the two of 'em went, rollin' and tearin' down the mountain, bawlin' and bellerin' like two mad bulls. Did you ever shoot a b'ar and have it roll down a hill, and holler? Yes? Well we started down after 'em. I remarked to Mr. Phillips that they were very tuneful gents, thinking probably he hadn't noticed it; but he was already laughin' fit to kill, and came near rolling down on the Duke.

"Finally John M. handed the Duke two more .405 soft-nosed pills, and that settled *him*. Then we started in to look for Blucher,—and a very dangerous thing to do; for by that time it was getting dark, and even in daylight, tracking up a wounded grizzly ain't none too safe. But we couldn't do any good at it, so we lit out for camp and got in about ten o'clock."

"Did you get Blucher the next day?"

"No, we never did get him. It rained all that night, and about daylight a big snow-storm came on, and we couldn't track Blucher, nor flush him a little bit."

THE HORROR OF THE ROCKS

"I THINK," SAID I, ONCE when there was a silence that needed breaking, "I'll tell you a joke on Charlie."

Charlie Smith looked at me quick and hard, quite mystified.

"Just before we left Goat Pass, Charlie and I once stopped to rest on the steep side of Bird Mountain, about half-way up. It was really very steep, and if a tenderfoot had once got well started to rolling, he would have bowled down about a quarter of a mile without stopping.

We dug our heels into the ground, leaned back against the mountain, and I led Charlie into telling stories. I got him to tell me about the most scary things that ever happened to him on the rocks,—how the recoil of his gun, in shooting at a mountain sheep, nearly knocked him off a ledge to his death; how he and Mack caught that first mountain goat kid, and other adventures.

"Well, by the time we were due to go on, Charlie's stories had scared me until I was stiff with fright, and he came very near having to carry me to camp."

"Humph! Well!" said Charlie, very energetically, "I'll know enough next time not to tell yarns to anybody while I'm on a mountain."

What I told the boys was more than half true. I was nerve-weary that day, and ankle-sore; and the stories that I drew out of my companion scared me quite as ghost-stories used to wreck my courage when I was a small boy.

The horror of the rocks has shaken the nerves of many a stout-hearted mountaineer, long after the event.

Once Charlie Smith and his former partner, daredevil Jack Lewis, had a narrow escape from a tragedy on the crags of Sheep Mountain. Charlie almost slid over the edge of a precipice, with Jack close by, and both were as badly scared as these bold men of the mountains ever can be. That night, when they reached their cabin, and went to bed in their double bunk, to sleep the sleep of the exhausted, Charlie was suddenly awakened by Jack, who with both hands seized him by his beard and hair, and pulled at him desperately.

"I surely thought," said Charlie, "that Jack would tear the very face off of me, he was that wild. He yelled, 'Charlie! Charlie!' and we rolled and tumbled around in that bunk until I thought he never would come to his senses. Finally I yelled at him so loud that he woke up, panting like a man who has been running. When I spoke to him, and asked him what he was dreaming about he said, 'My God, Charlie! I thought you were sliding off them rocks again, and I was tryin' to pull you back.'"

"Say, Charlie," said Mack, "what's the matter with tellin' how you-all came to scare Jack Lewis that way?"

"Oh, I've told that before, nearly a dozen times," said Smith, with an air of strong disapproval.

"Never mind, Charlie," said Mr. Phillips, "the Director has never heard it, and I'd like to hear it again myself."

"Go on, Charlie; go on."

THE SHEEP THAT COULDN'T BE CAUGHT

"Well," said Charlie, more cheerfully, "about five years ago an eastern Sportsmen's Association offered five hundred dollars for a live, full-grown mountain sheep ram; so Jack Lewis and I secured a permit from the government and started out to land that five hundred. It was in January. The thermometer was away below zero, and the mountains were covered with snow and ice. We discovered a band of sheep high up on a wind-swept ridge of Sheep Mountain, and tried to drive them down into the deep snow, where we could rope them; but the sheep were contrary, and took to the crest; and of course Jack and I followed them.

"We had just reached the very top of the mountain when I slipped and fell, and started to slide down, with the Elk River Valley as my nearest stopping-place."

"What did you *think* Charlie, as you were going down?"

"Oh, nothing much," he replied. "When I slipped and fell, I knew it was all over with me if I started to roll, or failed to stop myself in the first few feet of my slide. All I could re-member in the shape of a prayer was 'Now I lay me down to sleep,' a little rhyme my mother taught me when I was a kid. Just as I was sliding over the edge of the cliff, in a sitting posi-tion with my heels digging hard into the snow, I uncovered a trailing-juniper bush, which sprang up between my legs. Well, sir, when that bush sprang up, I embraced it like a long-lost brother. It stopped me all right, but all I could do was to just sit there, with my legs hanging over Kingdom Come. As quick as he could, old Jack threw down to me the end of one of the ropes we had brought along to rope the sheep with, and he snaked me back to the top. I tell you I was mighty glad to shake hands with him! His face was as white as a sheet!

"Finally, we corralled the sheep on that peak just above Pass Creek. The top of the peak is hollow, and from the valley it looks like an arm chair with the north side cut off almost square, and pitching straight down five hundred feet or more toward Pass Creek. We made the climb from below, Jack, who is perhaps the best mountaineer in British Columbia leading the way. As soon as he got his head and shoulders above the seat of the chair he saw a big ram close by, and prepared to rope him. As I was hanging onto the icy rocks at one side, I happened to cast my eyes over the precipice, plumb down into Pass Creek. The sight of it fairly chilled the marrow in my bones, and brought me to my senses. I yelled out to Jack, 'For God's sake, Jack, don't rope that sheep, or he'll pull us both off the mountain!' At that, Jack pulled up short, and as we clung to the rocks, the sheep stampeded. But the sheep couldn't get up the back or over the arms of the chair, so they came out almost over the top of Jack, one large ewe making a pass at him with her horns as she went by. After getting away, all the sheep ran south along the mountain, with the exception of the old ram, who circled below them to the north, and headed for Hornaday Mountain. He went down that awful mountain-side just a-tearin'. As we watched, we saw him plunge into a patch of deep snow in Pass Creek and go *plumb out of sight*! Then we thought we had him.

"We scrambled down from the crags, and as soon as it

was safe we put on our snow shoes, which we had been carrying on our backs for just such an emergency. As we ran down
to the creek, with Jack Lewis leading, one of his shoes came
off and he turned a complete somerset, breaking through the
crust and disappearing in the deep snow. I was so close after
him that before I could stop or swerve to one side, I piled in
on top of him. When we finally succeeded in getting out, the
old ram had broken his way to a safe footing on the cliffs of the
opposite side of the creek, where he stopped and looked back
at us.

"But it was something awful the way that sheep worked
to get through that snow. It was six or eight feet deep, and had
a slight crust on top. He would leap clear to the top of it, strike
the crust with his breast and send the pieces flying, forge forward a few feet, then sink again out of sight only to bob up
once more and try it again."

"So you lost him?"

"Sure. But we caught an old nanny goat that was sheltering in a cave, and hog-tied her without hurting her. We were
too exhausted to take her down that day, so after spending the
night very miserably by a little fire under the cliff-wall near the
mouth of the creek, we climbed up the next morning only to
find her dead. We thought she died of old age, she was so very
old and thin, and almost toothless."

Naturally, one tale of hardship brought forth another.
The mountains were full of them. The very creek upon which
we were camped had been the scene of a tragedy in the early
days. Seven white prospectors had gone in somewhere very
near to where we then were, camped, and never were heard of
more. Some think they were killed by Indians; but they may all
have been buried under a great snow-slide.

Some one told us of this lonesome tragedy:

THE MATCHES THAT WOULDN'T LIGHT

UP IN THE EDGE OF THE MOUNTAINS, twenty miles or so above the Sulphur Spring, there lived alone, in a lonesome little cabin, a trapper who was an old man. He was too old to live there alone, but the love of the life was strong within him, and he was quite content.

One bitter cold day in midwinter, when the snow lay a foot deep on the trail, he shouldered his pack of flour and coffee, and set out from the cabin of Wild-Cat Charlie to go to his own.

The labor of the journey at last proved too great for him. As his weary steps dragged more and more slowly through the snow, the cold assailed him at all points. Two miles from the shelter of his cabin, he threw down his pack. A mile farther on, he leaned his rifle against a tree and left it. Two hundred yards from his cabin he fell, but bravely crawled the remaining distance on his hands and knees.

He reached his cabin, entered, closed the door, and whittled some shavings with which to kindle his fire. The kindlings and the dry wood all were there. At last everything was ready for the match, and he essayed to strike it.

His fingers were so benumbed by minus forty degrees of cold that they were like sticks of wood. The first match broke short off, unlighted. So did the next, and the next, and the next.

It was beyond his power to strike the match that would have started the fire that would have saved his life. Days after, he was found lying upon the floor, on the remains of the matches that would not strike, frozen as hard as the rocks of the cruel mountains around his lonely cabin.

CHAPTER XVII

A GREAT MOUNTAIN
SHEEP HUNT

VARIATIONS IN SHEEP HUNTING—ARTISTIC VALUE OF SCENERY
IN HUNTING—JOHN NORBOE'S PERIL—CAMP NECESSITY—
REMARKABLE GOAT LICKS—SHEEP SIGNS—A VERY LONG STALK—
ATTACK IN A WIND STORM—MISSES AND HITS—MACK NORBOE'S
"BUNGERS"—THREE DEAD RAMS—A NIGHT OF TERROR

"Though far be the glacier-filled fountain,
    The foot of the hunter is free.
Though high be the ram on the mountain,
    The hunter climbs higher than he."

IN THE HUNTING OF MOUNTAIN SHEEP in British
Columbia, there are many variations. In the south, among
the house-roof mountains, it is possible that you may be
required to climb very high, amid real perils on the cliffs.
You may make tremendously long and steep climbs without
perils, or the sheep may run into your arms at an elevation
of eight thousand feet, as did the pair which Mr. Phillips
photographed. In northern British Columbia and Yukon

Territory, you can find sheep on low, hill-like mountains in high country; or you may, like Charles Sheldon, find them on slide-rock so fearfully steep that you cannot measure a sheep, even after you have killed it.

It is not all of hunting to kill game. The surroundings, and how you used them to outwit your keen-eyed quarry, sometimes are fully as interesting as the game itself. It is far from ideal hunting to tramp hour after hour through a monotonous, brush-filled forest, "head" the soggy-banked ponds and flounder through bogs for a final shot at a moose in a tangle of underbrush so thick you can see through it only a few yards. It takes a mighty fine animal to compensate one for mean hunting grounds.

But take mountains like ours, where at every mile there rises around you a new cyclorama of crag and peak, ridge and valley, timber, slide and glacier, and it takes a fine animal to draw your gaze from the pictures! To kill, in such a setting, a mountain ram, a goat or a grizzly bear is Hunting, indeed. With all her bison and tigers, buffalo and bear, India has nothing like it south of the Himalayas, not even in the Nilgiris. Judging by a thousand photographs, I should say that with all her multitudes of big game, Africa has nothing like it, anywhere. South America has her Andes, but alas ! they are deplorably barren of animal life.

To one who has seen the cyclorama, and the dead game lying on the mountain—as I did,—Mr. Phillips's hunt for mountain sheep in the Big Bend of Avalanche Creek was a fine performance, and it is a pleasure to help the Reader to see it as it was. It fairly illustrates one phase, and a difficult one, of mountain sheep hunting in those precipitous mountains.

It was undertaken for the special purpose of procuring one or two extra-fine rams, for a laudable purpose, and it was the appearance of the twelve rams on the summit sky-line on the evening of September 15th which led the hunters into that particular territory.

John Norboe returned from a look into that region on the very night the sheep were seen, and in terse but picturesque language he impressed his hearers with the idea that it was a bad country in which to hunt. Mack then remarked, with emphasis,

"Well, if *he* says it's bad country, you kin shore set it down that it's a terror!"

Said John, "Director, I was in a place this afternoon that I don't believe you would be willing to get into for a million dollars. In fact, money couldn't hire me to try it again myself. I started to climb up a bad place, and when I got away up, *I couldn't go on, and I couldn't get down!* For a while I just hung on, and wondered how many days it would take the boys to find my body."

"And how did you get out of it?"

"Well, at last I managed to take my shoes off, and hang 'em round my neck. Then I hung on till I got my nerve back, and finally I managed to climb on up. I haven't been so skeered in years. It's lucky I didn't have my gun with me. I'd shore a-dropped it!"

This was the country south-east of Phillips Peak.

On the morning of the 16th, Mr. Phillips and the two Norboes took the four-by-seven silk tent, a scanty supply of blankets and three days' rations, and marched off down Avalanche Creek. They planned to strike the sheep country from the south, and the idea was right. They tramped down Avalanche Creek to where it strikes Roth Mountain, beyond which it was unexplored. At that point it turns to the east, in a right angle, and in the bend of this elbow rise the Phillips Mountains. From that point they followed the stream eastward, crossed some immense rock slides, and finally entered a tract of heavy, moist and mossy green timber, two miles long. In the centre of this ribbon of timber, they found the tepee poles of what once had been a Stoney Indian camp; and there they pitched their own tiny tent for two, and called the place "Camp Necessity."

"There shore must be game about here," said John Norboe, as he kicked at a piece of mountain sheep skull. "Injuns hain't been campin' here for fun."

After a hasty luncheon, Mr. Phillips and Mack Norboe set off up the northern mountains, climbing up the face of a lofty ridge that rose like a gigantic roof a mile and a half from base to summit, and two miles long. At its western end this ridge terminates against a towering peak, with perpendicular walls. The eastern end stops abruptly in mid-air, forming a commanding point. On the southern face were two or three outcroppings of rock wall, precisely like dormer windows. It was from the eastern point of this ridge that Charlie Smith and I saw a very spectacular bear-hunt a little later on, when I came to know all that ground very well. This ridge is described because it presently became a storm-centre of some magnitude.

In climbing the ridge, the hunters steered well toward the west, in order to strike the cliffs that rose from that extremity. Half a mile up, they found the most extensive series of goat-licks that were seen on our whole trip.

They were situated in a scattered clump of stunted spruces, toward which well-worn goat-trails led from various directions. The earth was sufficiently impregnated with mineral salts that the goats—and sheep, also, beyond a doubt—were very fond of it.

The animals had dug under the roots of ten or a dozen spruce trees until they were undermined by great cavities, and the large roots, exposed in mid-air, looked like the bodies of boa constrictors and pythons. The rough bark of the spur-roots was covered with fine, soft white hair which plainly told the species of earth-eater most in evidence. The goats had worked under the trees because the earth was more moist there, and their mining operations were not disturbed by the sliding snow and rocks that annually assailed the unprotected surfaces of the mountain. The zeal and industry of the animals, and their strength also, was amazingly portrayed. They had dug out and thrown aside quantities of stones, which had rolled down the mountain side, and the whole place looked as disturbed and bare as if it had lately been worked over with mattock and rake. (In 1902, Messrs. G.O. Shields and W.H. Wright found on the west fork of the north branch of the Athabasca River a goat-lick of still greater proportions than those described above. Trails lead to it from a radius of five miles. A cut bank fifteen feet high has been eaten away, until trees and large stones have been undermined and thrown down the mountain-side. A man can ride on horseback behind some of the roots now exposed. The earth is described as a light, chalky clay.)

Mr. Phillips's excellent photograph of one of the goat-workings under a spruce tree is shown herewith. These goat-licks are fairly common throughout the mountains of British Columbia. There is one within two miles of Charlie Smith's ranch on Elk River.

On reaching the summit of the lofty ridge, the hunters found themselves at the foot of an unscalable wall between two hundred and three hundred feet high, with a slide-rock basin beyond, another transverse ridge beyond that, and no sheep in sight. On the north side, their first ridge dropped away very steeply to a V-shaped valley and a creek. The great ridge that rose beyond that was even taller than that on which they stood; and creek and ridge swung around the eastern end of ridge No. 1 at very nearly a right angle, debouching into Avalanche Valley half a mile below the new camp. The summit of Ridge No. I reminded me so much of the business centre of a cyclorama that I named it that, and called its eastern terminus Cyclorama Point.

Two other interesting incidents marked Mr. Phillips's first afternoon on Cyclorama Ridge. One was a goat performance, the other the discovery of good mountain sheep signs. The former is thus described in detail by Mr. Phillips:

"On rounding a small cliff that broke out of the side of the mountain, we discovered about fifty yards away to our left, a nanny goat, a yearling billy and a kid. In Mack Norboe's mountain language he called them an old lady, a little billy and a goatee. As goats are always interesting to me, on account of their propensity for doing queer things, we sat down to watch them.

"They had not seen us, and the old mother was busy licking the face of the cliff. Perhaps she was finding something alkaline. The young billy was growing his first whiskers, and in a dignified manner he resented certain playful advances on the part of the kid.

"After we had watched them for some time, the mother-goat winded us, and after a mild stare in our direction, started up the apparently vertical cliff, the young billy following her. The kid, not knowing of our presence, and being deserted by its mother, immediately set out on its own account to climb up a perpendicular chimney in the wall. The crack was about four feet wide, and inasmuch as there were no footholds discernible from where we stood, we expected to witness the ultimate downfall of the kid.

"The little fellow bounced nimbly from side to side, making jumps from two to three feet high. When about twenty-five feet up he made a spring across, struck on an apparently smooth wall, and seemed to lose his footing. The most surprising thing was that he shoved himself backward with his front feet, and alighted safely on the invisible foothold which he had left four feet below. He then bounced down from side to side, like a rubber ball, galloped like a hobby-horse under the base of the cliff, and scrambled up after his mother and older brother.

"When we arose and walked to the goats' point of departure, they looked down upon us from the cliff, with the indifference of conscious security. We were no doubt the first human beings they had ever seen, and of course they regarded us with curiosity. Possibly they thought we were bears of a new species, walking upright."

Quite near to the haunt of the goats, the hunters discovered four or five wild-animal beds which Mack thought had been made by sheep. This belief was confirmed by the finding of some sheep hair. From the character of the spot, and the absence of protecting cliffs, the sheep sign was supposed to represent a band of ewes, until presently the hunters found unmistakable evidence of the recent presence of a band of large rams, which evidently had lived for some weeks in that neighborhood. The contiguous ridges and slides were carefully examined, but no sheep were seen that day, and at nightfall the hunters returned to the little pulpit-like spot in the green timber whereon John Norboe had with great pains made a camp close beside an old Indian trail.

On the following morning the sheep-hunt opened early and with vigor. The three hunters packed their entire outfit upon their backs, and set out to make a hunt up the newly-found creek,—which later on for a good reason they elected to call Grizzly Creek,—and camp well northward of its valley. They started up that creek from its mouth, half a mile below their camp, but had not gone more than a mile through its tangle of down timber when they discovered their long-lost band of rams. They were on the western face of Cyclorama Ridge, under a point which sheltered them from the wind, and the wind was blowing half a gale from the hunters perilously near the sheep.

The plan of the hunt was quickly formed. John Norboe was sent down to Avalanche Creek, with all the outfit. Mr. Phillips and Mack stripped for a strenuous effort, and mapped out a long and severe detour to the eastward, away from the sheep, and around them. The circuit they actually made took them up to the top of the eastern mountain, northward under the shelter of its crest for two miles, then a long swing westward into the valley of Grizzly Creek. After that they climbed southward to the top of Cyclorama Ridge, and at last, after a four-mile struggle, stood above their quarry and dead to leeward of it. In looking over the summit, they were rejoiced to find that the sheep had not moved.

Keeping well below the crest of the ridge, the hunters moved eastward until they reached their chosen line of approach, then began to work downward under cover of some stunted spruces and aspens. When they gained the high, dormer-window point under which the sheep had been seen, the gale was so strong that it was almost impossible to face it. It was laden with so much dust that had been swept off the rocks, that Mr. Phillips's eyes watered so copiously he could scarcely see. They could hear dead timber crashing down in Avalanche Valley, and the quaking-asps around them were whipped almost to the ground.

Finally a fierce gust of wind bent down a clump of bushes in such a manner that a massive pair of ram's horns stood revealed to the anxious eyes of the searchers, and only seventy-five yards away! The next instant, the bushes sprang up again and masked the quarry. Then Mr. Phillips trained his rifle to bear on the spot desired, and waited for another gust. It came; the bushes gave way for an indistinct glimpse, and Mr. Phillips fired at the ram's shoulder. This is the hunter's own account of what followed:

"At the roar of the gun, the sheep broke away in all directions. Three ran south-west, across the slide and up the next ridge. I thought that the leading ram was the one at which I had shot. As he ran, I fired three more shots at him; but the wind either swayed me or drifted my bullets, for they only threw up dust beside him. After missing three times, I realized that I must get him with the fourth and last shot, or not at all; so I quickly sat down, took a knee-rest, and held to the left. With that shot I hit him high up in the shoulders, striking the spinal column, and killing him instantly. Fortunately he rolled only once, and lodged against a stump.

"While reloading my gun I sat watching the two three-year-old companions of my big ram, which were making frantic leaps up the ridge toward the high peak. Just as I finished loading, I heard Mack yelling in great excitement, fifty yards below me, 'Jack! Jack! Run here, *quick*. Two bungers!'"

Mack and Charlie always speak of rams with big horns as "bungers"—a very convenient term when breath is scarce, and rams are running.

"Running at top speed down the point, I soon saw two large rams, two hundred yards away. They were running north, through a patch of burned timber, quaking-asp and willows, which made it very difficult to get any kind of a shot. The speed with which those rams bounded over the down timber and brush was really wonderful. They seemed scarcely to touch the ground, and their white rump-patches gave them the appearance of two large pieces of paper blown along by the wind.

"The rearmost ram carried the larger horns, and at him I fired three shots, but without result. Again I sat down, and holding high above the white patch on the seat of his pants, fired again, just as he disappeared in a patch of green timber.

"There were originally eight rams in that herd, and

Mr. Phillips's Finest Mountain Sheep
THE CARNEGIE RAM.

of these, Norboe had seen two run down toward the creek. Immediately following my first shots, the herd had divided into three groups, which fled in three directions. After the excitement was over, I proceeded to make explanations to Mack, to account for the firing of nine shots and a score of only one ram. The old fellow looked at me with a merry glint in his keen gray eyes, and handed me my hunting-shirt.

"'You and your big gun shorely had a full-grown time stampedin' them sheep, and shootin' off a whole lot o' timber.'

"This observation was at the expense of my .405-calibre gun, Mack being an advocate of the .33 high-power gun. 'Them cannon guns,' he once said to me, 'gives me the buck fever whenever I unlimbers 'em, thinkin' of the roar, and the kick that's comin'! When you shoots standin', they shoves you around like a monkey on a stick; and if you sets down and turns 'em loose, they move a feller along the ground so quick that it ain't pleasant. If you're lucky enough to hit your game, it tears his hide open; besides which, them big explosions blasts down the standin' scenery, and scares the rest of the game plumb outen the country.'

"Presently John Norboe joined us, and together we climbed up the point to the body of the ram which I had killed. We photographed, measured, skinned and weighed him. His horns measured fifteen and one-half inches in basal circumference, and his weight on the director's scales was two hundred and eighty-five pounds. All this time the wind poured a strong blast along the side of the mountain. After we had finished our work, John Norboe took the skin, with the unskinned head attached, and a small quantity of meat, and started for camp, while Mack and I set out to investigate my bad shooting.

"On visiting the spot whereon Ram No. 1 had stood when I fired at him, we were surprised to find blood. This we trailed up, around the rocky point from which I had fired, and soon found where the sheep had fallen and started to roll. We found him far down, lying dead within a hundred yards of the brook, where he had lodged against a stout young quaking-asp. He was the leader of the band, we thought, and the others which ran north had hesitated after he was stricken, thus giving me a chance to fire at them, also.

"This sheep was a much larger ram than the first one. He was forty-one inches high at the shoulders, the way Mr. Hornaday measures animals, with the elbow pushed up, and he weighed three hundred and sixteen pounds. He was the largest ram I ever killed, or saw, although at that time he was not in fat condition. We thought that had he lived he would have put on another thirty or forty pounds by the time severe winter weather set in. My bullet struck him just behind the shoulder ranged back through his stomach, and passed out on the opposite side.

"After that we climbed up to see what had become of my third ram, and were very much surprised at finding him lying dead! I had killed my legal limit of mountain sheep, which was one more than I had intended! This one was five years old, with horns already fifteen and one-half inches in circumference, and his gross weight was two hundred and eighty-seven pounds.

"I felt very badly over this sheep, for I had intended to kill only two, one for the Carnegie Museum, and another for the director. But there was no time to spend on the mountain in regrets. Our long stalk, and the work afterward on the rams, had carried us well toward the close of the day. By that time the wind had abated, it was raining softly, and almost dark. Packing up all the meat we could carry, Mack and I laboriously worked our way down to Avalanche Creek, to the new camp which John had made.

"That was a damp and gloomy spot; and we named it Camp Necessity. We were profoundly tired, and ravenously hungry—having had no mid-day bite; but the delicious mutton chops which John Norboe had ready for us soon put us at peace with all the world.

"But not for long; for that proved to be a fearful night. It rained all night, and nearly drowned us out; but that was not the worst of it. The wind increased in violence, and came roaring down the narrow valley until the trees rocked under its force, and many tree-tops were snapped off and hurled to the ground. I could feel roots moving under our bed of boughs, like great snakes writhing, and was thoroughly afraid that a tree-top, or a tree, would be snapped off and sent crashing down upon us.

"At last I got so nervous I could lie still no longer, and crawled out of the tiny tent, ostensibly to mend the fire. John Norboe occupied my canvas sleeping-bag, outside.

"'Have you got a pipeful of tobacco, John?' I asked, for the sole purpose of rousing him a bit.

"'No, I hain't,' said John, 'but I know what's the matter with you!'

"'Well what?'

"'You're scared!,

"'Well, so are you!'

"'Say, Mr. Phillips, does this sleepin' bag o' yourn ever leak?'

"'No. Why?'

"'Becos it's full o' water that's run in at the top, and I've been a-hopin' it would run out below.'

"But at last the long night wore away without accident."

Two days later I assisted in working up those three fine specimens, especially in the work on the heads. In fact, I may say I was chief mourner; but it was a task of great interest, as will be noted elsewhere.

The Brooklyn Ram, Thirty Minutes After Death
SLIGHTLY DISTENDED BY GAS.

DIMENSIONS AND WEIGHT OF
MOUNTAIN SHEEP RAMS
SHOT BY JOHN M. PHILLIPS, SEPTEMBER 19, 1905

	No. 1, for Carnegie Museum.	*No. 2, for Brooklyn Museum.*
Age ...	*13 yrs*	*10 yrs*
Height at shoulders ...	*41 in.*	*40 in.*
Length of head and body ...	*69"*	*68-1/2"*
Girth, behind foreleg ...	*53"*	*52"*
Girth at middle of body ...	*57-1/2"*	*60"**
Girth at loins ...	*54"*	*48"*
Circumference of fore leg, at elbow ...	*13"*	*12"*
Circumference at hind leg, at knee ...	*—*	*21"*
Distance from elbow to head of femur ...	*33"*	*33"*
Circumference of neck, at throat ...	*27"*	*24"*
Point of shoulder to rear of rump ...	*—*	*44"*
Weight by scales ...	*316 lbs.*	*285 lbs.*

* THIS EXTRA LARGE MEASUREMENT PROBABLY WAS DUE TO GAS.

CHAPTER XVIII

MOUNTAIN SHEEP NOTES

THE CULMINATING POINT OF A SPECIES—MEASUREMENTS
OF RECORD HEADS—RANGE OF THE BIG-HORN—THE WHITE
SHEEP—THE BLACK SHEEP—FANNIN'S SHEEP—FIGHTING NOSES
OF OUR SPECIMENS—REINFORCEMENT OF THE NECK—CAPTAIN
RADCLIFFE'S OPINION ABOUT BROKEN TIPS—MEASUREMENTS
OF OUR SHEEP—COMPARATIVE DIMENSIONS OF SHEEP, GOAT
AND MULE DEER—COMPARISON OF SHEEP AND GOAT—ENEMIES
OF MOUNTAIN SHEEP—IMPENDING EXTINCTION IN BRITISH
COLUMBIA.

MR. PHILLIPS'S MOUNTAIN SHEEP RAMS were to all of us specimens of great interest. All three were carefully measured and weighed, and the skins of all were saved entire, for mounting. The oldest and largest ram, and the five-year-old, were presented by Mr. Phillips to the Carnegie Museum at Pittsburg, and the second in size was given to me, for presentation to the Brooklyn Institute Museum.

American literature is not so much overburdened with information regarding the mountain sheep of North America

254 CAMP-FIRES IN THE CANADIAN ROCKIES

that I need apologize for noting here a few of the most important facts regarding that group of animals. Be it known, therefore, that it is in the very locality in which we then found ourselves,—southeastern British Columbia,—that the true Rocky
Mountain Big-Horn, (now *Ovis canadensis*, but for eighty years
called *Ovis montana*), reaches its maximum development.

The culminating point of any important species, or the
locality in which it grows largest and carries the largest horns, is
a very interesting item of its life history. For the past five years,
or thereabouts, we have known that throughout the wide range
of the Big-Horn—let us say from the Grand Canyon of the
Colorado to the Liard River, a distance of two thousand miles—
the largest horns come from southeastern British Columbia and
southwestern Alberta, within a radius of two hundred miles of
Banff. I have had the pleasure of measuring,—in the severest
manner possible in taking such dimensions,—several very fine
heads owned by personal friends, to which I can add the splendid head procured for me in Banff by Mr. G.O. Shields. The
circumference measurements of these specimens were taken in
as perfect a plane as if each horn had been cut in two with a saw
on the line of the tape; and there is no better place in which to
place them before the Reader than here.

A "record head "of a big-game animal is one which by reason of its commanding proportions and superior qualities is
entitled to a place in every printed list of heads or horns which
undertakes to set forth the finest existing specimens of that
species. A record head is not necessarily the largest head "on
record." Usually, it is an impossibility to find "the finest head
in the world" of any given species, because so many qualities
enter in for judgment that it is almost impossible for any one
specimen to combine all of them. As a rule, the longest horns
lack massiveness, and the thickest horns lack in length. Real
grandeur is not often attainable by mere attenuation.

Massiveness, symmetry, texture and color are not to be ignored for the sole sake of inches on the tape.

All the heads listed below are, in my judgment, record heads, i.e., worthy of being recorded with the world's best heads of their respective species. To those who desire to make comparisons between heads of Big-Horn Sheep, here is a simple rule by which to reduce each pair of horns to exact terms:

COMPARATIVE HORN MEASUREMENTS OF SIX VERY LARGE HEADS OF OVIS CANADENSIS FROM SOUTHEASTERN BRITISH COLUMBIA

OWNER.	Circumference at base.	Circumference 18″ from base.	Circumference 1″ from tip.	Length on outside curve.	Widest outside spread.	Distance between tips.	Weight of dry skull and horns.	Remarks.
Madison Grant .	16⅝	15⅝	4¼	43½	22¼	20¼	36 lbs.	Fully dry. A very fine specimen.
John M. Phillips	17½	10½	2½	34½	21	17¾	—	Measured 18½″ in circumference when killed.
E. J. Taylor . .	17¼	13½	5	32	23¾	16	—	Measured 18½″ in circumference when killed.
J. E. Roth . .	16	15⅛	5⅞	42¼	21	15	—	Fully dry when measured.
W. T. Hornaday	16½	16	6¼	40½	17	17	38 lbs.	Fully dry when measured.

It is reasonably certain that each of these heads has shrunken at least one inch in circumference since they were killed. The measurements of freshly killed specimens are not comparable with any of the above.

Add together (1) the basal circumference, (2) the circumference 18 inches from the base, (3) the circumference one inch from the tip, and (4) the length on the outer curve; and divide their sum by 4.

It must be remembered that all sheep horns shrink in circumference with age. A large horn will in two years' drying shrink nearly or quite an inch in basal circumference; and there is no way to prevent it, in a mounted specimen.

North America contains six species of mountain sheep, which form two fairly distinct branches of the genus *Ovis*. The Big-Horn (*O. canadensis*) forms the stem of the first, and from it branch off the Mexican Sheep (*O. mexicanus*), of northern Mexico, and Nelson's Sheep (*O. nelsoni*), of southern California.

The stem of the other branch is formed by the White Sheep (*O. dalli*), and its branches consist of Fannin's Sheep (*O. fannini*, if it survives) and the Black Sheep (*O. stonei*).

It is interesting to note how much more persistent in its desire to migrate is the mountain sheep (genus) than the mountain goat. Here in British Columbia we found them inhabiting the same mountains, and on September 11 we actually saw sheep and goats in the same moment. In its eastward range, the goat now stops at St. Mary's Lakes, on the eastern slope of the Rockies, in Northwestern Montana, but the mountain sheep goes four hundred and seventy miles farther, to the Little Missouri River, in western North Dakota.

In going southward, the goat halted at the Teton Mountains, Wyoming; but the mountain sheep has gone on to the lakes of Santa Maria in Chihuahua, Mexico, and southwestward to the lower end of the Lower California Peninsula.

As the Big-Horn goes northward, it is finally replaced in northern British Columbia by the Black Sheep (*Ovis stonei*), a species which as yet is but little known outside the basin of the Stickine River, and the mountains which surround it. It is now certain, however, thanks to the explorations of Mr. Charles Sheldon, that the range of the latter species extends northward from the Stickine River to the Macmillan River, in latitude 63°. Just where the Black Sheep and Big-Horn come together, no one is as yet able to say; but it is very probable that the extreme northern and western boundaries of the latter species will shortly be determined.

A Prize Big-Horn Head (top)
Taken near Banff, Alberta, in 1903. No. 3 on the list.

Head of a Black Mountain Sheep, (Ovis stonei - bottom)
Killed near the Stickine River, northern British Columbia
September 1904, by J.R. Bradley.

The White Sheep (*Ovis dalli*), has been observed as far south as the Schesley Mountains, the first range north of the Stickine River. This means that in the southeastern portion of its range, the White Sheep is found in the territory of the Black Sheep. It is impossible to pursue this point any farther without forestalling the publication of the results of Mr. Charles Sheldon's very valuable scientific explorations, and studies of mountain sheep in some hitherto unknown portions of the great Yukon Territory. If *Ovis fannini* is eventually abandoned, as a distinct form, the author will be consoled by the knowledge that his description of that form is accredited by Mr. Sheldon as the original cause of his extensive explorations for sheep in the wild Northwest.

The Black Mountain Sheep is the darkest in color, or one may say the most nearly black, of all American wild sheep. North of the Stickine River it is not so black as it is farther south, where the blackness of its head, neck and body is very pronounced. In the majority of cases, its horns are so characteristic that any studious person should be able to recognize the species by them alone.

The front angle of the horn is very sharp, and near the base it actually overhangs the face of the horn. This feature is constant. In about nine cases out of every ten, the horns of the Black Sheep are distinguished by their widely-spreading spiral, and the great distance between the tips. Occasionally, however, a head develops horns with a more narrow spiral, like those of the typical White Sheep; but all such are exceptional.

The White Sheep has an immense range, covering half of Alaska, and practically the whole of Yukon Territory. It is all over pure white, save when stained by contact with wet earth or dulled by age. Occasionally an individual is found which has a few dark hairs in its tail, and others thinly scattered on its hind quarters. Of the original species, *Ovis dalli*, two subspecies have been described; but neither are separately discernible without a close examination of their skulls. In section, the horns of the White Sheep are very much like those of the Black Sheep, but those of northwestern Alaska show the flat spiral, and have the tips closer together. The exceptions are those which spread widely, like the typical horns of Black Sheep; and of that form Mr. Sheldon collected some striking examples.

Fannin's Mountain Sheep (*O. fannini*) was described by the writer from a Klondyke specimen in the Victoria Museum, marked by a well-defined blanket of gray hair on its back and sides, a dark gray tail, a brown stripe down the front of each leg, white abdomen, pure white neck and head, and horns like the White Sheep. Although other specimens exactly similar to the type have been taken, several others have shown a lighter phase, running farther toward the typical White Sheep. At present this species is being weighed in the balance, and when the studies of Mr. Sheldon's collection have been finished, its true character will be known. At present we can only say that it is a form standing between the white and black species.

The most remarkable feature of the three mountain rams shot by Mr. Phillips, and one which instantly attracted the attention of us all, was the manner in which their countenances were disfigured. Each of the two larger rams had on his nose, half way between horns and nostrils, an abnormal hump an inch in height above the normal outline. It reminded us of the old saying about "an inch on the end of your nose." To produce such an excrescence by hand, one would need to strike a mountain ram across the nose, half a dozen good blows with a hammer or a club, daily for about a week.

Fortunately the epidermis had not been beaten off, nor had there been any suppuration, and therefore the hair was intact. Of course those humps had been caused by fighting, long continued and oft renewed. When the horns of the combatants crashed together at their bases, the noses of the rams also struck together. On dissecting the heads, we found the skin over each hump quite free from the nasal bones, but underneath the skin there had formed a layer of tough gristle three-quarters of an inch thick, and apparently of a permanent character.

The accompanying photograph shows the appearance of the head of "the Brooklyn Ram"; but this hump was not so large as that on Ram No. 1.

On dissecting the heads of Mr. Phillips's oldest mountain rams, a hump on the top of the neck, partly covering the base of the skull, also attracted general attention. In each case the calloused excrescence was very large, sharply defined, and so slightly merged into the upper surface of the neck that it was the work of but a moment to detach one, bodily, with the knife.

I cut off the largest hump, and preserved it in alcohol. It was two and one-eighth inches high, six inches in length on the curve, and seven inches in width on the curve. The accompanying sketch shows the position and proportions of this strange growth. As found upon a freshly-killed animal, it has the density and toughness of a mass of soft rubber. Its composition is of tough white fibre and fat, and while very solid it is not as dense as a large tendon. As detached, the mass weighs sixteen ounces. It could easily be dismissed by calling it a nuchal callosity.

Naturally, this huge bunch of combined elasticity and toughness suggests a cushion, for the protection of something from severe shock or strain. It lies directly over the occiput and the first two cervical vertebrae, and is built upon the *ligamentum nuchi*, which lies upon the top of the neck, and forms the chief support of the head. Its anterior end spreads fan-shaped over the lambdoidal crest and the parietal bone, firmly grasping the rear upper surface of the skull. Of course

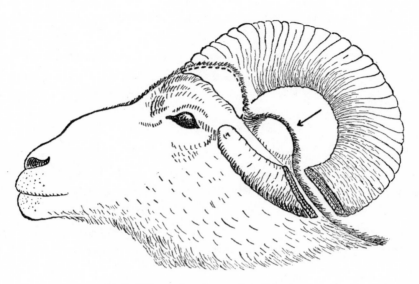

Nuchal Hump of our Largest Ovis Canadensis

the posterior end of this mass vanishes on the upper surface of the neck.

On young rams and ewes—with small horns—this strange reinforcement is not found. Evidently it is developed as an extra means of support for the heavy horns of old rams, and a provision against cerebro-spinal meningitis from overstrain on the spinal cord.

In the rutting season, and also shortly before it, two rival rams will choose a level spot, back off ten or fifteen feet from each other, and come together with a force like two heavy sledgehammers wielded by blacksmiths. The force of the impact sometimes throws both combatants upright on their hind legs, just as colliding locomotives often rear up as they crash together. It is then that the strain upon the neck of the animal is very great; and the wrench and shock are greatest at the point where the neck joins the skull. Small wonder, then, that Nature, in her infinite wisdom and patience, has reinforced the danger-point with a rubber-like ligament of such enormous strength that the neck cannot be broken by any blow from in front.

Captain C.E. Radcliffe, of the Life Guards, author of "Big-Game Shooting in Alaska," claims that mountain sheep do not break or broom the tips of their horns in fighting, as many sportsmen and naturalists have hastily concluded that they do. I entirely agree with him. When Mr. Phillips and I placed together the unskinned heads of those two big rams, with their massive horns base to base, just as we know that sheep horns strike in fighting, we saw that the tips of the two pairs were far distant from each other, and well out of harm's way. As sheep strike each other in fighting, head to head, it is a physical impossibility for the tips to be harmed. And even if a horn should be struck, it would need to be held tightly in a vise in order for its tip to receive a blow of sufficient force to break it off, or even to "broom" it.

Take it at any point you please, the horn of a living mountain sheep ram eight or nine years old is a very hard and tough proposition. Even with an old, dry horn, I think no man can take a hammer and break off its tip without first fixing the horn very firmly in a vise. I have recently tried the experiment, with sheep horns dry enough to be as brittle as such horns usually are, and it is my belief that no sheep can break off the tip of a horn save in a fall such as he never would take voluntarily. In leaping down rocky situations, no American mountain sheep could fall upon the tips of his horns without crushing his nose; and that no sheep would willingly do.

Captain Radcliffe says that he has seen mountain sheep rubbing the ends of their horns against rocks, and he believes that sometimes sheep purposely try to rub off the tips of their horns, because in their upward growth they interfere with the animal's vision, and constitute both an annoyance and a disability. (See *Shields' Magazine*, January, 1906.) Similar observations have been made by Mr. F.B. Wellman, of Banff, who shares Captain Radcliffe's belief regarding the purpose of the act. For myself, I cannot agree with these observers concerning the object of this act. It would require an immense amount of effort for a ram to rub away the ends of his horns.

The Big-Horn is almost strictly a grazing animal. His natural feeding-grounds are the high mountain meadows which lie from 1,000 feet below timberline up to the snow-line. In the mountains of British Columbia they feed mostly around the heads of the slide-ways, where the turf is seldom torn up by the avalanches. Close by are sheltering crags and rock walls that tower far above.

But, while the mountain sheep dwells among and near the cliffs, and knows how to utilize them to the utmost in making a "masterly retreat," he rarely ventures on the dizzy ledges that delight the soul of the mountain goat. The mountain sheep can climb, boldly and well; but, like a sportsman who has passed his fiftieth year-post, he does not care to climb high without good reason.

The sheep killed by Mr. Phillips had been feeding on bunch-grass, which grew abundantly on the side of Cyclorama Ridge. Charles L. Smith says that sheep are very fond of feeding on the "wild pea," or *hedysarum* (*H. Americanum*), the root of which is so acceptable to the grizzly bear.

The specimens of mountain sheep which we handled so soon after our work on mountain goats, naturally suggested comparisons between the two species.

COMPARISON OF MOUNTAIN SHEEP, MOUNTAIN GOAT AND MULE DEER

	Big-Horn Sheep. Adult Male.	Mountain Goat.* Adult Male.	Mule Deer.† Adult Male.
Height at shoulders	41 in.	39 in.	40 in.
Length of head and body	69 in.	61 in.	68-1/2"
Girth, behind foreleg	53 in.	53 in.	52"
Girth at middle of body	57-1/2 in.	57 in.	60"*
Weight by scales	316 lbs.	276 lbs.	285 lbs.

* THE WRITER SHOT AND MEASURED AN OLD GOAT THAT STOOD 42 INCHES HIGH AT THE SHOULDERS, BUT IT WAS SO OLD, AND SO THIN IN FLESH, IT WAS NOT WEIGHED.

†SHOT BY W.T.H. ON HELL CREEK, MONTANA, OCTOBER 9, 1901.

The Big-Horn Sheep is an animal of nervous-sanguine temperament, not so insanely foolish as the mule deer and white-tailed deer, nor yet so lymphatic as the goat. It is a far more graceful walker and runner than the goat, and also more agile and fleet of foot. A mountain sheep can run over rough ground, or leap through the mazes of down timber, as nimbly as any deer, and as rapidly. A goat runs on level ground with the grace and ease of a fat yearling calf, but not much more.

As will be seen by a glance at the measurements recorded in this volume, the adult male goat and sheep are of the same height, but the latter averages about twenty-five pounds (the weight of his horns!) heavier. The abundant hair on the legs of the goat makes those members seem thicker and shorter than

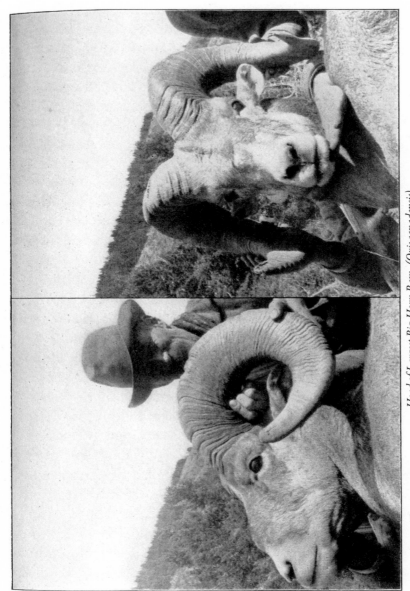

Head of Largest Big-Horn Ram, (Ovis canadensis).

CARNEGIE MUSEUM SPECIMEN (No. 1). THE HUMP ON THE NOSE IS DUE TO RECENT FIGHTING.

they are,—which is really great,—and this effect is increased by the abundant pelage of the body, neck and head. The more slender and shapely legs and finely erect carriage of the head make the mountain sheep a stately and handsome animal, while in appearance the goat remains a zoological curiosity.

The sheep is much more alert and suspicious than the goat, and most men who have hunted both animals believe that the vision of the former is much keener. This impression may be due to greater fear, and a tendency to flee at the slightest alarm.

The hoof of the goat is distinctly larger than that of a mountain sheep of the same age, and more square in outline. The goat's toe is broad, and the bottom of the hoof is a combination of ball and cup. The hoof of the sheep is more pointed, and its bottom is cup-shaped.

The natural enemies of the mountain sheep in British Columbia are the golden and the white-headed eagle, and farther south, the puma, or "mountain lion." In the western Kootenay country, a guide who was in the mountains in May saw a golden eagle bearing off a mountain sheep lamb. He followed the bird, and finally found its nest, and its brood of eaglets. Around the nest lay the skulls of several lambs, showing that the mother bird had been making a specialty of that kind of food for her young. The young eagles were promptly destroyed.

On the Shoshone Mountains in Wyoming, east of the Yellowstone Park, my one-time guide, Charles Marston, once saw a puma seize a mountain sheep ram by the throat, and hold on with a fierce grasp of tooth and claw while puma and ram rolled down the mountain side for a number of yards. The puma held fast to the throat, sucking the blood of the ram, until the latter expired. Then, to even up matters, Marston killed the puma. Beyond a doubt, in localities like Wyoming and Colorado, many mountain sheep have been killed by pumas.

Although I am no pessimist regarding the permanence of animal life, I am compelled to believe that unless several great provincial game and forest reserves are at once set aside in British Columbia, the mountain sheep of that province are doomed to speedy extinction. To the Stoney Indian, to the hungry trapper, and to every sportsman, that fine animal is so great a prize, both for its valuable trophy head and for food, that it will continue to be sought, everywhere, so long as the law permits the hunting of it. It is the boast of the Stoney Indians,—the boldest mountaineers in the Columbian Rockies,—that no big game can live in any country which they themselves inhabit. This is no idle boast, for they are great slaughterers of game.

While the killing of "bungers" (old rams) will not exterminate a species, there are men who will not always go without fresh meat when ewes and lambs are to be had for the killing. In total number, the sheep of southern British Columbia already are down to a *very low point*. Many an eastern sportsman has gone to that country to kill a big ram, worked hard, spent nearly or quite $1,000, and returned empty handed—because of the scarcity of sheep.

It would indeed be cause for great regret if any combination of circumstances should bring about in the splendid mountain lands of British Columbia, the extinction of the grandest mountain sheep in America.

CHAPTER XIX

A PANORAMIC GRIZZLY-BEAR HUNT

LUCK AS A FACTOR IN BEAR HUNTING—AN EXHAUSTING
CLIMB—A SILVER-TIP SIGHTED—MR. PHILLIPS AND MACK RUN
FOR IT—A SUMMIT STROLL BETWEEN THE ACTS—THE BALL
OPENS—A LONG CHASE—SNAP-SHOTS ONLY, AND AT LONG
RANGE—A GOOD LONG SHOT—MACK'S FUSILLADES—A FOOT-
SHOT BEAR, AND CHAFF FOR THE VICTORS.

IT IS STRANGE HOW LUCK works out things for hunters.

If we had had no mountain sheep specimens to finish on
the forenoon of September 23d, and had gone up the mountain some hours earlier, it is reasonably certain that we would
have missed seeing what we saw later on that eventful day.

Beyond question, luck has much to do with the net results in hunting, and particularly in the pursuit of the grizzly. Of course, after all has been said, it is the strong lungs
and straight powder that wins; but at the same time I pity any
hunter who is prone to be unlucky. Only yesterday a noted
grizzly-bear hunter said to me, "We saw twenty-one grizzly
bears on that trip, and we hunted hard, but we never got a

shot!" When I said, "Why, on earth?" he answered, with a fatalistic shrug, "Mostly on account of the tangle of rank, snow-dragged willow brush on the slides where the bears fed. It always took so long to fight our way up to where a bear was feeding that by the time we got there he was gone, and couldn't be found."

As an instance, however, of luck combined with effort, the events of our day were interesting.

Mr. Phillips was anxious that I should have a hunt for mountain sheep, and bring out for my own personal trophy collection a good Columbian head. Having already had a fine hunt for sheep in Wyoming, I was at first positively averse to killing even one more sheep. Finally, however, I concluded that he was right in assuring me that the taking of another ram would have no exterminating tendency, and I decided to kill one if the chance offered. Mr. Phillips and Mack felt sure that other sheep could be found on the mountain north of Camp Necessity, whereon the three rams had been killed, and they insisted that we ought to go up that afternoon to "locate a band for the director." We also wished to carry down a quantity of meat from the previous kill. After an early luncheon, Mr. Phillips, Mack, Charlie and I started up.

It was a hot afternoon. There was hardly a breath of air stirring, and the southern slope up which we climbed caught the full glare of the sun. After we got clear of the down timber, and were well started up, the going was by no means bad, even though the slope was as steep as usual.

On that occasion I acted very badly. The heat in my lungs became horribly oppressive, and the exertion of climbing was the hardest I had yet been called upon to make. At every step my knee-breeches caught on my knees, and caused a loss of fully ten per-cent of my horsepower. It was like an addition of eighteen pounds to my weight, until at last I gathered four safety pins from the party, and took a reef in each leg of my trousers, so that they ceased to drag.

As we slowly climbed, the perspiration ran off my face like rain, and soon I was in a Turkish-bath condition, plus my clothes.

"Take it easy," said my ever-patient companions. "There's no hurry. Rest whenever you get tired."

Mack Norboe led the way, choosing the route carefully with a view to making the climb as easy for me as the ground would allow. His easy "panther stride," as Mr. Phillips aptly called it, seemed absolutely tireless. About every two hundred feet upward, my lungs simply gave out, and I was forced to stop, and pant for my vanished breath. I was disgusted and mortified beyond endurance, and at last even became very angry,—but all to no purpose. The sun and the mountain were both inexorable, and my feebly-growing reputation as a mountaineer melted away forever. How I envied those three one-hundred-and-forty-pound men, in good training, who went up with ease and nonchalance that were almost maddening to see!

On the way up we passed the carcasses of two of Mr. Phillips's rams, and we saw where they were first seen, how they ran, where they fell, and how they rolled. That was a wonderful chance,—to get a bunch of large rams on that open mountain-side, where long-range shooting was practicable,—and the shooting had been exceedingly well done. As before noted, the sheep were far from safety rocks when the hunter opened fire.

At last we reached the top of that awful mountain, and sat down to rest on Cyclorama Point, where the great ridge stops short in its easterly course. Take a large visiting card, fold it lengthwise along the middle, back the western end of it up against a conical ink-bottle and you will have the topography, with the eastern point as our coign of vantage.

The top of the ridge was barely wide enough for a game trail, and the trail was there, leading back to the tall peak farther west. From the crest, the northern slope fell away even more steeply than the southern, but it was well covered with green timber. Far below us, a mile at least, a creek ran through a narrow valley, and on the farther side of that another mountain ridge, two miles long from bottom to top and three miles long from end to end, swept steeply upward. It was a crazy-quilt of green timber, brush, slide-rock and dead timber.

As usual when hunters reach the top of a lofty ridge, and a new prospect opens to view, every eye quickly swept the opposite mountain-side in quest of big game. Mack Norboe had not looked through his glasses for more than ten seconds when his low, deeply-resonant voice rumbled out of the depths of his chest.

"I see a big grizzly! Come here, and I'll show him to you." I went.

"He's right over there, in the open, near the east side of that patch of green timber," and in an instant more every eye had picked it out.

What we saw was an oblong speck of dull black, with a faintly-discernible wedge of a lighter tint driving into it from the left side.

"Are you sure it's a grizzly?"

"It's a silver-tip all right," said John Phillips. "I can see the light mark behind the fore-leg."

"He's eating berries," said Charlie Smith. "There now! He's standing on his hind legs!"

The bear was on a slide that had become overgrown with bushes, and quite near to an island-like patch of several acres of green timber,—an excellent refuge in time of trouble. West of that another slide ran down; and beyond that lay a tract of several hundred acres of green timber, in which the chase of an able-bodied bear, at four-thirty P.M., would be quite hopeless. The distance from the creek up to the bear was about half a mile, and as usual, the ascent was steep and tangled.

It was then twenty minutes of four o'clock, and it would be dark at six. Of course the hunt led directly away from camp. It would take first class work to get over to that bear, find it, and kill it before sunset, saying nothing of getting back to camp. It was a thrilling moment, and called for swift action.

"That bear is two good miles from here," said Charlie, breathing hard.

"Well, if we get him before night we've got to be a-ma-vin'!" said Mack very earnestly.

"Then get ready for a run!" cried Mr. Phillips. "Can you make it, Director?"

Now, I am no gambler; but I take pride in knowing one thing that every good poker-player knows,—when to "lay down" my hand.

"No, I think not. I would only be a hindrance to the rest of you, and I might be the means of your losing the bear. Go ahead; and I'll stay here and see you do it. I've got my grizzly, and that one is yours, in any event."

"I'll stay here, too," said Charlie. "Now, you fellows *light right out.*"

Meanwhile, Mr. Phillips was hurriedly removing from his person everything that could be spared, even to his pocket knife; for in a run like that about to be made, every ounce counts.

"Come on, Jack!" cried Mack. With his blue eyes glint-ing, and his face aglow he backed over the edge of the rim-rock, and dashed down into the green timber, with John leap-ing after him, like two deer escaping from a pen. The ground was soft, and they ran with great plunging strides, covering at least eight feet at every step. It was surprising that neither of them pitched headlong downward against a tree trunk. In five seconds the green shadows had swallowed them.

"I pity that bear, with those wolves after him," said Charlie, reflectively.

He sat down, as agreed, to watch the bear constantly, and to give semaphore signals, with his hat, to show the location of the animal whenever the time came to attack it. It had been agreed, as an estimate, that it would take the hunters an hour to reach the bear by the course they had mapped out as most likely to lead to success.

I decided to take advantage of this brief interval, in a still-hunt westward along the top of the ridge, in quest of sheep, and without the loss of a moment I left Charlie and set out.

It was a lovely hunt, prosecuted in a most orthodox manner, but it yielded nothing larger or more serious than a big and prosperous yellow-haired porcupine. Him I found in the green timber of the northern slope about fifty feet down. I learned of him through his querulous, whining talk. He said, "*Uh! Uh! Uh! Uh! Uh! Uh! Uh!*" over and over, in the thin, high-pitched nasal voice of a barn-yard hen who thinks she can sing in the sun, and attempts to prove it. The note starts low and faint, and increases in volume but not in pitch, until it can be heard a hundred yards or more. The note struck by that particular porcupine was the same as the third G above middle C on a piano.

After watching *Erethizon epixanthus* for a few minutes, I hastened on up the ridge, following the well-worn game trail that leads along the summit. After a swiftly covered stretch of two miles I reached the peak and precipice at the western end of the ridge, and briefly viewed the great rocky basin in which the valley terminates, against the sheer wall. Although I prospected some fine sheep rocks, I saw neither sheep nor deer; but a week later, when John and Mack stood in that same spot, enveloped in clouds, they heard a band of sheep walking over the slide-rock a few score feet below them, but safely hidden from view.

Having traversed the entire ridge, I wheeled about and started back almost on a run, to reach Charlie's lookout point by the time the hunters began their attack on the bear. I was not a moment too soon, for at twenty minutes past five, I heard John's .405 roar and echo in the canyon. The shot was quickly followed by five or six others, and it was clear that the battle was on.

Covering my remaining distance on a keen run, I joined Charlie on the rim-rock, just as the first fusillade ended. A little later, when we saw the bear break out of the timber island into the open slide, we thought it had escaped; but when we saw it roll, and then heard the roar of Mr. Phillips's big gun, we yelled our approval. But we were a trifle premature. We were terribly disappointed when the pursuing hunters, without a sound in reply to us, disappeared in the brush and timber. We knew they were following a wounded animal; and in thick and tangled willow brush, a wounded bear is what Sioux Indians call "bad medicine."

After quite a long interval, we heard more firing, and saw the boys running. We were able to locate them by Mr. Phillips's white undershirt. Presently we saw arms wildly semaphoring, and triumphant yells came pealing across the valley. By those tokens we knew that the bear was dead. We yelled back our approval and congratulations, but when I shouted "Is-it-a-*big*-one?" the wires immediately stopped working!

Charlie had not once seen the two hunters, and had no knowledge of their movements, until they opened fire. Even then, the distance was so great, and their clothing so perfectly matched with their surroundings, it was only because Mr. Phillips had taken off his outer shirt of gray flannel that we were able to locate him by his white undershirt. Besides, they

made the run in record-breaking time, and Charlie did not expect them to reach the bear so quickly.

John Phillips declares he and Norboe reached the creek at
the foot of the mountain in the quickest time they ever made.
Within ten minutes after they left us, they found a foaming
stream of ice-cold water.

"Last chance to drink!" cried Mack, throwing himself
flat upon the stones. Mr. Phillips did not dare to drink, for
fear of the effect it might have on his wind in the hard run
upward; but he flung himself down, and plunged his head into
the water. Dripping from the stream, he rose and dashed at the
steep slope of the northern mountain, gaining a few seconds
on Norboe.

For several reasons, the hunters dared not run directly
toward the bear. It might detect them, and if it took alarm before they could get in a fatal shot, they would have a hard time
chasing it up hill. So they bore away westwardly, to make a
long detour through the big tract of green timber that would
bring them out above their quarry. Like all mountain-climb-
ing through green timber, they had to work hard for all they
won. They went up fully a mile before swinging eastward, and
then another mile before reaching their game.

Once when they reached a small open slide, they halted
in the opening, and with their binoculars looked across at
Charlie. He was sharply defined on the skyline, but made no
sign of any kind. They waved to him, frantically, many times;
but he saw them not, and of course made no signals. They
were desperately eager to know whether the bear had moved,
and if so, whither. They scolded, and waved, and fumed, and
waved some more; but Charlie sat with his binoculars glued
to his eyes, as impassive as Farragut on his pedestal. With
all his faithful watching, Charlie says, "I never saw hair nor
hide of 'em until after the ball opened!" So the hunters had to

·proceed without the aid of their semaphore station; and this was Mack's final growl:

"From the way Smidty's glued to them glasses, you'd think he'd never seen a b'ar afore! It's up to us to find and kill that b'ar, wherever it is."

They steered southeast through the green timber, keenly observant of everything in sight, hoping to discover the bear before it saw them. Vain hope! It had moved westward into the timber islet, passed through it and out into the slide way that bounded its western side. It was heading for the large tract of timber, and was almost in it, when it detected the on-coming hunters. Whether it saw them, or heard them, or smelled them, no one can say; but I suspect that it both saw and heard them. Charlie says that suddenly it wheeled about, and raced back toward the island of green timber. When the hunters in the timber first caught sight of the bear, it was running from them at full speed, and was half way across the brush-covered slide way. Mr. Phillips, who was leading, caught sight of it, through the overhanging spruce boughs, and instantly fired. The bear flinched slightly, but ran the faster. Immediately he sent forward three more balls, and Mack, seeing that the bear was running well, joined in the *mêlée*; but all this seemed only to accelerate the animal's speed.

The bear won its race for life to the edge of the green timber, and plunged into its shadowy depths. "Come on, Jack!" yelled Norboe, "Let's git out of this timber, and catch him when he runs across the open slide." And he plunged down the bank.

At the edge of the open ground, Mr. Phillips sat down and waited for a shot. Very soon the bear broke cover, on the farther side of the timber islet, nearly four hundred yards away. With a careful long shot, holding high and ahead, he caught the animal high up in the flank. The bullet ranged forward and lodged in the opposite shoulder; and the bear rolled heels over head in the brush.

This made five shots that Mr. Phillips had fired, which emptied his gun. As he began to reload, Mack broke past him on a keen run. He has been in at the death of many a bear, and his motto is, "When you git a b'ar down, git in quick, and *keep him down!*"

"Hold on, Mack! *Wait!*" yelled Phillips; and without waiting to finish his reloading he sprang to his feet and raced after his excited comrade. Half way across the slide, Mr. Phillips ran into a clump of snow-bent willows, and fell headlong. When he regained his feet and looked ahead, he saw that Mack was in a like predicament. Many a fine bear has been lost through an excess of snow-bent willow brush on the slides where they feed.

While Mack was wallowing in the brush, John overtook him, and together they raced through the timber, and out upon the slide beyond, to the spot where the bear had fallen. Alas! Their quarry had disappeared! But the hunters knew from the blood-stained trail, and a wide swath of broken weeds, that the grizzly was dragging its hind-quarters, and could not be far away. They tried to send Kaiser after it, but he flatly declined to go alone. Norboe then followed the trail down the timbered point toward the creek, while Phillips scouted lower down on the brush-covered slide in order to head off the bear from the heavy green timber beyond.

They had gone but a short distance when Mack, reaching an elevated point at the end of the timber, and looking across the slide down to the bank of the creek, caught glimpses of the bear a hundred and fifty yards away, in some willow bushes. His companion was in a low spot, half way between himself and the bear. Immediately he began firing, over Mr. Phillips's head, and emptied his .33-Winchester of the eight shots it contained. John, floundering on the slide below, could see nothing on account of the high willows, and during the fusillade kept yelling, in desperation, "Hold on, Mack! Wait till I get there! Don't kill him! I want to photograph him!"

The only thing in the West that can excite Mack Norboe beyond control is an unfinished grizzly bear; and so he kept on firing.

When they finally reached the bear, they found it dead. Then its sex changed; for it proved to be a female.

Mr. Phillips had shot it as described above, while Mack had put one of his eight shots through its back. The greatest joke of the whole trip was that the bear had three bullets through its right hind foot, two in the left, and one in a front paw; and *all of them had entered from below!*

As soon as the last firing ended, the long-distance shouts of the hunters told us of their triumph. We were barely able to see them with our glasses, but we yelled back our pleasure in their success. By that time, the day was nearly done, and in order not to be benighted in the down timber, Charlie and I turned, and began a swift retreat down the mountain. He set a racing pace, but I showed him that when piloted in the proper direction, I am a very good mountaineer. But even going down hill, the side of the mountain seemed almost endless, and I was glad to see through the heavy shadows of the green timber the gleam of the camp-fire, and hear Huddleston's cheery "Hello."

Half an hour later, we were astonished by the arrival of John and Mack, hot and tired, but triumphant. They came to camp down the creek on which they had killed the bear, and both complained bitterly of the treatment they received from its down timber and rock-slides. By this we knew that both must have been very bad.

The boys told of their bad shooting with great glee, and we chaffed them long and uproariously over their foot-shot bear.

Mr. Phillips Regrets the Impending Extinction of the Grizzly Bear

Mr. Phillips thought that some of the holes in the feet might have been made during the first attack, when the bear rushed up out of the slide. She was then running diagonally away from them, and they could catch only occasional glimpses of her. There was no such thing as a fair shot, and a proper lead. In the difficult snap-shot firing which followed, she simply ran away from the bullets.

Inasmuch as both the boys are excellent shots, particularly when big game is afoot, I became deeply interested in finding out how that bear got so many shots in her feet, from below. It is quite true that when a bear is galloping away from a hunter, the soles of the hind feet are thrown so far up in the air that a bullet fired from behind, and from a lower level, might strike them. But it seems that Norboe last saw the bear alive, and fired the eight shots which finished her as she lay on her back, in a tangle of brush, at the edge of the creek. He said, "Well, she laid thar on her back, and waved her hind feet at me till she looked like a spinnin' wheel covered with b'ar feet; and I shore shot at all I saw!"

It is my opinion that the majority of those feet were shot by Norboe, in the last assault, when there was nothing else in sight at which to fire. Altogether, it was one of the most remarkable results in shooting that I ever examined.

The pelage of this bear was very fine and beautiful, being long, abundant, and of rich colors. Judging from the skin, Charlie Smith and I guessed the weight of the bear at between four hundred and four hundred and fifty pounds, but she scaled only three hundred and twenty pounds, gross. When stretched upon its frame, the skin looked so handsome that Mr. Phillips decided to offer it to the Carnegie Museum, at Pittsburg, to be mounted for a place in a future group of grizzly bears. Eventually it was so offered, and promptly accepted.

CHAPTER XX

AVALANCHE AND SLIDE-ROCK

THE "SNOW-SLIDE"—AN IDEAL MOUNTAIN SECTION—
CREEK BURIED UNDER SLIDE—ROCK-TIMBER WRECKED BY
AVALANCHE—SLIDES AND WILD ANIMALS—HOW SLIDES
ORIGINATE—TWELVE SLIDES IN ONE MILE—SLIDE-ROCK—HOW
MOUNTAIN PEAKS CHANGE TO STEEP SLOPES—AN OBJECT
LESSON IN FALSE NOTCH.

OUT IN BRITISH COLUMBIA THEY call them "snow-slides," or merely "slides," because there are so many of them it takes too much time to say "avalanche." But, call it what you may, the snow-slide is the logical sequence of steep mountains and abundant snow.

Take your own house-roof in winter, pile upon it a foot of snow, then send a January thaw with water running on the shingles. The thundering rush, the shiver, and the ultimate crash which you hear tells the story of a miniature snow-slide. Take one of those microscopic slides, magnify it ten million diameters, send it half a mile down a very steep incline, with the speed and power of an express train, and you will have an ordinary snow-slide, such as occur by the thousand every spring in the house-roof mountains of British Columbia.

From man's view-point a snow-slide is awe-inspiring, and in its open season, profoundly dangerous. As viewed by Nature, it is one of her ordinary processes, very quick and useful in paring down steep mountains, and filling up narrow valleys. Incidentally, they furnish early pastures for the mountain flocks, and the best of hunting grounds for men who come with rifles to take toll of the wilds.

The eastern mountain-side on Avalanche Creek was an ideal section for the study of Nature's methods as manifested in slides. The story of the avalanche was written out along miles of roof-like slopes, and divided into many chapters. I spent hours in climbing over them, and in trying to read aright the things written there.

One incident that awakens one to a realizing sense of the majesty, and at times the terrors, of the forces exerted in that spot is finding the brawling waters of the creek disappearing under a *hill* of slide-rock nearly forty feet high! The avalanches have rushed this great mass down from the Phillips Mountains, and piled it clear across the valley. But for the open-work character of this great natural dam, which permits the waters of the creek to run under it in its original bed, the valley above it would now be a lake, thirty feet deep at the spot whereon our camp stood. As the perpendicular face of the eastern mountain is split off and thrown down by water freezing and expanding in its millions of crevices, the annual spring snow-slide gathers up a few thousand tons or so, rushes it down the icy slope at express-train speed, and spreads it a quarter of a mile wide over the surface of the existing hill. It is mixed with thousands of tons of snow, as a matrix, but ere long the latter melts away, and there remains only an innocent

The Might of a Snow-Slide

A TIMBER-WRECK ON AVALANCHE CREEK.

looking hill bestrewn with fresh slide-rock the size of paving stones. As usual, the slide-rock surface is immaculately clean, gray, sharp-edged, and cruel to man and beast.

About two miles farther down there is another manifestation of a very different character, and as a revelation of power, it is enough to send a thrill of awe through a pack-horse. I watched its effect on Kaiser, and am sure he was deeply impressed by the sight. He sat near me on a high log, and looked over the wreck until called away.

About ten years ago, an avalanche came down a long and very steep mountain-side, through a thick patch of green timber. Tall spruce trees, two feet in diameter and seventy-five feet high, were swept down bodily, root, stem and branch, as if they had been so many stalks of green corn. The mass of snow and ice which did this, for in it there was but little rock, must have been twenty or thirty feet thick when it struck the heaviest of the green timber, and solid as ice. As it went along, it tore up every tree, sapling and bush, leaving in its path not one stick of wood the size of a chair-post, and smashed the whole mass into the bottom of the valley. You can find it there now, piled twenty feet high above the bed of the creek, as shown in Mr. Phillips's excellent photograph.

Trees eighteen inches in diameter were snapped in two; and one, with a stem as big as a large telegraph pole, was bent like a bow. It is partly in view in the left of the picture. The bark has weathered away from all these logs, and the tangled mass of smooth gray trunks now tells the story of the avalanche, just as the white bones on the Montana ranges once told the story of buffalo slaughter.

No wonder the timber-haunting mule deer jump and fly at break-neck speed whenever a mischief-loving hunter rolls a big rock over the edge of a cliff into their cover. They very wisely "fear the awful avalanche." For the same cause, bears and lynxes also madly fly for tall timber, to the hilarity of many a hunter. They are wise to side-step quickly whenever they hear a roar higher up.

But the mountain sheep and goats are different. They dwell mostly where the snow-slides start, and they fear the latter very little. A goat cares naught for a falling rock, and to him an avalanche is an incident of passing interest, no more. Mr. W.H. Wright tells me that he once rolled several rocks directly over a goat that was feeding close to the foot of a mountain wall, and the animal coolly went on with his luncheon.

In order that I may here place before the Reader an exact and authoritative statement regarding the genesis and exodus of avalanches in the Canadian Rockies, our mountain savant, Mr. Charles L. Smith, has kindly written this:

SNOW-SLIDES, AND THEIR DANGERS

"BUT FEW PEOPLE, EXCEPT THOSE living in a mountainous country, have any idea of the tremendous force of a snow slide. There are two kinds, one of which we call a 'dry slide,' and the other a 'wet slide.'

"On account of the wet and heavy condition of the snow, the wet slide has the greatest force, carrying before it everything that offers any resistance, except solid rock. These descend chiefly in the spring, the time varying according to the weather. After repeated freezing and thawing, the snow becomes granulated and coarse, so much so that it has little or no adhesive qualities, even under slight pressure. When in this condition, it is extremely dangerous to disturb it, as the slightest jar, or anything touching it, often will set thousands of tons of it in motion. Once it is under way it runs like water, at least as long as the ground is steep, and it meets with no firm resistance. But once it reaches flat ground it stops, and the pressure from behind quickly becomes so heavy that it is at once formed into solid ice, and anything caught in it is instantly frozen.

"One would naturally suppose that large standing trees could withstand a few feet of this moving snow, but such is not the case. Four or five feet is sufficient to break the largest trees, or tear them out by the roots, brushing them from the mountain-sides like so many straws. If the roots hold firmly, the tree is broken off near the ground.

"In some respects the wet slides are not so dangerous as the dry slides, for the reason that they do not travel so fast, and do not spread out over so much ground. They follow more closely the bottoms of the ravines, never leaving their beds except in very short turns. On a sharp curve, the snow will leave the bed of a ravine and spread out on the long side of the turn for a height of from fifty to a hundred feet; and woe to any living thing that is caught in its toils!

"When the snow is in the proper condition, a very small thing indeed will start a wet slide. A stone no larger than an egg, falling from some overhanging rock, or a handful of wet snow slipping from a shrub, is all that is required to set acres of the sodden stuff in motion. Once started, its power is resistless, and it descends with a mighty roar that may be heard for miles, carrying everything before it. When it is under full headway and strikes standing timber, it sweeps it down like grass before a sickle. The trees fall backward like grain before the reaper, and are carried down and ground to kindling-wood. In many respects the dry slide differs from the wet slide. It comes down only in very cold weather, when the snow is fresh and light. While it does not have the crushing weight of the wet slide, it is by far the most dangerous to human life. Generally it is started by the settling of the snow. In all high mountains where snow falls deep, one will notice that in passing over a body of newly-fallen snow, sometimes it will suddenly drop, as it were, with a swishing sound, and settle from one half to two inches. When this happens on very steep ground it will slide, and more especially if there is crusted snow underneath, affording it a smooth surface to start upon.

"A dry slide travels more swiftly than a wet one for the reason that it completely fills the air, and creates a driving wind equal to a tornado. When in sweeping down a steep drop it reaches a sharp turn, it will spread out and run up on the mountain-side sometimes five hundred feet; or, diving into a canyon, it will dash up the opposite side for scores of feet, carrying with it large trees and stones. Often a dry slide is half a mile wide, and any one caught .in its path is almost sure to be either instantly killed, or buried in the blinding, seething mass of snow, and smothered.

"If a hunter should be crossing the path of an oncoming slide, even if it were but a few hundred feet wide, he could never hope to reach safe ground; but if one is in a steep gulch and near a turn, by acting quickly one may possibly have a fair chance to escape by good judgment and quick action. One must always climb up on the short side of the turn, no matter what obstacles are in the way. In such a situation, a man's impulse would be to take the wrong side because it is always more clear of brush; but this open ground is only a snare, and the fact of its being clear should always teach us to keep away.

"Where a gulch is straight for a long distance, the one in peril may then choose the shortest way out. The dangers of these slides are not so much from starting the snow one's self, as in being caught while crossing the foot of the slide-way, at the base of the mountain. The dry slides are so swift and terrible that the wind caused by them sometimes uproots timber some distance away.

"Slides on southern slopes are less liable to start by being disturbed high up, except immediately after storm, or in the early spring. As they are affected by the sun they soon become crusted, but on the northern slopes, where the sun does not strike, they are liable to start at any time."

In the mountains of southeastern British Columbia, the spring months are beset with perils. The open season for avalanches is from February 1 to May 15, and during that period many men,—sometimes whole parties together,—have been destroyed. In the early spring of 1905 a bear hunter from New York City lost his life in the Fort Steele district. While crossing the head of a steep slide way, the snow gave way under his feet, he fell, and started an avalanche which carried him down and buried him under an enormous mass of snow and slide-rock.

Usually it is prospectors and bear hunters who lose their lives in snow-slides, but occasionally a settlement is overwhelmed. The awful catastrophe at Frank, in 1902, wherein nearly a hundred persons lost their lives, is still fresh in the minds of all persons who are interested in the great Northwest.

It is a bold man, and it needs to be a hardy one, also, who goes a-hunting or prospecting in the summit ranges of the Canadian Rockies during any portion of the winter or spring. In my opinion, those high interior ranges were not made for winter use, and it is unfortunate that the best bear-hunting is to be found only at the worst season of the year. In May, after the bears have left their dens, the mountains are yet full of snow, particularly in the valleys and the green timber. Although the majority of the slide-ways are clear, the valleys are a-soak in snow-water which is colder than ice, and every camp is a wet one. Naturally, the guides and hunters go about with water-soaked feet and wet clothing, and if they do not have to sleep in wet blankets, they are lucky.

A Great Snow-Slide

THE TOTAL LENGTH OF THIS SLIDE IS ABOUT TWO MILES.

DRAWN BY CHARLES B. HUDSON, FROM PHOTOGRAPH BY PHILLIPS.

The rheumatic tendencies in all this are very great, and it is no wonder that Charlie Smith, and many other mountain men who hunt bear in the spring, are afflicted by that painful malady.

I was greatly impressed by the axe-like straightness with which an avalanche cuts its way through a mountain· side forest. You never see a slide way with ragged edges, or an occasional tree standing upon it. To-day I cannot remember any slide way stumps. No army of laborers ever cut a railway line through a forest with straighter sides than the snow-slide cuts for itself. Trees and brush are swept away, root, stem and branch, and the earth remaining is left all ready for cultivation. Nature then proceeds to plant it with the seeds of yellow willow, trailing juniper, aspen, *hedysarum*, snow lily, fire-weed, wild onion, and various grasses.

Naturally, these clearings become so many sun gardens, and as the new vegetation develops, it attracts the ground-squirrel, chipmunk and snow-shoe rabbit, insect a few and birds a-many. It is upon them that about nine bears out of every ten are found, feeding, and either shot or shot at, from the timber on one side.

A very common agent for the starting of avalanche is the "snow comb "which often forms on one side of sharp mountain-top, and overhangs like a gigantic cornice. Sometimes this overhanging comb is forty or fifty feet thick, and hangs with wonderful tenacity. A snow comb is always a thing to be dreaded and shunned. If the climber is upon its crest, it is liable to break away under his feet, and dash him to destruction in the crush and smother of an avalanche. If he is below it, its fall upon him is equally fatal. These formations start many an avalanche; and sometimes they are so compact and hard that a huge section of a snow comb will roll down a mountain-side intact.

A Snow-Comb at Timber Line

THIS CORNICE OF SNOW OVERHANGS A PRECIPICE, BELOW WHICH THE SNOW IS ABOUT TWENTY FEET DEEP.

The steeper you find a mountain roof, the greater will be the number of slides upon it; but the more numerous they are, the narrower they are. On the mountain-side opposite our camp on Goat Pass, there are twelve slides in a mile, all very much alike and very nicely spaced. Between twelve gullies there run up twelve fingers of timber and stunted bushes,—on a dozen little ridges, like the teeth of a comb. Near our camp on Avalanche Creek, there were ten or twelve slides on one side within a space of three miles, but they were much wider, and more irregular. As I remember it, the one which piled up the forty-foot hill of slide-rock over our creek was fully a quarter of a mile wide at its base.

Often we passed over fields of slide-rock so vast and far removed from their parent cliffs, we were forced to wonder how they were formed. The most extensive was that found in the big bend of Avalanche Creek, which rounds off the south-western angle of Phillips Mountains. Where our pack-train crossed it, on "the bloody trail," it was fully half a mile wide, and I think it was half a mile from bottom to top.

As we toiled over the great fields of foot-breaking gray limestone,—hard as flint, pointed to pierce, edged to cut and immaculately clean—we could think only of snow-slides as the agencies which had conveyed them so far down from the summits. The *principle* of slide-rock is clear enough; but even with one's imagination working over time, it is not easy to fig-ure out the transportation of such enormous *quantities* of it. Naturally, the place for slide-rock is near the foot of the cliff from which it fell, and not three thousand feet away, in a mass equal to that of the pyramids of Gizeh, and half a mile wide.

Take, for example, the spot whereon we killed our first goats. Originally, the ridge on which we stood when we fired was topped by a cliff. The cliff turned to slide rock and fell away until there remained a ridge so low that no more

The Pack-Train on a Great Field of Slide-Rock
The "bloody trail," on Avalanche Creek, angle 30°

294 CAMP-FIRES IN THE CANADIAN ROCKIES

slide-rock was given off. Then soil and timber began to cover the ridge, and there being no proper conditions for avalanches, the slide-rock remains to-day as it fell so long ago. Gradually it is being covered with soil and brush, and young spruces; and finally "green timber" will grow upon it, and cover it with an evergreen mantle.

On the summit of the mountain roof which Charlie Smith and I climbed in False Notch, the manner in which Nature pares down mountain peaks by the manufacture of slide-rock, was plainly written out. At the very spot where we climbed, there once had been a rocky cliff, joining the two peaks which still exist. Originally the two peaks must have been merely parts of one grand precipice, as high as their summits are to-day.

But it seems that the centre of this great cliff was softer, or at least more friable, than either end; and at that point there began a great slide-rock factory. Gradually the face of the cliff cracked off and fell in ragged fragments; and the annual snow-slides that went thundering down into the basin, carried with them great quantities of talus from the foot of the cliff. As the face of the cliff fell away, and its summit receded farther and farther, the slide-rock built a new slope upon the mountain, rising higher and higher toward the summit. At last the perpendicular cliff wall entirely disappeared, and in its place we have to-day that frightful slope, paved with naked slide-rock which is merely so much wreckage from the cliff and peak. To-day, instead of a precipice to crown the summit, the slide-rock slope extends on up to what once was the other side of the peak. There it cuts the western precipice, and ends in a knife-edge summit, "three feet wide in some places, and in some it's twenty."

The accompanying sketch shows the situation, both as it was and as it is. The peak to the left is slowly sharing the fate of its opposite neighbor, but its summit wall is yet well preserved.

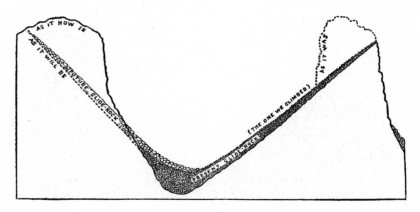

An Object Lesson in False Notch.
THE MAKING OF SLIDE-ROCK, AND THE DESTRUCTION OF PEAKS.

Quite rapidly the sharpest peaks and the sheerest walls of the Canadian Rockies are weathering down, and becoming talus and slide-rock. And rapidly, also, are the avalanches filling up the valleys with slide-rock and soil, and tree-trunks torn from the steep slopes. Eventually the sharpest of these peaks will be rounded off into great knobs, like Bird Mountain and Bald Mountain; and their rounded tops will be crowned with thick skull-caps of broken rock. These mountains are yet young. If the world does not grow cold too soon for them, even the tallest of the peaks between the Elk and the Bull may yet be broken down to timberline, and their rounded tops may be covered with green timber.

Regard them where you may, and how you may, these summit ranges tell wonderful stories of Nature's daily toil in her rocky mountain workshop.

CHAPTER XXI

THE SMALL NEIGHBORS OF THE BIG GAME

ANIMAL LIFE ON THE SUMMITS—THE LITTLE CHIEF "HARE"—A
FOUR-FOOTED HAYMAKER—THE FATE OF "LITTLE MIKE"—THE
COLUMBIA RIVER GROUND-SQUIRREL—A TINY CHIPMUNK—A
PLETHORIC GROUND-SQUIRREL—THE YELLOW-HAIRED
PORCUPINE—THE PINE SQUIRREL—THE PACK-RAT—THE HOARY
MARMOT—THE WOLVERINE—THE TRAPPERS' EVIL GENIUS—
SPECIES OF DEPREDATIONS—CHARLIE SMITH GETS SQUARE
WITH AN ENEMY—A WOLVERINE CAUGHT ALIVE.

FROM OUR FIRST MOMENT ON the summits, we were
keenly interested in the small mammals and birds which dwell
with the goat, sheep and grizzly bear. Amid such riotous abundance of mountain-side, peak and valley, every bit of animal
life attracts grateful attention. The vastness of the mountains
makes one feel so small that even a chipmunk or a little chief
"hare "is welcomed on the basis of brotherhood in the great
Family of Living Things. The only occurrence on our trip
that bordered upon calamity concerned Little Mike, the Pika,
whose story will be set down later on.

On the summits, small mammalian life is not really abundant. I was disappointed by the discovery that it is possible to tramp and climb for hours at a stretch without sight or sound of a four-footed creature of any kind save the goat. This scarcity is doubtless due to two causes: the martens and wolverines, and "the long and dreary winter." When we reflect that from October until May, almost eight months, the frozen earth is locked fast under a thick layer of ice and snow, it needs no philosopher to suggest that only the toughest and wisest animals can survive the great annual test of endurance. The bookshelves of our libraries and our homes actually yawn for a volume which will tell us, fully and truly, how the small creatures of the summits live through the awful winters which we, in our comfortable homes, shiver to think of. As yet we have only begun to learn how a few of the rodents manage to pull through. Those of the summits surely must lie for months in a torpid state, more dead than alive.

No doubt I am to blame for not having been more diligent in devoting time and labor to investigations of the home life of the small rodents with which we came in touch. Perhaps I lost some opportunities which could have been improved; but really, I think not. During the month that we were in the mountains, it was a physical impossibility to do more than we did. My total sum of hard climbing in hunting for big game, specimen-making, meat-drying, sketching and note-taking left me no time for the pursuit of small creatures, either with digging tools or traps. Whenever I wished to spend half an hour digging out some interesting burrowing creature, it always chanced upon a mountain-side or summit whereon there were no tools with which to dig. In digging out mountain rodents, one needs a good, healthy grizzly bear as an assistant.

From my first day on the slide-rock, I became deeply interested in the remarkable little creature which makes its home in those rugged fields. I say "in" those fields, because his life *upon* them is only a trifling incident. It is the Little Chief "Hare," Pika, or "Crying Hare,"(*O-cho-to'na prin'ceps*) which is not a real hare at all. Its three or four species and subspecies occupy a Family box all alone, and for mammals it surely is in the top gallery. It looks like a timid, little, one-third-grown gray rabbit, with white ear rims; and it has neither speed nor activity. It lives solely by its wits, in an atmosphere reeking of grizzly bears, wolverines, martens, weasels, eagles and hawks. It ranges from just below timberline up to the line of perpetual snow.

When you stalk silently into the head of a great rock-walled basin, over coarse and jagged slide-rock, to the spot where the first cupful of water starts down to form a creek and take a name, you listen as well as look. As you slowly pick your way along over the roughest of all rough hunting-grounds, you hear a queer little sound, like the "cheep" of a monster cricket. It comes from the depths of the slide-rock somewhere,—anywhere,—and it says deliberately but plaintively, *"Che-ee-ee-p! Chee-ee-ee-p! Cheep!"* It is a piercing, high-pitched squeak, like the third D above middle C on your piano. If you wish to see the owner of the insect-voice, sit down at once, remain perfectly quiet, and watch sharply in the direction of the sound. It is quite useless to try to locate the voice precisely until you see the owner of it.

In a reasonably small fraction of an hour, you will see a small gray form, about seven inches long over all, but quite tailless, gently slip into daylight atop of a chunk of slide-rock which affords a level resting place. If it has a large round ear, with a white rim, it is Pika, the haymaker of the slide-rock. In September, and I know not how many other months, he hops out to the edge of the slide-rock where things grow, cuts a big mouthful of weedy plants a foot long, carries them to the mouth of his den, and lays them down atop of a flat rock, to cure. He brings more, and more, until he has amassed a pile three inches high. All the stems are laid the same way, neatly and systematically, and they are to lie there until they dry sufficiently that when finally taken into the den and stowed away they will not mould. If a rock cuts off from the hay-pile the rays of the descending sun, the Pika will promptly move his hay into the direct sunshine.

On the day that Mr. Phillips and I first climbed to the top of Goat Pass, we found in the stunted timber on the steepest part of the mountain-side, three little piles of Pika-food, lying across the top of a fallen log, curing in the sun.

While we were measuring, skinning and weighing my first mountain goat, a Pika squeaked to us many times. At last it came out of the slide-rock about a hundred feet below us, and sat on a flat-topped stone viewing the world. We watched him with our glasses as long as our time would permit, then I went down to take a look at his ranch. As I approached, he turned about, and vanished.

On a flat-topped stone, with table area about the size of *Country Life* lay the little squeaker's hay pile, freshly cut, and in quantity a double handful. It contained no grass,—just weed-like plants, with thick stems and large leaves. About one-half the bunch consisted of squawroot (*Senecio triangularis*), the root of which makes a good spring salad that is much in favor with both white men and Indians. There was a good showing of the same pasque flower (*Pulsatilla occidentalis*) which the mountain goat loves. Of a plant from the Saxifrage Family, there was what chemists call a "trace," and that was all.

I set to work to follow up the rock burrow of our Pika by removing stones; but the task was not successful. Underneath the big chunk of slide-rock on which the hay-pile lay drying, I found more fodder of the same kind, almost dry enough to store away. It had been drawn under the rock so that the elements could not sweep it away, and a little later would have been carried farther in. But I could not reach the end of the home burrow. Cavities ran in several directions, and the more stones I pulled out, the more I lost the trail. Finally I gave it up, and contented myself with bringing away some specimens from the collection of the small creature who knows not only to make hay when the sun shines, but also *where* it shines.

From first to last, I think I saw half a dozen Pikas, and heard twenty crying from the safe depths of the slide-rock. Naturally, they live where the rock has fallen in large blocks, furnishing crevices and runways large enough for them, but too small for the marten or wolverine. I think the bears do not trouble them,—which must be for the reason that it is useless to try. No doubt the grizzlies fail to get them from the same cause that operated against me—too many rocky ramifications per Pika.

The only serious accident on our whole trip occurred during our last day at Camp Necessity. A Little Chief "Hare" was the victim, and Mr. Phillips was chief mourner.

On the last climb which was made by Mr. Phillips and Mack Norboe, they expended much time and labor in catching a Pika alive, "for the Zoo." They came into camp fairly radiant over a difficult task and a new triumph, and at once placed in my hands the black leather case of Mr. Phillips's new binocular. A small hole had been drilled in the cover of it.

"There, Director! We've brought you a new kind of an animile, to take to New York. We've got Little Mike in there! We worked nearly two hours to catch him. When Mack grabbed him, he fought like a little tiger, and bit Maxie through his glove. After we put him in the box he chippered and scolded a long time; but he's quieted down now."

When I saw the smallness of the air-hole that had been drilled for the animal through the thick leather, my mind was filled with dread; and I hardly could muster up courage to open the lid. But no time was lost on that account. When I looked in, poor "Little Mike," as Mr. Phillips called him, was curled up in the bottom, stone dead.

For several days Mr. Phillips was fairly racked by regret and remorse. That small creature's death haunted him nearly to Minneapolis, and he continually wondered whether "poor Little Mike "smothered because they did not give him enough air. I think the animal was hurt internally when captured, or else died of a "broken heart," as even bear and deer sometimes do when caught and crated.

The Columbia River Ground-Squirrel, (*Citellus columbianus*), is the special prey of the grizzly bear. On the grass slides and meadows at timberline, we saw at least fifty holes that had been dug by bears in quest of those animals. In southeastern British Columbia this creature is called a "gopher," but that term is a misnomer. The real gophers are very short and thick-bodied villains, with large claws and cheek-pouches, and they belong to a family well removed from the Squirrel Family.

The Ground-Squirrel mentioned above looks somewhat like a common gray squirrel with a half-length tail; but in reality its pelage is marked with fine cross-bars. It has the habits of a spermophile, and when alarmed sits up at the mouth of its burrow, very erect and post-like. Evidently it does not burrow deeply, for none of the holes dug by the grizzlies descended more than four feet, and the majority of them did not exceed a depth of three feet. The question is, as winter approaches do they burrow on down below the frost line, or do they hibernate in shallow burrows, in a torpid condition, as does our common chipmunk, with six heart-beats to the minute and a blood circulation that is scarcely perceptible?

We saw several examples of the very small and dark-colored Buff-Bellied Chipmunk (*Eutamias luteiventris*), and killed one which we did not mean to kill. While passing over a meadow on the bank of Kaiser Lake, our dog flushed the tiny creature, several yards from its burrow. In the mix-up that followed, of chipmunk, dog and men, the frightened animal leaped upon Mr. Phillips's leg, and then upon mine, seeking refuge from the dog. We all cried out "Save it! Save it!" and I tried to shelter it in my clothes. But it sprang off, and was seized by Kaiser. As quickly as we could we rescued it; and when I took it in my palm, it turned over, bit my finger until it bled, then died happy. As laid out it measured only four and three-fourth inches in length of head and body, tail three and one-half inches.

A solitary example of the Ashy-Mantled Ground-Squirrel, with the appalling Latin name of *Callospermophilus lateralis cinerescens*, was the handsomest rodent we observed. From the top of the loftiest ridge trodden by any one during our trip, whither Charlie Smith and I had gone on a "side hunt" from Camp Necessity, we looked far down into the maze of mountains and valleys, basins and slides that make up Wilson's Creek. Momentarily we expected to see big game of some kind, and we were hunting very carefully, through a scattered growth of stunted spruces. At last Kaiser stopped short, elevated his nose and sniffed significantly to windward. Was it sheep, or grizzly bears? All ready to burst with readiness, we waited for the foe, Kaiser sniffing crescendo, and pointing down the mountain.

At last we saw the game. It was a big, fat Ashy-Mantled Ground-Squirrel, marked on each side with a very broad light-colored band between two equally broad black ones. Its sides seemed ready to burst from good feeding. As we all stood motionless, he galloped up within five yards of us, saw us, and stopped to look. For fully three minutes he stared at us and we at him, and no one moved. Then he made a rush of about six feet, dived into his burrow and disappeared. We tried hard to dig him out, but the ground was so hard and stony we had to give it up.

The Western Yellow-Haired Porcupine (*Er-e-thi'zon ep-i-xan'thus*) was sufficiently numerous that we saw six, all on Avalanche Creek. On September 11, at the close of our great day with goats on Phillips Peak, we overtook two porcupines waddling along the trail a mile above our new camp. At first they refused to turn off and permit us to pass, so we leisurely strolled along at their heels for nearly two hundred yards. They walked as rapidly as they could, but their legs were clumsy, and their best speed was slow. Finally they arrived opposite a drift of logs, over the bed of the creek. Quitting the trail abruptly, they shambled down the steep bank, scrambled into the thickest chaos of logs, and flung themselves down in most absurd fashion, under the logs and out of sight. That night we were fearful that the spiny wayfarers would take to the trail once more, and land in our tents; but they refrained from troubling us.

I expected that the Oregon Pine Squirrel (*Sci-u'rus hud-sonius richardsoni*) would be plentiful on those mountains in September, but they were not. I do not recall that we saw more than one, a very cheerful and saucy individual who inhabited a big spruce at Camp Hornaday. Every morning he would awaken very early, perch high in the big spruce nearest to our tent, and bark and scold at Kaiser, the horses, the cook, and every living thing in sight. His truculent chatter, heard daily for many days, now is associated with the smell of boiling coffee, and the sizzle of goat steaks in the frying-pan. On general principles he objected to our presence there, but whenever he saw Kaiser he became positively abusive. When very angry his bark was like the yapping of a small fox.

This squirrel, which is very like our eastern red squirrel, has a habit which implies genuine reasoning powers. It collects mushrooms—which it does not eat when fresh—puts them in the sun, and *dries them* until they are acceptable. The average eastern hunter does not readily believe that the half-dozen or more mushrooms which he finds lying in a row a-top of a log, or grouped on a rock, or fixed in the forks of young conifers, were really gathered and placed there by red squirrels, to cure. But it is true. Charlie Smith says that the dried product is stored for winter use.

The Pack-Rat (*Ne-o-to'ma cin-e're-a drummondi*) has already been mentioned. Although this droll and interesting creature inhabits the mountains quite up to timberline, it chanced that we saw none after leaving Smith's ranch. Jack Lewis declared that when he and Mr. Phillips were benighted on Sheep Mountain, and he fell asleep by the smouldering camp-fire, a Pack-Rat tried to steal his cap from his head. It is really strange that the Pack-Rat of the British Columbia mountains is just as mischievous and ingenious as his brethren in the Florida pine woods, nearly 3,000 miles away. The northwestern animal secretes a very disagreeable odor, which is emitted under excitement, perhaps in the line of self-defence.

The Hoary Marmot, or Whistler (*Arc-to'mys pru-i-no'sus*) was constantly looked for, and expected, but seen only once on the entire trip. I saw one run out of sight around a spur-root of a mountain, just below timberline, as hurriedly as if he knew there were guns about. This creature is merely an over-grown, grizzly-gray, mountain woodchuck, who is so careful of himself that it is practically impossible to procure living specimens at a sum even remotely corresponding to their exhibition value. Several men have endeavored to catch specimens for us at $15 each, but thus far not one has been taken on that basis.

The Snow-Shoe Rabbit must be counted with the small mountain-dwellers of the Order *Glires* (Rodents), but they were so rare that I did not see even one specimen. Mr.

Phillips saw one, at the big bend of Avalanche Creek, on Roth Mountain. Their great rarity is probably due to the martens, lynxes and wolverines. As those fierce fur-bearers disappear via the trap line, all the rodents of the mountains should become more abundant.

Of all the carnivorous animals (Order *Ferae*) inhabiting the region which was ours for a month, the Grizzly Bear, or Silver-Tip, stands first; and he has already been set forth. The Black Bear inhabits the same territory as the Grizzly, but around Phillips Peak it appears to be less abundant. The Cinnamon Bear is merely a color phase of the Black Bear, but, remarkable to say, it is absent from all the territory of the latter east of the great plains. The question why this is so, is still unanswered.

The Puma, or Mountain "Lion," (*Felis concolor*) inhabits the Elk River valley, but its tenancy hangs on a very slender thread. The most interesting fact that can be mentioned regarding it is that we were then at the northern limit of a species which has the longest geographical range of any large feline animal,—from Phillips Peak to Patagonia.

We have fallen into the habit of regarding the Puma as a hardy, snow-defying animal, most at home in the western Rockies. But this view is entirely wrong. In reality *Felis concolor* is more at home in the tropics of northern South America than on the snowy wastes of the American Rockies. The Puma is to Colorado as the tiger is to Corea.

We saw no Pumas, nor even puma tracks; but in 1904 Charles L. Smith caught one near the Sulphur Spring, and another was taken shortly after on Pass Creek.

Although no specimens of the Canada Lynx, or *Loup Cervier*, (*Lynx canadensis*) were seen during our September on the summits, our guides were more fortunate later on. During their trapping operations, in November, they caught two fine, large specimens. One was taken on Avalanche Creek, and very well photographed by Mr. Smith in the trap. This animal is distinguished from its nearest relative, the "bob-cat" of the North, by the very long black pencil on the tip of each ear, its enormous feet and legs, and its uniform color of pepper-and-salt gray. American lynxes of lower degree are more or less spotted, and have either very small ear-pencils, or none at all. The bay lynx, red lynx or bob-cat-of which there are two or three forms, which hope-lessly run together-is much more common than the fearsome Canadian species.

The Wolverine, Carcajou, or—as the Indians of Washington call it—the Mountain Devil, is quite at home in the Elk River mountains, but his shrewdness is so great that he is seldom seen outside a trap. Unquestionably, this is the most interesting small mammal of the northwest. In some places it is called the Skunk-"Bear."

If you meet a strange trapper and desire to take a measure of his moral leanings, ask his opinion of the moral character and mental capacity of the Wolverine. I have heard trappers solemnly declare that no matter how much any one may ma-lign this particular devil, its character always is much blacker than it can be painted.

The Wolverine is the largest, the strongest, most vicious and most cunning member of the Marten Family. In compari-son with the size of its body, its teeth are of enormous size and power. It is about as large as a fox terrier, and ten times as savage as a bad bull-dog. It is built on the plan and specifications of a Malay sun-bear, and has the same evil eye, wedge-shaped head, splay feet and truculent manner. It has long hair, ivory-white claws, and a mean-looking tail that looks as if it had been cut off half way, and healed up with a wisp end. The animal runs with its tail down, but when it stops to look back, up goes the

The Western Yellow-Haired Porcupine (top)
A DANGEROUS ANIMAL IN CAMP AT NIGHT.

Canada Lynx, in Trap (bottom)

tail, skunk-like. In spying out the land, a Wolverine often rises high on its hind legs.

A full-grown Wolverine stands about twelve inches high at the shoulder, its head and body are about thirty inches, and tail ten inches, exclusive of the hair. The general color of this animal is dingy or smoky brown, but there is a large light-colored patch on the side. On the head the hair is short and close, but on the body, neck and tail it is long and flowing. Its eyes are black, and so are its legs, but its claws are conspicuously white, and very large.

The Wolverine is a fairly good climber, and game hung in a tree is not safe from its destructive jaws. Mr. J.W. Tyrrell once outwitted the wolverines of the Barren Grounds by erecting a cache on four very high posts, then trimming the posts and peeling off all the bark, after which he nailed six cod-hooks to each post. The Wolverines tried very hard to climb up to that cache, but failed.

The Wolverine is a great traveller; but Mr. J.W. Tyrrell says that those he chased on the Barren Grounds could not run very fast, and he easily outran them. Charles L. Smith says that this animal has the widest individual range of any carnivorous animal with which he is acquainted, not even excepting the grizzly bear. He says that from its home den a Wolverine will travel from twenty to thirty miles in each direction. Like all the short-legged marten-like animals, it travels by a series of long bounds; or, in other words, it goes at a gallop. Its specialty is following up a line of marten traps; and on this point my good friends Charlie Smith and the Norboe brothers became quite wrought up. This is the substance of what they told me:

A Wolverine will follow the trail of a trapper, visit every one of his marten traps (or any others, for that matter), spring every trap, steal every bait, and take out every marten that has been caught. If the marten is not dead, it is killed and torn out

The Wolverine, in Trap (top)
The Wolverine, in New York (bottom)

of the trap; and if dead and frozen, it is seized by the body and violently jerked until the trapped leg is torn off the body, and the skin spoiled. The dead body will then be carried some distance, a neat hole will be dug straight down into the snow for perhaps two feet, and the dead marten is cached at the bottom. Then the snow is replaced in the hole, tamped down and neatly smoothed over on the surface, after which the Wolverine defiles the snow over the grave, and goes his wicked way.

By these signs, the trapper knows where to dig for his stolen marten. J.R. Norboe once recovered four martens out of six that had been stolen by a Wolverine on one line of traps.

In the Elk River Valley, C.L. Smith once had about seventy miles of traps, and every mile of his lines was gone over by Wolverines. He said, "They caused me a great deal of loss, and at last they nearly drove me crazy." He once set a trap for a Wolverine, and put behind it a moose skull bearing some flesh. The Wolverine came in the night, started in at a point well away from the trap, dug a tunnel through six feet of snow, fetched up at the head—well behind the trap—and dragged it in triumph through his tunnel and away.

The female Wolverine has four young at a birth, and they are born in December. The mothers are more fierce and troublesome in February and March than either earlier or later, for it is during those months that they are required to work hardest in feeding their young.

Contrary to the statements of the earlier writings upon the Wolverine, the three trappers in our party united in expressing the opinion that this animal is not a gluttonous feeder, and that the amount of food it consumes is proportionately no greater than that of other members of the Marten Family—marten, fisher, mink, otter, etc. The Edwards Brothers, animal showmen, have today a captive Wolverine which they have kept for twelve years, and its daily ration of meat is only half a pound.

To a trapper, the Wolverine's crowning injury and unpardonable insult is the invasion of his cabin, during his absence. Then it is, with the trapper far from home, and his all-too-scanty winter's store of flour, bacon, coffee and sugar laid bare and at his mercy, that the eternal cussedness of *Gulo luscus* rises to the sublime. He rips open every sack and parcel, scatters flour, coffee, sugar and grease in one chaotic mass upon the cabin floor, and wallows in it, with ghoulish glee. He goes to the bunk, and with fiendish persistence tears the blankets to shreds. The stove is about the only thing in the cabin that goes unscathed. At the last, he defiles to the utmost every edible that he cannot carry away, and departs.

Charlie Smith tells with much fervor how he got even with a Wolverine which made several unsuccessful attempts to raid his cabin. One morning before starting out on his trapline, he buried a trap directly in front of his cabin door, and set the door slightly ajar. Just inside the door, he placed some meat. Then, on the roof peak of his cabin, at one end of the structure he rigged a balanced pole, like a well-sweep, drew down the small end, and under it very carelessly hung a deer's head, in a small tree. Directly under the head he set a trap, and attached it to the end of the pole.

He figured out the mental process of the Wolverine in this wise: He will suspect the trap in front of the door, and avoid it. But he will discover the deer's head, and say, "Aha! This fellow has forgotten that I am about!" and straightway he will stand up on his hind legs and reach for the head, with his front feet against the tree.

The Wolverine came, and saw, and thought, and did precisely as the trapper had figured it out that he would; and that night when Charlie came home, he found his cunning enemy hanging high in the air, "and dead as a wedge."

In the United States, the Wolverine is now so rare that it is almost non-existent; but it is not extinct. In British Columbia, and northward thereof far into the Barren Grounds, it is generally distributed, though it is nowhere really numerous. Rarely indeed is one ever seen afoot by hunter or trapper, save in the far north. In all C.L. Smith's years of trapping, he has seen only three; and curiously enough, two of those he saw, and shot at, were at the carcass of my first goat.

After we left the mountains our three guides returned to the scene of our late adventures, and went to trapping. Smith worked Avalanche Creek, Mack Norboe took his old cabin on Bull River, and John Norboe went to Lake Monro. I think Charlie Smith had the most fun.

Within a hundred feet of the spot where he, Phillips and I sat on the bank of the creek and ate our luncheon on the day we first went bear hunting down to Roth Mountain, he caught a big and savage Wolverine, once more scoring against his ancient enemy. To make sure that a captured animal should not chew himself out of his trap, he rigged his favorite engine of destruction—a spring-pole—and to the end of this attached the chain of his trap. The Wolverine sprung the trap, the trap sprung the pole, and Gulo had nothing to do but to wait for Charlie.

When Charlie came, he found the Wolverine held by two toes only, and therefore practically unhurt. This was great fortune, and at once the trapper resolved to earn an additional increment by sending the animal alive to the New York Zoological Society. He had no cage, nor was it possible to make one on the spot. Single-handed and alone, he tied the jaws of that raging musteline demon, tied its legs and feet, also, made the Mountain Devil into a package, took it on his back, and carried it through a foot of snow, down the creek six miles, to his cabin.

There he made for the beast a rough cage of poles, and later on he and his partners *carried* cage and contents out to the wagon road in Elk valley. The labor and hardships they endured in this task are almost indescribable. They slept on the snow, without shelter, with the temperature at 20 degrees below zero.

But at last they won out; and the Wolverine at last reached New York, alive and well. It was the first specimen of that species to reach the Zoological Park, and was treated with the utmost consideration. Two photographs of it are reproduced herewith.

CHAPTER XXII

SMALL NEIGHBORS OF THE BIG GAME-CONTINUED

THE PINE MARTEN—THE COYOTE—MULE DEER—WINTER BIRDS
ONLY—FRANKLIN GROUSE, OR "FOOL-HEN"—WHITE-TAILED
PTARMIGAN—HARLEQUIN DUCK—WATER OUZEL—EAGLES AND
HAWKS—CLARK'S NUTCRACKER, CANADA JAY AND MAGPIE.

THE PINE MARTEN (*MUSTELA AMERICANA*) is now
the most important and valuable fur-bearing animal of British
Columbia. Fine, dark pelts are worth as high as thirty dollars
each; but the lighter ones run as low as three dollars. The beaver
and otter are done, at least in southeastern British Columbia,
but of Martens there are yet a goodly number. During their
October and November trapping (1905) in the mountains between the Elk and Bull Rivers, our three guides caught fifty-
three Marten—a very fine catch for so short a period.

The Marten is an animal of about the size of a half-grown
red fox, and looks like one. In head and body it is seventeen
inches long, and its tail is seven inches. Ordinarily its body is
brownish-yellow, but the legs are two or three shades darker.

It has three kinds of hair. From the standard color, the coat of this animal shades darker until it becomes almost black.

The Marten is in every sense a predatory animal, and a very savage one, but it is not a double-dyed villain, brimful of malice and mischief, like the wolverine. In the wilds it is a great hunter, but it seldom turns poacher and poultry-killer. It hunts in the daytime, and cannot properly be called a nocturnal animal. It is an expert tree-climber, and it is said that Martens catch red squirrels out of their own tree-tops. Charlie Smith has shot five or six Martens out of trees, on Bull River. In descending a tree, a Marten goes head first, like a squirrel.

We found Marten signs quite up to timberline, and we know that in the autumn they eat mice, for we saw proof of it. Of course they feed upon small mammals and birds of every kind they can catch. In summer they eat berries of several kinds. In winter they live chiefly by catching mice under logs, where the snow does not drift in and pack tightly. By means of these open places under logs, and their runways under the snow, the mice move about quite freely, and thus serve the Marten with many a warm luncheon, of small dimensions. When pressed for food the Marten digs down beside a fallen log until he reaches the open space under it, and there he travels to and fro, practically under the snow, for considerable distances.

Even where they are abundant, Marten are rarely seen until they are trapped. Once however, on Bull River, after a fire in green timber, eight martens were seen in one day, just below the fire line. This animal is a good traveller, and runs rapidly, by long bounds which cover from three to six feet at a leap.

In temper the Marten is very savage, and also finely courageous. When caught, it fiercely glares upon the trapper, and growls its hatred. So strong is its appetite, and so dull its sense of pain, that even with one foot crushed in a steel trap, it will accept food and make a hearty meal, growling angrily all the while. When caught in a steel trap it does not lie down and give up, but snarls and fights to the end.

One Marten was seen on our trip, near the spot where the cycloramic bear-hunt occurred. Mr. Phillips saw it start to run along a fallen log, and instinctively took aim at it, when Mack Norboe cried out in great alarm,

"Hold on, Mr. Phillips! Don't shoot! Don't shoot! *That pelt will be worth twenty dollars next month!*"

That Marten went its way unharmed—until the trapping season.

The absence of wolves was very noticeable. We saw not one Gray Wolf (*Canis nubilis*), and the only Coyotes (*Canis latrans*) encountered were the two young animals which Mr. Phillips found on the Sulphur Spring meadow, one of which he killed. But of course wolves are more in evidence later in the year.

Mr. Charles L. Smith related a very curious fact, bearing upon the mental capacity of the Coyote. He said that already the Coyotes of the Elk Valley have so well learned the deadly character of traps and poison that now it is almost impossible to kill a wolf with either. So very wise and suspicious are the Coyotes now that a hunter may hang up a dressed carcass of a deer, and leave it in the woods, actually surrounded by hungry wolves,—and they will walk around it for days without daring to eat a mouthful.

The Mule Deer is yet found in southeastern British Columbia, but it is no longer numerous. Its delicious venison has brought upon it the rifles of all hunters and trappers, and we found it quite as scarce as mountain sheep. I think our party saw a total of twelve head; but we killed only one. In October and November the snows drive the deer down from the mountains into the valleys of such streams as the Elk River, where the hunters find them rather easy prey.

A Dark-Skinned Marten, (Mustela americana – left)

A Typical Marten Trap (right)

THE TRAP IS FULLY EXPOSED, AND THE BAIT IS PLACED BEHIND IT.

THE OTTER ENTERS AT THE OPENING LEFT FOR HIM, AND JOYOUSLY TREADS UPON THE SMOOTH, CLEAN PAN OF THE STEEL TRAP.

We saw no White-Tailed Deer; but there are in that corner of British Columbia a few representatives of that species.

Farther west, in the lower valley of the Fraser River, the Columbian Black-Tailed Deer (*O-do-coil'e-us columbianus*) is abundant, but I believe none are found in the Fernie district.

In 1901 a Moose was killed in the Elk Valley, near the Sulphur Spring, by Mr. Charles L. Smith, but since that time no other Moose have visited that region.

Of bird life we saw much less than I expected, for I had thought that the late-ripening berries of the summits would attract and hold a goodly number of the more venturesome birds. But the berries *had no effect whatever upon bird life*, and throughout the entire trip, I did not see even one migratory bird which was lingering to feed upon them. Even as early as September I, nearly all the migratory birds had vanished. My bird notes relate only to certain birds which we saw, and positively identified. We saw half a dozen species which we could not identify.

The Franklin Grouse, or "Fool-Hen" (*Ca-nach'i-tes franklini*) is the first game bird which greets the hunter as he enters the mountains, and when he departs it is the last one to speed the parting guest. As already recorded, we flushed about twenty of these birds in the heavy jack pine forest of Elk Valley, just below the Sulphur Spring. Later on we found them elsewhere, up to an elevation of about 5,000 feet; but above that we saw no more of them. It is a bird of the valleys and heavy timber, rather than of the mountain-sides.

The Sooty Grouse (*Den-drag'a-pus ob-scu'rus*), Blue Grouse or Pine Hen lives higher up, but it is so rare we met with only two flocks. At an elevation of about six thousand feet Charles L. Smith killed a fine specimen by throwing a stone at it, as it sat upon one of the lower branches of a tree. This bird is a subspecies of the well-known Dusky Grouse of the southern two-thirds of the United States west of the great plains. In the Shoshone Mountains I found it living close beside the mountain sheep, and almost fearless in the presence of man.

Above the timberline, the White-Tailed Ptarmigan (*La-go'pus leu-cu'rus*) was delightfully common. On the evening of September 6, about an hour after the three goats ran past our campfire on Goat Pass, four of these birds flew into our camp, and created another diversion. Mr. Phillips shot one for close examination, and as a small contribution to the frying-pan. Later on we found two flocks on the bald, rocky summit of Bird Mountain, a most weird place in which to find members of the Grouse Family.

The Ptarmigan is a brave bird, or it would not choose as its home the rugged rocks and storm-beaten slopes above timberline. Although its flesh is excellent, and on the mountaintops a great delicacy, we were not at all keen in seeking it. We did not need more than a sample of Ptarmigan, and that was all we took. They were such queer little creatures, and so companionable on the summits, we had not the heart to pursue them for food.

It is natural for people to be specially interested in birds and mammals which live under conditions fraught with great danger, or with difficulty to the party of the first part. Take the Harlequin Duck, for example—a bird so fantastically painted by Nature, with white bars and stripes and splashes on a bluish background, that the finished effect suggests the painted markings of a clown.

This bird loves rough water, and in the Elk River and its tributaries you will find it from early spring until the end of September. It breeds in that region. If you see it at all, it will be in the roughest water, perhaps standing upon a stone in the centre of a roaring rapid, or bobbing like a cork on the boiling flood at the foot of some cascade. Standing on a dry shelf in a museum, or lying as a dry skin in the black obscurity of a smelly drawer, the Harlequin Duck is not seen at its best. But place it in its natural haunts—a roaring mountain stream, in a setting of rocks, enamelled with evergreen timber,—as shown in Mr. Phillips's beautiful photograph, and this is a grand bird. Even the best diamond needs a proper setting in order to show off at its best.

The Water Ouzel,—in habits the strangest of all passerine birds,—is also a bird of the mountain torrents. This is the little creature which looks like a short-tailed catbird, or a big gray wren, which always nests beside a foaming mountain torrent, and occasionally amuses itself by diving into an icy cold pool, and *walking upon the bottom!* I have seen them fly off the edge of a rushing stream, in November, and plunge into the icy waves, *for fun,*—just as a feverish city sparrow bathes in a fountain-basin in mid-August.

We found a Water Ouzel's nest on Avalanche Creek. It was a mile above Camp Necessity, and the elevation was about 6,000 feet. The nest was situated in a horizontal crevice, a foot wide, at the base of a smooth wall of rock, and only eighteen inches above the turbulent waters of the stream. To me it seemed strange that a summer freshet had not swept away the little home. Mr. Phillips endeavored to photograph the nest, but the effort was not successful.

The nest was of very simple construction. It consisted merely of a broken wreath of moss, lying upon the bare rock, and backed up against the inner wall of the crevice. With the Carnegie Museum in his mind, Mr. Phillips removed it; and lo! there was nothing but a meaningless handful of dried moss.

Under a log in a snow-slide I saw one Wren, which I think was a Western Winter Wren (*An-or-thu'ra biemalis pacificus*).

A few Golden Eagles were seen on the summits, always hunting around the peaks, or the tops of the ridges. The

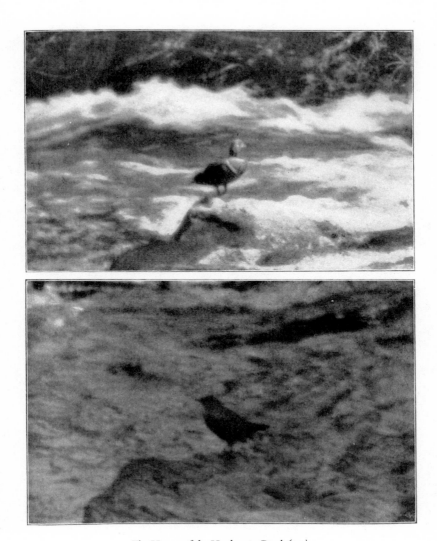

The Haunt of the Harlequin Duck (top)
The Water Ouzel (bottom)
THE BEST RESULT OF MANY EFFORTS IN PHOTOGRAPHING THIS REMARKABLE BIRD.

mountain goat kids were then too large to be carried off by eagles, and it is probable that the latter were seeking ptarmigan, pikas, ground-squirrels and hoary marmots. But Eagles were by no means numerous, and I think that altogether we saw only eight or ten.

Hawks were more numerous. A brown-gray species, which I failed to identify, was frequently observed flying low along the mountain-sides, hunting with the utmost diligence for the small creatures of the slopes. At times these birds flew slowly along, not more than three feet above the earth, their keen eyes searching sharply for "gopher" and chipmunk.

No British Columbia mountain is complete without Clark's Nutcracker (*Nu-ci-fra'ga columbiana*; commonly called "Clark's Crow"), and the Canada Jay (*Per-i-so're-us Canadensis*, also called "Whiskey-Jack" and "Moose Bird") and a river valley without a Magpie (*Pi'ca pica hudsonia*) is desolate. It is disappointing to find a hunter's cabin with no Magpies about it, and a mountain camp without the Canada Jay is out of joint. In their own proper places we saw all three of these birds. First came the Magpie, the most beautiful and showy of the trio, which was plentiful around our camp at Sulphur Springs, and around Wild-Cat Charlie's cabin. To my mind, this is the most beautiful and picturesque of all the American members of the Crow Family, and throughout most portions of its range it should be permanently protected by law. There are times, however, when this bird becomes a nuisance to domestic animals.

In the higher altitudes, the Nutcracker and Canada Jay are the big-game hunter's most intimate feathered friends. In the wildest basins and on the steepest mountain-sides, you will see them hang upon the heaven-pointing tips of the last dead pines and spruces, and hear their weird, squawking cries. It is fitting that the birds of the summits should be widely different from those of the plains, and that the sound of falling slide-rock, and the whistle of the wind through the pine-tops should forever be associated in the hunter's mind with the queer *"Keewock"* of Clark's Nutcracker.

CHAPTER XXIII

DOWN AVALANCHE CREEK, AND OUT

CUTTING OUR WAY OUT—A SIDE TRIP TO HIGH SUMMITS—
DISCOVERY OF LAKE JOSEPHINE—A CAMP FOR THREE—A
LOFTY HUNTING GROUND—MY LUCK AGAINST THE STORM-
CLOUDS—A BODY-RACKING DESCENT—THE STRUGGLE FOR A
TRAIL OUT—MR. PHILLIPS AND I GO OUT ON FOOT—THE JACK
PINE, DOWN AND UP—RUNNING LOGS OVER DOWN TIMBER—
OUT AT LAST.

BELOW CAMP NECESSITY, THE VALLEY of Avalanche
Creek was in a frightful state. It was full of "down timber,"
through which no trail ever had been cut. Our guides knew
that to cut our way out to Elk River Valley would be a serious
undertaking, but it was voted less laborious and more expe-
ditious than to retrace our route, and swing back twenty-five
miles northward. To retrace our steps would mean a total loss
in distance of at least fifty miles, half of it over very bad trails,
with much climbing; so the guides and the cook voted to chop
out a trail down stream in order to save the horses.

At the beginning it seemed like a three days' task, and

it afforded an interval that Charlie Smith and I made haste
to spend in a hunt up to the summits south of our camp. He
said, "There is some mighty fine country up there. I have seen
it from the south, but I don't believe any white man ever has
been in it,—at least not in my time. There ought to be grizzly
bear and sheep up there, and mule deer, too!

"We took the 4 x 7 silk tent, an axe, a small tin pail, a
small piece of bacon, a little chocolate, sugar, bread and a can
of tongue; our rifles, a small camera, one blanket, and that was
all. Knowing that it would be a hard climb up, and one equally
difficult coming down, we left behind every ounce that could
be spared. Charlie even declined to take a blanket, but with
needle and thread I quickly converted my best blanket into a
first-rate sleeping-bag, and took it on my back.

We went up the bed of a creek that came plunging down
into Avalanche Valley, just below our camp; and of all the
down timber! The narrow valley was filled with it; and being
unable to go under it, or through it, we had to go over it, by
walking the logs as they lay. It was both difficult and dangerous. I had one hand free, but how Charlie could risk it with a
heavy pack on his back, a sharp axe in one hand, and a rifle in
the other, was a mystery. We not only had to run the logs, but
it was necessary to climb at the same time; and the combination was far from easy.

At last we climbed above the down timber, and entered
upon slide-rock; and over that we climbed on up through a
gloomy notch in the rocks. Beyond that lay a basin filled with
green timber, which Charlie scrutinized. "By the amount of
water coming out of that basin," said he, "I think there must
be a lake in there, somewhere."

In the Adirondacks, and other places wherein water
is plentiful and cheap, we speak of any small body of it as a
"pond;" but in deserts and on mountain summits, where a body

of water of any size is something to be petted and made much of, people call it a "lake." And very properly, too; for no meek and lowly "pond "is a proper associate for Nature's grandest works. One of the most beautiful lakes in the Elk River country is Lake Monro, a few miles north of Goat Pass—named in honor of Mr. G.N. Monro, of Pittsburg, who has hunted big game in this region.

Charlie was right. We found a lovely sheet of water, walled in by a dense green stockade of spruces and balsams. Toward the south and west, a high cliff of rock loomed up, and southeastward were several immense ridges with broadly-rounded tops.

The lake is a gem of green and blue, lying in the lap of Nature. For a few yards outward from the shore the shallow water showed the clear green of an emerald, but suddenly it plunged into unknown depths and became "deeply, darkly, beautifully blue."

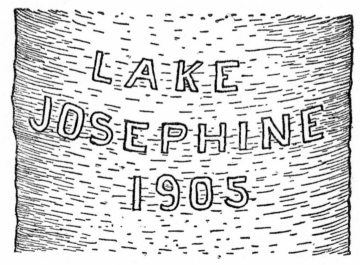

Near the outlet of the lake, we found big tracks coming up from the blue water, and at the head of it we found where the maker of those tracks had gone in. About two weeks previous

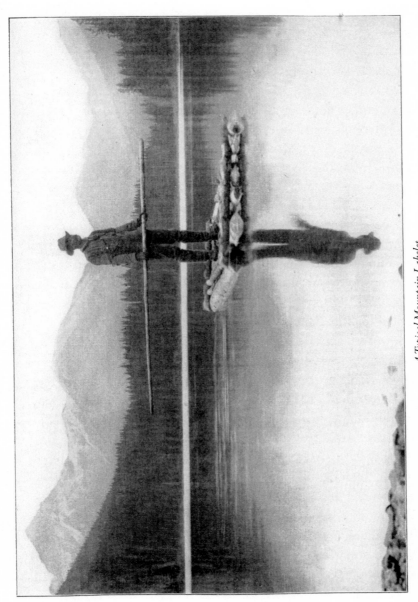

A Typical Mountain Lakelet

LAKE MONRO, A FEW MILES NORTH OF GREAT PASS.

to our visit a large bull elk had entered the southern end of the lake, and swam the entire length of it. Having read this bit of history, I formally christened that body of water, in honor of my wife, and filed her claim on the side of a fine young balsam that stood on the southern shore.

Then it began to rain, and we made haste to pitch our tent, cut spruce boughs for our bed, and collect a huge pile of wood for the camp-fire; for it was nearly night.

People may paint and photograph camps and campfires, until doomsday; but after all they are mostly tame and spiritless. One might as well try to paint the perfume of orange blossoms, or the charm of a lovely woman's manner, for all are equally futile. But those who have camped in the lap of Nature, far from the haunts of man, far beyond the last trail and the ultimate tin can, can realize without any pictures the composite sensations of awe, of triumph, and of rare satisfaction which filled our souls as we lit our camp-fire, and settled down for the night.

Our tent was small, even for two men; but in view of the rain that steadily pattered down, and dog Kaiser shivering as he lay tightly coiled on the dry needles at the foot of our sheltering spruce, we cordially invited him to come into the tent, for the night. Kaiser always was *persona grata*, and it was no hardship to share with him our bed, as well as our board.

When not exercising, it was stinging cold; and Charlie was blanketless. To remedy that, he left the front end of the tent wide open, and built across it bows, and only six feet away, a perfectly gorgeous camp-fire six feet long by three feet high. The heat of this radiated into the tent, and warmed it very well, save to a man lying down; who naturally lay under the warm air, rather than within it.

Charlie's rest was continually broken by the necessity of replenishing the fire; and when lying down, he should have had a good blanket. The first night, I was new to the situation, and watched to see how my comrade would get on with no blanket. The second night, I knew all about it; and after a watch below I made Charlie get into my one-blanket sleeping-bag, get warm and go to sleep, while I took the watch on deck. Every half hour I had to get out and mend the fire; and then Kaiser would quickly jump my claim, and settle down in the warmest spot of my bed. When I dislodged him, and settled down for another shivery half-hour, he would insinuate himself into my arms, and I found the warmth of his body grateful and comforting.

True to the general keynote, we found those mountains quite different from every other spot we had visited. The big, rocky peak that formed a quarter-circle around the western side of the basin of Lake Josephine seemed to be a sort of culminating point. From it and its spur-like ridges, great basins were scooped out in every direction, and creeks innumerable headed and ran down north, east and south. From the bald top of a vast ridge southeast of the lake, we seemed to overlook the world.

The crest of Cyclorama Ridge, on which Mr. Phillips killed his three rams, was so much below us that we looked down upon it, and saw it clean and bare, while we were in snow. Southward, fully a thousand feet below us, a big valley of many slides and much green timber ran down, due south. Charlie said it was Wilson's Creek, whereon Mr. Phillips had killed several grizzly bears.

It was a glorious country for big game; but just at that moment, the sheep and deer and grizzlies happened to be elsewhere. We found goats on the cliffs, and, as described fully elsewhere, saw a big billy promenade across the face of that awful precipice as coolly as if he were cropping *pulsatilla* on a sky pasture. On the summit of the highest point trodden by us, we met an ashy-mantled ground-squirrel. East of our camp, a whole mountain-side was covered with huckleberry bushes hanging full of ripe berries, on which we fed sumptuously more than once.

The night before we were to return to Camp Necessity, it began to rain and snow, and after studying the weather Charlie said, very seriously,

"We'll find ourselves in a foot of snow at daylight to-morrow!"

"Charlie," I said, "my luck won't have it that way! When I go hunting, bad weather doesn't strike until after I get in."

"Well, this time I'll back the clouds against yer luck," said Charlie.

We spent a very anxious night, but at daylight we had only the same two inches of snow that we had at sunset. We ate our last mouthfuls of grub, spent our last films in trying to photograph Lake Josephine, and then set out—or I should say set *down*—for Camp Necessity. The valley route was impossible, because of the wet snow on the logs, so we went down the crest of the ridge west of our little creek.

It is easy to over-estimate the height that one climbs, and magnify the difficulties of an ascent; but, as truly as I live, that descent seems like one of the most trying experiences that I ever went through in hunting. We went down at a frightfully steep pitch, through green timber and dead timber, clinging like frightened monkeys to every branch, and bush, and twig that we could grasp, to keep from pitching headlong. There were ten thousand fallen trees to climb over,—but we didn't climb over quite all of them. Every fallen tree was wet, every root and stone was slippery. I got three hard falls on soft earth, and each time thankfully went forward to the next. It seemed to me that we went down about five thousand feet,—at least twice as much as we climbed up in going to Lake Josephine,— but I know that the distance was nothing like that. To my last day, it will be to me a profound mystery how we climbed up so easily, and scrambled down so far, and so hard. During the lower third of the descent, the tangle of down timber on that awfully steep mountain-side was most trying. It made one think of tangled hair.

Soaking wet, we reached Camp Necessity about noon, and were glad to get into dry clothing. The cutting of the trail had been steadily going forward, but instead of being nearly at an end, three miles were yet unopened, and the work was slow and toilsome. To save Charlie Smith from heavy axe-work, which he was then in no physical condition to perform, Huddleston, our cook, pluckily volunteered to change work with Smith; and he flew at the chopping of tough jack pines as if he liked it.

On the following day, Mr. Phillips and I packed up all our skins and heads, and made them ready for the trail. The last photographs of the camp were taken. When the Norboes and Huddleston dragged wearily into camp, at night, they sadly confessed that the trail-cutting was far from being finished. At least two days' work remained, possibly three. Being already behind my schedule time, and urgently anxious to get in touch with a telegraph wire, I proposed to Mr. Phillips that we break through on foot, and walk to Michel by the end of the following day. It was only twenty-five miles, or thereabouts, but getting down and out of Avalanche Valley made it equal to forty on a fair trail.

At daylight on the morning of September 29, John and I took our rifles and one camera, and set out. The only incident of the promenade worth mentioning is the down-timber feature.

Thus far I have said little about "log-running" in getting over bad down timber. What we did previously in that line was like child's play in comparison with that forenoon's record. To be appreciated, down timber must be experienced; for seeing is not all of believing.

Fallen jack pines are the curse of British Columbia. They hinder all enterprises, and help none. They never decay, and the longer they lie the tougher they are. They are too small to convert into lumber, and too hard to chop into cordwood. They are too big for fishing rods, and too small for masts. After a time, a jack pine stem becomes practically indestructible. To burn one off the face of Nature requires more good kindling than the burnee would make, if sawn and split. A jack pine stem is so tough that you cannot break a section of the tip as large as a walking stick.

If you try to break off a tip, to use for some good and lawful purpose, it will lure you on to strive until you are exhausted, and then when you say something bad and let it go, it will fly back and hit you in the eye.

When the wind begins to blow hard, dead jack pines that are standing are more dangerous than grizzly bears. Then the boldest hunter will quit the trail, and break for open ground. Even when the wind is not blowing, it is dangerous to walk through jack pines that are dead standing, for they have a sneaking way of silently letting go at the roots, and falling across anything or anybody that can be hurt. A dead jack pine is a woody degenerate, neither beautiful nor useful, and forever menacing the peace of the world until some well-directed fire reduces it to its lowest terms.

The lower reaches of Avalanche Valley are to-day suffering from a fearful attack of jack pines. Once the mountains on both slopes were covered with that misbegotten tree; but about ten years ago they were swept by fire. The trees were killed, but not burned. They fell down-hill, so that travel on the mountain-side is everywhere a practical impossibility. In the bottom of the valley they fell across each other in every direction, and piled up higher and higher, until the uncut residuum is absolutely impassable for horse, deer, or any large

Packing Up The Trophies

hoofed animal except man. There are places where the criss-crossed logs are only four feet high, but there are others where they are ten, fifteen, or twenty.

To get a horse through, a course must be so cut out that the highest uncut log is low enough that a horse can step over it; and such a trail winds in the wildest and dizziest zig-zags ever laid out by man. A worm fence, or a streak of chain light-ning, is an air-line in comparison with it. In advancing one mile you travel three or four.

The foot-slogger who is unhampered by a pack-train can get over the infernal tangle by walking on the topmost logs. He goes first in one direction and then in another, as the good ones,—no, I mean the least bad ones,—happen to lie. The stems are bare of bark, and smooth as a floor, but plentifully provided with tough, mean limbs to catch in your clothes and otherwise throw you down. There is hardly a square yard below that is not criss-crossed by logs, and if you lose your balance and fall, you plunge down upon an assortment of tree trunks and limbs as hard as iron, and lying all sorts of ways about.

When your foot-log is near the ground, you jog along quite joyously, but at six feet or more above mother earth, a fall means broken bones. Broken bones in the mountains spell calamity, to yourself and to your whole party. Doctors are im-possible, and to carry a man out over those mountain trails is a task that the strongest party manager may well shrink from.

In getting out of Avalanche Valley, we had no choice but to walk logs for several hours and several miles. Without the hob nails in our shoes, it would have been quite impossible. It would have been much easier and safer without our rifles, but for a hunter to abandon his rifle means the last extrem-ity. While the dew was on the logs, we gave our undivided at-tention to the struggle to get on and yet keep from falling. As the morning drew on, and the dew dried up, we became more

The Tangle of "Dead" and "Down" Timber, Avalanche Creek (top)
Log-running over "Down" Timber (bottom)
A HARD FALL MEANS BROKEN BONES.

confident, and went faster. It was very funny, but we planted our feet just as a mountain goat does when walking a ledge,— very firmly and stiffly at each step, to get a sure foothold on the smooth wood.

Although I had lost eleven pounds since entering the mountains, my weight was still one hundred and seventy-four, and I dreaded the disgrace of broken bones on the last day. Many a time as we crossed logs that were fully ten feet from the ground, it seemed impossible that we should be permitted to get out without a break. But we did. We got so much in practice that we pegged along not only rapidly but recklessly, and took chances that were better not taken twice. Toward the end of the log-running, Mr. Phillips had a bad fall, and came very near Calamity. He did not fall far, but his foot was caught and held so firmly that he was glad to hang on and without moving wait for me to come up and help him to release his foot and rise. At first we both thought that his ankle was "gone."

A little later I grew careless, and fell a short fall with great violence, but fortunately landed full length upon some small stems. I thought my rifle stock was smashed to bits, but it came up unbroken.

At last, however, we got out of the down timber, out of the five-mile forest of young jack pines that lies below it, and down into the valley of Elk River.

All's well that ends well.

CHAPTER XXIV

CAPTIVE MOUNTAIN GOATS

RECORD OF CAPTIVE GOATS EXHIBITED-PERILOUS CAPTURE
BY SMITH AND NORBOE-AN EASY CAPTURE-A GAME WARDEN IN
TROUBLE-FIRST SPECIMENS FOR NEW YORK-OTHERS FROM FORT
STEELE-SHIPPING ANIMALS BY EXPRESS-THE AUTHOR BECOMES
TRAVELLING COMPANION FOR FIVE GOAT KIDS-TRAITS IN
CAPTIVITY-A GLANCE BACKWARD.

UP TO THIS DATE, THE entire history of the mountain goat in captivity is very brief. Although quite a number have been caught in various places, only a very few have lived long enough to change hands and be seen of men.

The first living mountain goat ever captured or photographed (s.f.a.k.) was a big male captured near Deer Lodge, Montana, about 1880, and taken alive to that town. For sixteen years I have been in possession of a dim photograph of that animal, taken as he stood with two ropes around his neck. "Deer Lodge Billy" lived only a short time. His alleged weight of 480 pounds is quite beyond belief.

In 1899 two goats were purchased of Dick Rock by

Charles W. Dimick, and exhibited at the Sportsmen's Show, in Boston. They lived on a farm in New England for about one year longer, then died of lung troubles.

In 1902 the Philadelphia Zoological Society came into possession of two fine young goats, which lived in the Gardens of that Society for two years, and then suddenly passed away.

In 1901, the Zoological Society of London purchased a typical full-grown male goat which had been captured in 1898 in the Fort Steele District of southeastern British Columbia, and reared to maturity in its home country. By its owner it was personally conducted to London, and on arriving there it elected to live. At this date (1906) it is believed to be yet alive; and I may add that it is living proof in support of the author's theory that the only perfect way to secure American mountain sheep and goats that can survive on the Atlantic coast is by having young animals reared to maturity in their home country.

In the spring of 1904, seven goat kids were captured near Banff for the New York Zoological Society, and most carefully cared for, but all died shortly after they reached Banff. During that same season, however, four other goats were caught for us, and also a mountain sheep lamb, all of which survived. The mountain sheep lamb, and two of the goat kids, were caught by Charles L. Smith and R.M. Norboe. As we climbed up Goat Creek into the mountains, we passed the very spot where one of the kids was taken, and Mr. Smith described to me the manner of it. It was, I think, the most hazardous and recklessly daring feat in mountaineering ever performed by any one known to me, and I shudder every time I think of it.

On that particular occasion, R. M. Norboe accompanied Smith into the mountains, for the purpose of capturing kids. They found a female goat, with a kid only a few days old, near the top of a lofty and very precipitous peak on the north side of Goat Creek. They climbed the mountain, scaled the peak to

Risking his Life for a Kid
DRAWN BY CHARLES B. HUDSON.

its summit, and finally succeeded in driving the mother goat and her kid upon a narrow ledge which terminated against an unscalable wall.

Rope in hand, Charlie Smith followed the mother goat and her young along their narrow shelf of rock almost to the end of the *cul-de-sac*. But there the pursuit ended. From that point onward the rock wall overhung so much that ten feet away from the goats a human being could go no farther. Below was a perpendicular drop of hundreds of feet, but the rocks above sloped sufficiently that Norboe was able to come within about ten feet of his partner.

"Mack," said Smith, "go and cut a pole about ten feet long, strong enough to swing this kid, give it to me, and I'll soon have him."

While his partner went to cut the pole, Smith sat down on the ledge, with his feet hanging over eternity, and waited. When the pole arrived, and had been passed down to him, he bent his lariat upon the end, and left a suitable noose hanging free. When all was ready, he bade Norboe climb down as near to him as possible, and when the word was given he reached forward, noosed the kid around its neck, swung it out over the abyss and up to Norboe, who took it, and carried it to a place of safety. Then Smith gingerly arose, edged his way back along the eighteen-inch shelf, and in safety reached the rocks above.

As we looked up at the frightfully dangerous spot whereon Smith risked his life for a mountain goat kid three days old, the thought came back to me, for about the one-hundredth time, "What a pity that visitors to zoological parks and gardens cannot know all the life stories of the animals!"

The second goat kid captured for us by Mr. Smith was obtained more easily. While hunting bear in May, 1904, near the head of Goat Creek, Mr. Phillips and Guide Smith saw a mother goat and a very young kid. They were lingering near

A Newly-Captured Mountain Goat Kid (a week old) and its captor, Charles L. Smith

A REST IN THE GREEN TIMBER, NEAR CAMP.

the mouth of a cave, high up in the rocks, quite as if the cave had been the birthplace of the kid. On the following morning, Mr. Phillips encouraged Smith to make a trip to the cave, and if possible capture the kid. Mr. Smith eagerly accepted the opportunity, hastened to the spot, and found both the mother goat and her young very near the ledge they had occupied on the previous day. As the hunter approached, the mother goat retreated with her kid into the cave. Smith followed, easily drove out the nanny and captured the kid.

Carrying the little creature tenderly in his arms, Charlie finally sat down to rest in the heavy green timber a mile above camp, and there Mr. Phillips found him and took his picture, as shown herewith.

A little later, a mountain sheep lamb was captured, and it and the two goat kids were safely settled for a period of several months at Mr. Smith's comfortable ranch on the bank of Elk River. The three animals were kept in a small yard made of poultry netting, and watched and tended by Mr. Smith's father. During the entire summer, those animals were not out of the father's sight in daylight for more than an hour at a time, and as a result, they lived and throve.

At first their food consisted of condensed cream, properly diluted with water; and after that they were fed on cow's milk, given in small quantities, but frequently. Very soon they began to eat grass, cabbage and dry bread, and after that, crushed oats. As they grew older, hay became acceptable to them, and soon formed, with cabbage, their principal diet.

During the summer Mr. Smith had various adventures with his strange little beasts, and one incident which he described in a letter to his friend Mr. J. E. Roth, of Pittsburg, presently found its way into print.

It appeared in *Shields' Magazine* under the caption...

A GAME WARDEN IN TROUBLE

"I HAD SOME EXCITEMENT LATELY in the exercise of my duties as game warden. Mother started in to violate our good game laws. Father had turned the pet sheep and goats out for exercise, and, as the day was fine, Mother stepped out and left the hall door open. The sheep, being near at hand, thought it a good time to explore new territory, so went in at the door and up the stairs on the run. Mother heard the racket, and, arming herself with a broom, did willfully, and, disregarding the game laws, pursue the said sheep.

"After an elaborate stalk, she found it in my room, standing in the middle of my bed, and she made a charge. The sheep dashed around the room, over books and flowerpots, and down the stairs, four steps at a time. The dining-room door was open, and the table was set for dinner. As it was the highest bit of scenery in sight the sheep took refuge in the middle of it, and cleared a space on which to make a final stand. Mother, being the wife and mother of a hunter, and being descended from a long line of that ilk, did, regardless of the law, still pursue; but, before she could make her way down stairs, the doughty big-horn had cleared the table of every dish, with contents, and they lay scattered around as if the place had been struck by a Kansas cyclone. "The mater made a charge on *Ovis canadensis*, but failed to bring him down. She then called in the pater, and, after some persuasion, the irate big-horn was taken away.

"About that time I arrived on the scene, and with dignity proceeded to read Mother the clause in the game laws which says: 'You shall not pursue, or cause to be pursued, etc., etc.,' upon which she informed me that I was the one who had caused the sheep to be pursued by allowing it to come near the house, and that she would fine me the price of a new set of dishes, and sentence me to go without my dinner. As she had the law in her own hands, I had to submit.

"This is the second time I have been turned down as game warden, and I think I shall resign."

It is quite useless to transplant from the Rocky Mountains to the Atlantic coast either mountain sheep lambs or goat kids only two or three months old, and expect them to survive. To such delicate animals, the shock of such a change is too great. They are easily upset. The longer they can remain in their home country, the better; and it is very unwise to move them before they are six or seven months old. Even then it cannot be managed successfully save by an attendant to travel with the animals, and care for them on the way.

In October, 1904, Mr. B.T. Van Nostrand, a Brooklyn sportsman on a hunting tour to the Columbian Rockies, personally conducted two mountain goat kids for us from Fort Steele to New York, and the animals arrived in perfect condition. A month later, Charlie Smith brought to us from his Elk River ranch the two goats and the sheep, mentioned above. They, also, arrived in good health, and the five novelties from the Rockies were duly placed on exhibition in the New York Zoological Park.

All went well until in August, 1905, when the goats began to have trouble with their digestive organs. One by one they were attacked by gastro-enteritis, the incurable curse of all North American hoofed animals on the Atlantic coast near tidewater, and in September, 1905, all four of the goats went the way of all flesh.

But we were not wholly bereft. Before I started for British Columbia the Zoological Society learned that its standing order for more goats was ready to be filled at Fort Steele, with five animals. Accordingly I arranged that they should be delivered to me at that point, and by me be personally conducted to New York.

On October 1, our three guides and cook, after several days of awful trail-cutting through down timber, finally succeeded in getting our pack train out of the mountains and into Michel. We worked until midnight, packing up and shipping eastward our boxes of museum specimens and trophies. On October 2, I went to Fort Steele, received the five little goats from James White,—who showed real feeling at parting from his pets,—and the long run home began. So many persons have asked me how we get our rarest wild animals, I am tempted to add a few lines regarding the transit of *Oreamnos*.

A bear cub seven months old, a wolf, or a puma, can endure to travel alone, and take chances of being watered and fed by kind-hearted express messengers. In all our seven years of animal-gathering by express, we have not lost an important live animal in transit through the neglect of express messengers. True, our printed shipping labels loudly appeal for "plenty of air," "Do not let them die of thirst!" and "Feed moderately." At St. Paul we have a half-way house, where an agent attends to the wants of all animals coming to us through his express company.

Bear cubs are tough, and can travel alone; but mountain goat babies cannot. They must be cared for three times a day, as regularly as it is possible for an able-bodied courier to break into the express car where they travel. It is a serious undertaking.

The five little goats were shipped in two light and roomy crates, in which they could turn about very freely. On the top of each crate was a hinged trap-door, which fastened with a padlock. The cracks of the crates were so narrow that no goat could thrust a leg through and have it broken off. I had four bags of freshly-cut clover, a bag of crushed oats and bran, and two watering pans. The food supply was furnished by White, and was supposed to be in accordance with what the goats had previously been fed upon.

They liked the clover, but the bran and oats they scorned to touch, save with their feet. Whenever I offered a panful of the ground feed they would smell of it, taste it once, and then, biff! a stocky black hoof would strike the pan fairly in the centre, and knock it into oblivion. After half a dozen snubs of this kind, I ceased to offer objectionable food, and in Fernie made haste to buy a bagful of cabbage. The goats accepted the amendment, and three times a day they stowed away cabbage most gratefully.

Morning, noon and night, those five little white hobby-horses were ravenously hungry; and every day at noon they were very thirsty. How they would have suffered had they been dependent, throughout the whole of that long trip, on such casual attention as busy and overworked baggagemen and express messengers could have given them! I think that without the care of an attendant they would have died before reaching New York; and I felt grateful to myself for having had sufficient intelligence to provide a convoy for each shipment of goats coming to us.

The green clover began to heat in the bags, and in the bottoms of the crates at night. Every morning the uneaten grass which served as bedding was very hot, and the goats were very uncomfortable. Not a moment was lost in throwing overboard that material. The importunate billies and nannies stamped impatiently, whined with queer little nasal squeaks, and pawed vigorously at the sides of their crates. It is a good thing for an uncomfortable animal to disturb the peace until its wants receive attention. Sometimes when the trap-door top was opened, an impatient kid would hop out, and require to be gathered up and re-introduced to his narrow temporary home.

In travelling on fast trains, I had great difficulty in getting into the proper express car and back again. Overland express cars have no end doors, and often two or three cars were between the smoker and my goats. Stops at stations were few and brief, and I had to figure carefully in order to make my three trips and get back without being left by the blind steps of closed vestibules.

On the return trip, my time was so fully taken up in caring for my small goats that I did practically nothing else, and made for Mr. Phillips a highly intermittent companion. But the five goats finally reached the Zoological Park alive and in riotously good health, and up to this date (July 1) not one of them has had a sick day. We "point with pride" to them as the first flock of their kind ever achieved by a zoological institution. Their queer ways and occasional antics are both amusing and instructive.

Regarding human society, and the human touch, they are nervous little creatures, and also irritable. At your, earnest invitation, they will gingerly approach your outstretched hand, and sniff at your finger tips. Then they stamp with their front feet, say "*Umph!*" in a falsetto nasal squeak, toss their heads and whirl away. Four out of the five refuse to be petted, save by force. The fifth is barely tolerant of a friendly and well-known hand. But none of them run and wildly bang themselves against the fences as do so many deer when at close quarters with man.

It is exceedingly interesting to see them leap against their barn, or upon elevations, or climb on the arrangement that has been built for their amusement. But it is unwise to hope that in New York these delicate young creatures will live long. If any one of the five is alive two years hence, we will rejoice, and call it good fortune.

And so has ended, in our mountain goat corral; in the mammal hall of the Carnegie Museum; and in this volume, our trip to a wonderland of fine mountains and grand game. The animal life of our hunting-ground was not appreciably affected by our rifles. Excepting our grizzly bears, we shot no females. We made thorough use of everything we killed, we left behind us no wounded animals, and excepting the mule deer, we converted each animal shot by us into a preserved specimen. Four museums now have specimens from our twelve head of game.

May heaven keep my memory of it all as fresh as the breezes that blow on Goat Pass, as green as the pines and spruces that clothe the lower slopes of those delectable mountains.

FAREWELL.

WHILE READING THE PROOFS of the last of the preceding pages, a letter from Charlie Smith brought the unwelcome news that Dog Kaiser is no more. In July last, while in pur suite of a field-mouse, he leaped in front of a mowing-machine on his master's ranch, and was killed.

To every sportsman and guide who knew Kaiser in camp and on the trail, his untimely death has genuine sorrow. There never lived a more perfect hunting-dog for big game; for he was a dog who made no mistakes. His senses were keen, he knew when to pursue, and when to save himself by a proper retreat. On the trail of large game, he would obey a strange sportsman as readily as his own master; and few hunting-dogs will do that. He never was permitted to range free, or to chase any hoofed game save when it was to be photographed.

In breed, Kaiser was part collie, and partly plain hunting-dog. As a hunter of intelligence, obedience, skill and courage, he contributed much toward the success of a number of sportsmen and naturalists, and in the annals of big-game hunting and photography, he fairly earned a place.